THE SPIRITUALITY OF VATICAN II

Conciliar Texts Concerning the Spiritual Life of ALL Christians

Assembled and Annotated by
WILLIAM A. KASCHMITTER, M.M.

OUR SUNDAY VISITOR, INC.
Huntington, Indiana 46750

Nihil Obstat:
Rev. Lawrence Gollner
Censor Librorum

Imprimatur:
✠ Leo A. Pursley, D.D.
Bishop of Fort Wayne-South Bend
December 11, 1974

The Nihil Obstat and Imprimatur are official declarations that a book or pamphlet is free of doctrinal or moral error. No implication is contained therein that those who have granted the Nihil Obstat or Imprimatur agree with the contents, opinions or statements expressed.

ISBN: 0-87973-868-5
Library of Congress Catalog Card Number: 74-29344

Cover Design by James E. McIlrath

Published, printed and bound in the U.S.A. by
Our Sunday Visitor, Inc.
Noll Plaza
Huntington, Indiana 46750

868

DEDICATION

To His Holiness

POPE PAUL VI

Who regards it as his principal duty to see that the ideas and ideals of Vatican II are put into practice.

The teachings of Vatican II "constitute a *Summa* for our time, a very rich, authoritative compendium of doctrine and guidance for its needs." (Pope Paul VI, General Audience, February 4, 1970. English Language *L'Osservatore Romano*, February 12, 1970, p. 1).

"The volume containing the Council's Constitutions and Decrees can serve as a book of spiritual reading and meditation. It has beautiful passages full of wisdom and historical and human experience. They deserve meditation and can become food for the soul." (Pope Paul VI, General Audience, St. Peter's Basilica, September 30, 1970. English Language *L'Osservatore Romano*, October 8, 1970, p. 12).

ACKNOWLEDGMENT

All direct quotations from the Second Vatican Council documents contained in this book were taken from *The Documents of Vatican II*, published in 1966 by America Press. I wish therefore to thank the directors of America Press for their gracious permission to use these texts.

W. A. Kaschmitter, M.M.

CONTENTS

INTRODUCTION

"The Constitutions and Decrees of the (Second Vatican) Council can serve as a book of spiritual reading and meditation." So declared Pope Paul VI in a public audience held in St. Peter's Basilica, September 30, 1970. (*L'Osservatore Romano*, October 8, 1970).

"We are still meditating on the Council's teaching," he had already said the previous February. "We are convinced that they constitute a *Summa* for our time, a very rich, authoritative compendium of doctrine and guidance." (*L'Osservatore Romano*, February 12, 1970).

"Anyone willing to see the Council as the work of the Holy Spirit and of the responsible organ of the Church, will take up the Council's documents assiduously and respectfully and use them as nourishment and law for his own soul and for his community." (*L'Osservatore Romano*, July 23, 1970).

It is the author's hope that priests and others will find this concordance useful in locating appropriate material for both private meditation and public instruction.

"God the Father is the origin and purpose of all men." (*Pastoral Constitution on the Church in the Modern World*, 92). On the basis of this fundamental doctrine, the Council has elaborated a very complete doctrine concerning man's duties to his fellow-men. (Cf. 688, 690, 682). The ancient Chinese saying, "All within the Four Seas are brothers," is a Christian truism. In fact, the Council gives more space to the "horizontal" aspects of its teachings than to the "vertical." It lays a more solid foundation for welfare work and aid to developing countries than can be found in any humanitarian theory of our overly humanistic age.

"Essential anthropocentrism" is how some have labeled Vatican II claiming that this is most clearly expressed in the Pastoral Constitution on the Church in the Modern World. No matter what the thought of those who use the term, deep truth lies beneath the surface. One need only check the topics referred to in the index under such captions as

7

"Development," "Social Welfare," "Better World," "Works of Charity," etc. For example check these numbers which follow:

> God loves the world He made (114);
> If you don't love people, you can't love God (682, 741);
> Love everything and everybody (537);
> If you have something, share it (700);
> He who needs help should get it (700, 742);
> Help people to help themselves (701);
> The poor and needy have dignity (695, 696, 742);
> Work on all levels (local, national, international) for a better
> world (702);
> Man is social by the will of God (487); Social virtues, part of
> home training (659);
> Social virtues are of the essence (759);
> Human fulfillment, rights and duties (758);
> Promote public opinion on justice, on sharing (760).

God focused His love on man: witness His creative, redemptive and
sanctifying action on man's behalf. The universe had to come from
somewhere, to get out of nothing; and since He made it out of nothing,
He had to have His own reasons for doing so. No creature, including
man, sufficiently accounts of itself for its own existence.

Man-oriented the Pastoral Constitution on the Church may be, since
it aims to stir man into taking a hand in his own salvation, yet this same
Constitution restates the most God-centered of teaching: "One of the
outstanding causes of human dignity is man's call to union with God.
He was invited to converse with God, from the very circumstances of
his origin. Were he not created by God out of love and constantly
preserved, man would not exist. (*Modern World*, 18).

"Only God meets the deepest longings of the human heart; never
completely satisfied by what this world has to offer." (*Modern World,*
41). "God calls man to a union with Himself in a sharing of divine life;
life unending and beyond corruption." (*Modern World,* 18). "Man is
called by God as a son by his father to commune with Him and share
His happiness." (*Modern World,* 21).

Man is a miracle — of God's making; what man has made of himself,
that's the problem of life.

The truth is that "the imbalances under which the modern world
labors are linked with that more basic imbalance rooted in the heart of
man." (*Modern World,* 10).

Vatican II is not unaware of the vast changes in contemporary life
resulting from the social, scientific and technological advances of recent
times. Yet, in the face of modern development, "an ever-increasing
number of people are raising the most basic questions, or are recogniz-

8

ing them with new sharpness. . . . Beneath all changes, the Church maintains, there are many realities which have their ultimate foundation in Christ. . . . Hence the Council wishes to speak to all men . . . to cooperate in finding solutions to the outstanding problems of our times." (*Modern World,* 10).

Vatican II might well be rated the most Holy Spirit-conscious, i.e. the most spiritual-minded Council since the time of the Apostles, which phrased its conclusions: "The Holy Spirit and we . . . have decided . . ." (Acts 15:28).

To *Lex orandi, lex credendi* — how one prays shows what one believes, add: *Lex vivendi,* one's life-style; and you have a good summary of Vatican II teaching.

The confusion and unrest that have followed the Council are not to be blamed on the Council. "More inclined, it would seem, to affirm man than to deny God, some of our contemporaries extol man so extravagantly that their faith in God lapses into a kind of anemia." (*Modern World,* 19).

"Fidelity to Christ — that is everything; that's what should be characteristic of the post-conciliar period. We are vital (living) members of Christ's mystical Body and in that Body we shall have our everlasting reward." (Pope Paul VI, *L'Osservatore Romano,* July 23, 1970).

AUTHOR'S CAUTION

About nine-tenths of the text of this book is made up of direct quotations from the documents of Vatican II. These are given in quotation marks and are identified as to the conciliar documents from which they are taken.

The other tenth represents merely what the compiler has read, heard or experienced during the past six decades and must be judged on its own merits since it is not explicitly based on conciliar teachings.

A friendly critic has suggested that such personal contributions should not be included in a book concerning the spirituality of Vatican II since they are too subjective. This objection is certainly worthy of consideration. On the other hand, it would seem that spirituality in its basic dimension as a relationship between God and the soul necessarily involves the subjective attitude of the individual and his reaction to his relationship with God.

Attitudes and reactions can be as varied as the problems with which the individual is faced. As Catholic press director in occupied China, the compiler was faced with such problems that he felt positively relieved when he was interned as an "enemy national" for the duration of World War II along with 6 bishops, 350 priests, 150 Sisters, 40 Brothers, 200 Protestant missionaries and 1100 civilians. As temporary pastor of the camp he often felt that he had escaped from the frying pan only to fall into the fire. Faced with the turmoil that has afflicted much of the Church since the close of Vatican II, he felt the need of authoritative and objective guidelines to supplement all subjective standards of spirituality and it is for this reason that he undertook the preparation of this book. The point must be made, however, that even the objective guidelines provided by Vatican II will be useful only insofar as they are integrated with the subjective attitudes and reactions of the individual.

Whether the compiler was really justified in including extraneous elements into this concordance of Vatican II texts must be left to the judgment of those who may use this book. The important thing to remember is that the author's observations must be judged on their own merits.

1. God

GOD IN GENERAL

1. Someone has said that it is only through God that man can understand himself. Again it has been said that it is only through himself that man can attain to a really effective understanding of God, however imperfect that understanding may be.

2. Men who have been all but crushed by burdens which they had to bear alone because others could not, or would not, help them, have found light and solace and strength by going back in spirit to that eternity that was (and is) before time began. God alone — Father, Son and Holy Spirit — then existed. Matter, men and angels were reality only as images in the mind of God and came into existence only because He willed it.

3. What was God Himself doing then, what kind of inner life did He live during that eternity before His external works began? There was then no one to know Him, no one to love Him, nor was there anything towards which He could show His kindness, His love, His Providence. His life was purely internal but it was infinitely great, infinitely glorious, infinitely happy. With His infinite Intelligence, He knew Himself with all of His infinite perfections perfectly. In some mysterious way, understood only by Himself, this self-knowledge has from all eternity had an identity of its own as the "Word" or the "Son" of God which distinguished Him from Him Who "spoke" the Word or "begot" the Son, namely God the Father Who is described by Vatican II as "the origin without origin." (*Missions,* 2).

4. Father and Son gaze eternally upon each other's infinite perfection and find each other infinitely lovable. Here is the origin of that infinite Love which proceeds from both the Father and Son and is the Holy Spirit.

5. Sacred Scripture and theology both teach us that God created man

13

according to His own image and likeness. To some extent, therefore, man can be described as a living image and likeness of God and by analyzing himself man can arrive at some vague knowledge of his Creator.

6. It is from God that man has received his powers of knowing persons and things and of loving what is (or seems to be) worthy of love and man knows from his own experience that his only *real* happiness is rooted ultimately in love. If man therefore concludes from this experience that God's own infinite happiness is rooted in that mutual love of Father and Son which is the Holy Spirit, his conclusion, though inadequate, cannot be altogether wrong.

7. Even in man, in spite of all of his limitations, there is an element of goodness which makes him wish to share his happiness with others insofar as that is possible. He can understand, therefore, that God with His infinite Goodness also wished to share His happiness with others. In that eternity which existed before time began, however, no other being existed with whom it would have been possible for God to share His happiness. Ultimately, therefore, it was this desire on the part of God to share His happiness with others that moved God to create men and angels.

CREATION

8. Vatican II speaks to us of the "fountain of love" within the Father (*Missions,* 2) and tells us that "by an utterly free and mysterious decree of His own Wisdom and Goodness, the eternal Father created the whole world." (*Church,* 2). It is through the Word that God created everything (John 1:3) and keeps all things in existence. (*Revelation,* 3). It was through the Word also that the Father chose us before the foundation of the world and predestined us to become adopted sons. (*Church,* 3). As the Council says again: "Man is called as a son to commune with God and to share in His happiness." (*Modern World,* 21).

9. It is not only the Father and the Son but the Holy Spirit also Who is involved in God's plan with regard to man, for "The Spirit too has been bestowed on us by the Father, that living the life of God, we might love God and the brethren who are all of us one in Christ." (*Opening Message*).

10. Such were some of the thoughts and plans in the mind of God before time began and it was with these thoughts in mind that He created man according to His own image and likeness. It was through the Son of God that man was created and when the divine likeness in man was "disfigured from the first sin onward" (*Modern World,* 22) it was

the Son "Who is the Image of the invisible God" that was sent into the world to become a "perfect man" and to restore that divine likeness.

11. It is customary for Christians to speak of heaven as our eternal home but when we consider the part the Father, Son and Holy Spirit took in bringing us into existence, keeping us from falling back into nothingness and planning to let us share in their own life, love and happiness, it seems logical for us to say that our real and final home is the Blessed Trinity itself.

GOD REVEALING HIMSELF TO US

12. If we are to commune with God, live His Life and share His happiness, we must know Him and must know also how to achieve our ultimate destiny in Him. Happily, God has used various means with which to make Himself known to us.

13. Insofar as we were ourselves made to the image and likeness of God, we are ourselves, to some extent, a part of God's self-revelation to ourselves and to others. The Second Vatican Council tells us that "God, Who through the Word creates all things (John 1:3) and keeps them in existence, gives men an enduring witness to Himself in created realities." (*Revelation,* 3). In the same document (*Revelation,* 6) the Council goes on to explain that "God, the beginning and end of all things, can be known with certainty from created reality by the light of human reason." (Rom. 1:20). The Council goes on to say, however, that it is through revelation "that those religious truths which are by their nature accessible to human reason, can be known by all men with ease, with solid certitude and with no trace of error, even in the present state of the human race." (Quoting Vatican I.)

14. It is with this doctrine in mind that many of the spiritual writers have urged us to look upon the universe as a book that was written by God Himself to teach His children many useful truths about their heavenly Father. Astronomers tell us that they have discovered stars that are eight billion light years removed from our earth. This challenges us to reflect on the omnipotence of that heavenly Father Who created such a great house for His children. The fact that He built that house many billions of years ago challenges us also to think of God's eternity — and the eternity of happiness He has in store for us. Comparing this length of time that God allowed to elapse before placing man on this little earth of ours again reminds us not to be too impatient if the results we seek to achieve are not achieved overnight.

15. Looking out on the universe from their own point of view, some

of the mystics see in it a kind of self-drawn portrait of God Himself. Gazing eternally at that Image of Himself which is His Son, God sees in Himself infinite perfections which are indeed inseparable in the simplicity of His divine nature, but which can be thought of separately for our instruction. In God there is supreme and infinite existence. The inorganic universe existing in its immensity is but one line in the self-portrait God has drawn for the education of men and angels. In God there is unlimited power. Men today are just learning of the enormous power hidden in the atoms of the universe. In God there is life and by the plants of the world, God teaches us much about life. In God there is infinite knowledge and intelligence. In animals we see the lowest form of knowledge attained through bodily senses. Man not only possesses sensile knowledge but also intelligence by which he has been made "a little less than the angels."

16. The mystics' view of the universe seems fanciful at first, but calls attention to the fact that everything in the world had its beginning in the mind of God and was so much esteemed by Him that He willed to create it even though it required an exercise of His omnipotence to do so.

17. Men never cease marvelling at the great discoveries still being made about the secrets of nature, the constitution of matter and the harmony existing in what scientists like to call the "laws of nature." The ascetic reminds us that all of the physical sciences are but faint and very imperfect copies of that natural order that God in His infinite knowledge and wisdom imposed upon the whole physical universe. Some of the ascetical writers therefore like to describe the earth, the sun, the moon and the stars as the "alphabet blocks" used by God in His "kindergarten" for the education of His children.

18. In their sermons, some preachers also like to compare the universe as a whole to the greatest masterpiece of some painter or sculptor who refuses to sell this masterpiece. The artist, they tell us, wishes to keep the masterpiece in his own house so that his children can come to a deeper knowledge of their father and appreciate the love he shows by keeping this greatest work as a gift to them and as an expression of his hope that they may understand him better.

19. Addressing itself to the scholars of the world, Vatican II says that those who apply themselves to the various disciplines "can do very much to elevate the human family to a more sublime understanding of truth, goodness and beauty and to the formation of judgments which embody universal values. Thus mankind can be more clearly enlightened by that marvelous Wisdom which was with God from eternity, arranging all things with Him, playing upon the earth, delighting in, the sons of men." (*Modern World,* 57).

16

GOD SPEAKING TO MEN

20. Not content with having given men a universe filled with object lessons concerning Himself, God also planned to teach them the way of heavenly salvation. From the start He "manifested Himself to our first parents. Then, after their fall, His promise of redemption aroused in them the hope of being saved (Gen. 3:15) and from that time on He ceaselessly kept the human race in His care in order to give eternal life to those who perseveringly do good in search of salvation. (Rom. 2:6-7). Then, at the time He had appointed, He called Abraham in order to make of him a great nation. (Gen. 12:2). Through the patriarchs and after them through Moses and the prophets He taught this nation to acknowledge Himself as the one, living and true God, provident Father and just Judge, and to wait for the Saviour promised by Him." (*Revelation,* 3).

21. For the guidance of individuals in their daily lives, men have a conscience of which Vatican II says that "man has in his heart a law written by God." It is "the most secret core and sanctuary of a man. There he is alone with God Whose voice echoes in his depths." (*Modern World,* 16).

GOD REVEALING HIMSELF IN CHRIST

22. It is through Jesus Christ, however, that God has revealed Himself most fully to us. For the Father "sent His Son, the eternal Word, Who enlightens all men, so that He might dwell among men and tell them the innermost realities about God. (John 1:18). Jesus Christ, therefore, the Word made flesh, sent as 'a man to men' speaks the words of God. (John 3:34). . . . To see Jesus is to see His Father. (John 14:9). For this reason Jesus perfected revelation by fulfilling it through His whole work and making Himself present and manifesting Himself: through His words and deeds, His signs and wonders, but especially through His death and glorious resurrection from the dead and final sending of the Spirit of truth." (*Revelation,* 4).

2. Man

23. "What is man? About himself, he has expressed and continues to express many divergent and even contradictory opinions. In these he often exalts himself as the absolute measure of all things or debases himself to the point of despair. The result is doubt and anxiety." (*Modern World,* 12).

24. Endowed with light from God, the Church can offer solutions to these problems "so that man's true situation can be portrayed and his defects explained while at the same time his dignity and destiny are justly acknowledged.

"For Sacred Scripture teaches us that man was created 'to the image of God,' is capable of knowing and loving his Creator and was appointed by Him as master of all earthly creatures that he might subdue them and use them to God's glory. 'What is man that thou art mindful of him or the son of man that thou visitest him? Thou hast made him a little less than the angels, thou hast crowned him with glory and honor: thou has set him over the works of thy hands, thou hast subjected all things under his feet' (Ps. 8:5-6)." (*Modern World,* 12).

MAN A MYSTERY

25. "The truth is that only in the mystery of the Incarnate Word does the mystery of man take on light. For Adam, the first man, was a figure of Him Who was to come, namely Christ the Lord. Christ, the final Adam, by the revelation of the mystery of the Father and His love, fully reveals man to man himself and makes his supreme calling clear. It is not surprising then, that in Him all the aforementioned truths find their root and attain their crown." (*Modern World,* 22).

26. "Such is the mystery of man, and it is a great one, as seen by believers in the light of Christian revelation. Through Christ and in

Christ, the riddles of sorrow and death grow meaningful. Apart from His gospel, they overwhelm us. Christ has risen, destroying death by His death. He has lavished life upon us so that, as sons in the Son, we can cry out in the Spirit: Abba, Father!" (*Modern World*, 22).

27. "God the Father is the origin and purpose of all men." (*Modern World*, 92). "God has a fatherly concern for all men and has willed that all men should constitute one family and treat one another in a spirit of brotherhood. For having been created in the image of God, Who, 'from one man has created the whole human race and made them live all over the face of the earth' (Acts 17:26), all men are called to one and the same goal, namely, God Himself." (*Modern World*, 24). "His Providence, His manifestations of goodness, and His saving designs extend to all men (Wis. 8:1; Acts 14:17; Rom. 2:6-7; 1 Tim. 2:4) against the day when the elect will be united in that holy City ablaze with the splendor of God, where the nations will walk in His light." (Rev. 21:23 ff). (*Non-Christian Religions*, 1).

DIGNITY AS SONS OF GOD

28. "By baptism men are plunged into the paschal mystery of Christ, they die with Him, are buried with Him, and rise with Him. (Rom. 6:4; Eph. 2:6; Col. 3:1; 2 Tim. 2:11); they receive the spirit of adoption as sons 'by virtue of which we cry: Abba Father' (Rom. 8:15), and thus become those true adorers whom the Father seeks (John 4:23). (*Liturgy*, 6).

29. The Holy Spirit dwells "in the hearts of the faithful as in a temple. In them He prays and bears witness to the fact that they are adopted sons." (*Church*, 4).

30. "An outstanding cause of human dignity lies in man's call to communion with God. From the very circumstances of his origin, man is already invited to converse with God. For man would not exist were he not created by God's love and constantly preserved by it. And he cannot live fully according to truth unless he freely acknowledges that love and devotes himself to his Creator." (*Modern World*, 19).

31. Speaking to the world in general, Vatican II tells us that man is called not only to commune with God but actually "to share in His happiness." (*Modern World*, 21).

32. Men have said that God's own happiness is rooted in that mutual love of Father and Son which is the Holy Spirit. It has also been said that the process by which men are to share in God's happiness is for men to love the Father in union with the Son, to love the Son in union with the Father in the strength of that love which is the Holy Spirit.

33. It is true according to Vatican II that men of good will can, under certain conditions attain to salvation without the baptism of water, but it is Christ's desire that all should be given this "patent of nobility" as children of that supreme Lord Who is the Creator of the universe. As if to ratify this "patent" in the name of all three divine Persons, Christ sent His apostles into the whole world to impress the sacramental character of baptism on every one in the name of the Father and of the Son and of the Holy Spirit. (Cf. References to "baptism" and "sons of God" in the index.)

THE NATURE OF MAN

34. When men design any kind of machine or instrument, the form, the qualities and the general nature of the things made are determined by the purpose for which they are made. The same can be said of man.

35. Speaking to the whole world in its Pastoral Constitution on the Church in the Modern World Vatican II declared: "Man is not wrong when he regards himself as superior to bodily concerns, and as more than a speck of nature or a nameless constituent of the city of man. For by his interior qualities he outstrips the whole sum of mere things. He finds re-enforcement in this profound insight whenever he enters into his own heart. God, Who probes the heart, awaits him there. There he discerns his proper destiny beneath the eyes of God. Thus, when man recognizes in himself a spiritual and immortal soul, he is not being mocked by a deceptive fantasy springing from mere physical or social influences. On the contrary, he is getting to the depths of the very truth of the matter." (*Modern World,* 14).

36. Made for the purpose of sharing God's own life, love and happiness for all eternity, man has an intellect which can not only know and understand the things of this world, but can thereby come to know much about the God Who created him. With that same intellect, man can understand the indivisibility and the immortality of his own soul. With a heart that is made for love, man can understand something of the life and love of God. Enlightened also by what God has taught us about Himself, man can enter deeply into God's own Mind and Heart and can see why it is that God should value each one of His children more than He values the whole universe.

FREE WILL

37. Along with intelligence by which he can, to some extent at least,

understand what God understands, and a heart that can love what God loves, man has a will which can either act in conformity with what God wills or act contrary to the Will of God.

38. Free will is one of the greatest of the natural gifts bestowed on man by the Creator and in this respect, too, man is made to the image and likeness of God Who "by an utterly free and mysterious decree of His own Wisdom and Goodness created the whole world." (*Church*, 2).

39. With regard to this free will, Vatican II again spoke as follows: "Only in freedom can man direct himself toward goodness. Our contemporaries make much of this freedom and pursue it eagerly; and rightly so, to be sure. Often, however, they foster it perversely as a license for doing whatever pleases them, even if it is evil.

40. "For its part, authentic freedom is an exceptional sign of the divine image within man. For God has willed that man be left 'in the hand of his own counsel' so that he can seek his Creator spontaneously, and come freely to utter and blissful perfection through loyalty to Him. Hence man's dignity demands that he act according to a knowing and free choice. Such a choice is personally motivated and promoted from within. It does not result from blind internal impulse nor from mere external pressure.

41. "Man achieves such dignity when, emancipating himself from all captivity to passion, he pursues his goal in a spontaneous choice of what is good, and procures for himself, through effective and skillful action, apt means to that end. Since man's freedom has been damaged by sin, only by the help of God's grace can he bring such a relationship with God into full flower. Before the judgment seat of God each man must render an account of his own life, whether he has done good or evil." (*Modern World*, 17).

42. Applying this doctrine concerning free will specifically to the problem of faith, the Council also declared that "it is one of the major tenets of Catholic doctrine that man's response to God in faith must be free. Therefore no one is to be forced to embrace the Christian faith against his own will. This doctrine is contained in the Word of God and it was constantly proclaimed by the Fathers of the Church. The act of faith is of its very nature, a free act. Man, redeemed by Christ the Savior and through Christ Jesus called to be God's adopted son, cannot give his adherence to God revealing Himself unless the Father draw him to offer to God the reasonable and free submission of faith." (*Religious Freedom*, 10).

43. Perhaps no word has been involved in as many conflicts and disturbances in human history as has the word "freedom." One might even go so far as to say that if conflict were at all possible in the heart of the

Blessed Trinity, the question of giving freedom to men might well have brought on such a conflict. Among men, much conflict is brought about by defects in our thinking processes. Different men grasp the premises of a problem differently and the processes by which they arrive at their conclusions also differ. The Mind of God sees every aspect of a given problem as well as the interrelationships of all of those aspects with perfect clarity in a single glance. Discursive thinking is utterly unnecessary to God, but His thinking and His "conclusions," if one may be permitted to use the word with regard to God's thinking, are completely in accord with the most rigid demands of the most rigorous logic.

44. To understand God's thinking with regard to the freedom He gave to men at least a little more clearly we might imagine a hypothetical debate on that subject carried on between God's Wisdom, His Justice and His Love. One might imagine that when God thought about the creation of man (as He does eternally) the question was raised as to whether man should be endowed with free will. One can then imagine that Love spoke up with ardor in favor of the plan. Love's argument would have been that such freedom was absolutely necessary if man was not to be a mere automation, but was to be able to gain merit and win a place for himself among all of God's creatures by his own efforts. To make this argument more intelligible to ourselves, we might think, for example, of a man like Lincoln who, by his own efforts and in spite of many hardships, won a place of distinction by rising successively to the ranks of a small businessman, a lawyer, a legislator and a president.

45. One can imagine that after listening to this plea made by Love in favor of endowing men with free will, Wisdom might have warned that if men were given free will they might abuse their freedom by acting contrary to the purpose for which they were created and thus commit sin.

46. In answer to such a warning we can imagine that Justice spoke up to declare that if men did commit sin, they would have to be punished. One can then imagine that Justice would turn to Love with the question: "How can you reconcile yourself with the idea of punishment for those you love?"

47. In response to this objection one can imagine that Love, speaking with all the ardor of its own infinite generosity, answered that "If men sin, I myself will go to Bethlehem, to Calvary, to every altar in the world and into every human heart that will receive me in order to bring all of the straying sinners back to the pursuit of their eternal destiny." Hearing this declaration, one can imagine that Wisdom and Justice, admitting defeat in the debate, agreed to the final decision: "Let us endow man with free will."

48. This "debate" is of course, purely imaginary but from what God

has revealed about Himself it would seem that the points made reflect God's thinking about human freedom with substantial accuracy.

MAN'S BODY

49. The history of Christian spirituality shows how varied the atti tudes of even some of the Saints were towards the value and function of the human body. St. Paul told the Corinthians that their bodies were members of Christ and temples of the Holy Spirit, but he also spoke of chastising the body and bringing it under subjection. Some spiritual writers, influenced, perhaps, more than they realized by the teachings of the Manicheans, seemed to look upon the human body as totally evil. Speaking to the world in its Pastoral Constitution on the Church in the Modern World, Vatican II distinguishes between those who under- value the human body and those who idolize it. (*Modern World*, 41).

50. In the same document, the Council gives us its own estimate con- cerning man's body which is remarkable both for its practical common sense and for the deep mystical significance it attaches to the human body. This statement reads:

51. "Though made up of body and soul, man is one. Through his bodily composition he gathers to himself the elements of the material world. Thus they reach their crown through him, and through him raise their voice in free praise of the Creator.

52. "For this reason man is not allowed to despise his bodily life. Rather, he is obliged to regard his body as good and honorable since God has created it and will raise it up on the last day. Nevertheless, wounded by sin, man experiences rebellious stirrings, in his body. But the very dignity of man postulates that man glorify God in his body and forbid it to serve the evil inclinations of his heart." (*Modern World*, 17).

53. Seeking a deeper understanding of God's innermost thoughts concerning man, mystics have long since pointed out that man, made up as he is of body and soul, can be looked upon as a representative of the whole of creation. His body contains inorganic elements in common with the whole material universe. It also has vegetative life in common with the entire plant world as well as sensile cognition and bodily emo- tions in common with the animals. United to an immortal soul, the body is to share in the joys of the beatific vision in heaven for all eter- nity. In the Body of Christ, the whole universe is thus to be united vicariously with the creative Word of God eternally by virtue of the hypostatic union. All things came forth from God through the Word. Through that same Word all things must go back to God. In man, the five senses provide the basic perceptions on which the intellect can rise

as upon a ladder to the knowledge of God while the bodily emotions can serve as a stimulant for that spiritual love by which man is to share in the life of the Trinity which is his eternal home.

54. This teaching of the mystics seems to throw additional light on what Vatican II said when it declared: "God saw all that He had made and it was very good. This natural goodness of theirs takes on a special dignity as a result of their relation to the human person for whose service they were created." (*Laity,* 7). This same mystical teaching helps us to understand better that other text of Vatican II in which we are told that at the end of the world "the human race as well as the entire world which is intimately related to man and achieves its purpose through him, will be perfectly re-established in Christ." (*Church,* 48).

GOD'S ATTITUDE TOWARDS MAN

55. With the help of their laboratory equipment, research workers in the field of medicine can isolate cells, microbes, etc., from various parts of the human body in order to investigate their activities, strengths, weaknesses, etc. Such studies make it possible for the practicing physician not only to make a correct diagnosis of the illnesses of his patients, but also to prescribe the necessary treatments. The important thing for the practicing physician is to deal with the disease germs, not in isolation, but in the human, bodily environment in which they are found.

56. It was not the purpose of Vatican II to do the "laboratory work" needed for the spiritual health of mankind but rather to diagnose the spiritual strengths, weaknesses, etc., to be found among men in actual life. The greatest of all possible strengths, of course, are those which are granted by God Himself, while the weaknesses are those resulting from man's limitations, especially when man seeks to isolate himself from God. It was customary, therefore, for Vatican II to deal with God and man, not as isolated from each other, but as interrelated. For that reason a single paragraph or even a single sentence may deal with subjects as diversified in the spiritual sphere as blood, nerves, etc., are in the physical sphere.

57. This diversity is exemplified in the following paragraphs in which God's own self-revelation, His purpose in creating man, man's destiny and his relationship with the Trinity, etc., are all brought out.

58. "In His goodness and wisdom, God chose to reveal Himself and to make known to us the hidden purposes of His Will (Eph. 1:9) by which through Christ, the Word made flesh, man has access to the Father in the Holy Spirit and comes to share in the divine nature (Eph. 2:18; 2 Pet. 1:4). Through this revelation, therefore, the invisible God

24

(Col. 1:15; 1 Tim. 1:17) out of the abundance of His love, speaks to men as friends (Ex. 33:11; John 15:14-15) and lives among them (Bar. 3:38), so that He may invite and take them into fellowship with Himself. This plan of revelation is realized by deeds and words having an inner unity: the deeds wrought by God in the history of salvation manifest and confirm the teaching and realities signified by the words, while the words proclaim the deeds and clarify the mystery contained in them. By this revelation, then, the deepest truth about God and the salvation of man is made clear to us in Christ Who is the Mediator and at the same time the fullness of all revelation." (*Revelation*, 2).

59. Basing itself on the gospels, Vatican II constantly insists on the necessity of faith but tells us that "it is one of the major tenets of Catholic doctrine that man's response to God in faith must be free." Faith, however, is a supernatural act for which God's supernatural help is necessary. "Man, redeemed by Christ the Savior and through Christ called to be God's adopted son, cannot give his adherence to God revealing Himself unless the Father draw him to offer to God the reasonable and free submission of faith." (*Religious Freedom*, 10).

MAN AS A PARTNER OF GOD

60. Every supernatural action performed by man is an example of man's cooperation with God. In endowing man with many and splendid natural faculties and powers, God intended to exalt men to the dignity of a partner with God in the natural sphere also. "God is Savior and Creator, Lord of human history as well as of salvation history." (*Modern World*, 41). Referring to the efforts men have made down through the centuries to better the circumstances of their lives, Vatican II tells us that "such human activity accords with God's will. For man, created to God's image, received a mandate to subject to himself the earth and all it contains, and so to govern the world with justice and holiness; a mandate to relate himself and the totality of things to Him Who was to be acknowledged as the Lord and Creator of all." (*Modern World*, 34).

61. "This mandate concerns even the most ordinary everyday activities. For while providing the substance of life for themselves and their families, men and women are performing their activities in a way which appropriately benefits society. They can justly consider that by their labor they are unfolding the Creator's work, consulting the advantages of their brother men, and contributing by their personal industry to the realization in history of the divine plan." (*Modern World*, 34).

62. "When, by the work of his hands or with the aid of technology,

man develops the earth so that it can bear fruit and become a dwelling worthy of the whole human family and when he consciously takes part in the life of social groups, he carries out the design of God." (*Modern World,* 57).

63. Referring to the function of parents in transmitting human life, Vatican II also says that God wished thereby "to share with man a certain special participation in His own creative work." (*Modern World,* 50).

64. The Council also urges the laity to "labor vigorously so that by human labor, technical skill and civic culture, created goods may be perfected for the benefit of every last man, according to the design of the Creator and the light of His Word. Let them work to see that created goods are more fittingly distributed among men and that such goods in their own way lead to general progress in human and Christian liberty." In the same section, the Council urges the laity to combine to remedy conditions which "are customarily an inducement to sin" and to work for reforms that "favor the practice of virtue." (*Church,* 36).

65. In its Pastoral Constitution on the Church in the Modern World, Vatican II describes man as a "mystery, and a great one." (*Modern World,* 22). "Although he was made by God in a state of holiness, from the very dawn of history, man abused his liberty at the urging of personified Evil. Man set himself against God and sought fulfillment apart from God. Although he knew God, he did not glorify Him as God, but his senseless mind was darkened and he served the creature rather than the Creator.

66. "What divine revelation makes known to us agrees with experience. Examining his heart, man finds that he has inclinations towards evil too and is engulfed by manifold ills which cannot come from his good Creator. Often refusing to acknowledge God as his beginning, man has disrupted also his proper relationship to his own ultimate goal. At the same time he became out of harmony with himself, with others, and with all created things.

67. "Therefore man is split within himself. As a result, all of human life, whether individual or collective, shows itself to be a dramatic struggle between good and evil, between light and darkness. Indeed, man finds that by himself he is incapable of battling the assaults of evil successfully, so that everyone feels as though he is bound by chains . . ." (*Modern World,* 13).

68. "Within the individual person there too often develops an imbalance between an intellect which is modern in practical matters, and a theoretical system of thought which can neither master the sum total of its ideas, nor arrange them adequately into a synthesis. Likewise an imbalance arises between a concern for practicality and efficiency, and

the demands of moral conscience; also, very often, between the conditions of collective existence and the requisites of personal thought, and even of contemplation. Specialization in any human activity can at length deprive a man of a comprehensive view of reality." (*Modern World*, 8).

69. Summing up the spoken as well as the unspoken pleas of the human heart, Vatican II tells us that "man will always yearn to know, at least in an obscure way, what is the meaning of his life, of his activity, of his death." (*Modern World*, 41). In the very next paragraph of the same section, the Council tells us that "only God, Who created man to His own image and likeness and ransomed him from sin, provides a fully adequate answer to these questions." (*Modern World*, 41).

70. The Council was well aware also of the demand for "fulfillment" which is heard so often in our day. As if in answer to that demand, the Council also declares that "the Church truly knows that only God, Whom she serves, meets the deepest longings of the human heart which is never fully satisfied by what this world has to offer." (*Modern World*, 41).

71. In answer to the question as to what man is, the Council also declares that "since it has been entrusted to the Church to reveal the mystery of God, Who is the ultimate goal of man, she opens up to man at the same time the meaning of his own existence, that is, the innermost truth about himself." (*Modern World*, 41).

72. A detailed discussion about how the Church can fulfill her function in this respect belongs to a later chapter of this book. Concerning the question as to how man is to attain his goal, suffice it here to quote a fourth statement made by Vatican II.

73. "The highest norm of human life is the divine law — eternal, objective, and universal — whereby God orders, directs, and governs the entire universe and all the ways of the human community, by a plan conceived in wisdom and love. Man has been made by God to participate in this law, with the result that, under the gentle disposition of divine Providence, he can come to perceive ever increasingly the unchanging truth. Hence, every man has the duty, and therefore, the right, to seek the truth in matters religious, in order that he may with prudence form for himself right and true judgments of conscience with the use of all suitable means." (*Religious Freedom*, 3).

3. Redemption — Salvation — Justification

74. Man sinned. Throughout that long eternity before time began, God had thought of all men and cherished the plan of allowing men to share eternally in God's own nature, His life, His love and His happiness. Unlike men whose earthly life is measured in decades and who strive to carry out all of their plans in years, days, hours or minutes, God "worked" quietly for billions of years in preparing a dwelling place for men in the universe which was also to serve as a book in which men could discover much of the truth about their Creator.

75. God was in no way surprised when man sinned. It was love for men that had prompted God to grant them free will so that they could gain merit and earn for themselves a greater share in God's life, love and happiness. Deceived by the tempter and seeking "fulfillment apart from God" (*Modern World,* 13) man chose self rather than God and would have lost both if God had not intervened in order to save him. Happily, God "did not abandon men after they had fallen in Adam, but ceaselessly offered them helps to salvation in anticipation of Christ the Redeemer." (*Church,* 2).

76. Man had abused his free will to choose self rather than God but with God's help man could still use that free will to reverse his first choice and choose God instead of self. From the start God had "manifested Himself to our first parents. Then, after their fall, His promise of redemption aroused in them the hope of being saved and from that time on He ceaselessly kept the human race in His care in order to give eternal life to those who perseveringly do good in search of salvation. Then, at the time He had appointed, He called Abraham in order to make of him a great nation. Through the patriarchs, and after them through Moses and the prophets, He taught this nation to acknowledge Himself as the one living and true God, provident Father and just Judge, and to wait for the Savior promised by Him." (*Revelation,* 3).

77. God not only "wishes all men to be saved and come to the knowl-

edge of truth" (*Liturgy*, 5) but his plan in creating man was "to dignify men with a participation in His own divine life." (*Church*, 2). In this plan, conceived in eternity, men were to be "called sons of God, and truly be such." *(Message to Humanity)*.

78. With such premises, it was not surprising that according to God's "logic," a divine Person should be sent to win rebellious men back to their God and Father. It was logical also that the Person sent on such a mission should be the Son. It was through Him that "God made all orders of existence" (*Missions*, 3) and therefore it was through Him also that men were made to the image and likeness of God. The Son is Himself the "image of the invisible God" (*Church*, 2). When therefore the image of God was marred in men by their sins it was logical with divine logic that the Son should be sent to restore that image in men. The Son's intimate connection with men is further stressed by Vatican II when it tells us that before time began the Father "foreknew and predestined" all the elect "to become conformed to the image of His Son, that He should be the first-born of many brethren." (*Church*, 2).

79. If it was logical that the Son of God as Image of the Father should be sent to restore God's image in sinful men, it was equally logical that the Holy Spirit should also cooperate in the work of saving men. The Spirit is the mutual love of Father and Son and it is in this personified Love that man is to be united with the Father, Son and Holy Spirit eternally in heaven and thus achieve the destiny for which he was created.

80. The Father "so loved the world that He gave His own Son to save it" *(Message to Humanity)* but it was through the action of the Holy Spirit that Christ became man. (*Missions*, 4). "Thus, too, Christ was impelled to the work of His ministry when the same Holy Spirit descended upon Him at prayer." (*Missions*, 4). Referring to the continuous action of the Holy Spirit, Vatican II tells us that "Christ completed His work by His death, resurrection and glorious ascension and by the sending of the Holy Spirit." (*Revelation*, 17).

81. These texts of Vatican II reveal once again the intimate relationship existing between man, the three Persons of the Blessed Trinity and Christ Who was established by God "as the source of salvation for the whole world." (*Church*, 17). His humanity is "the instrument of our salvation." (*Liturgy*, 5). Through Christ the Father aimed to "snatch men from the power of darkness and of Satan." (*Missions*, 3). Aside from Christ, there is no salvation. (*Missions*, 7).

CHRIST THE MEDIATOR

82. Vatican II reminded men of the fact that "the Father so loved the

world that He gave His own Son to save it." *(Message to Humanity)*. In the Pastoral Constitution on the Church in the Modern World, the Council also reminded us that "each of us can say with the Apostle: the Son of God 'loved me and gave Himself up for me.' " *(Modern World, 22)*. As is indicated by the very word "Jesus," Christ is indeed the Savior but the very nature of His work, Sacred Scripture, and the piety of the faithful have brought it about that He is also looked upon as a "Mediator" and a "Redeemer."

83. God sent His Son into the world as a Mediator "in order to establish peace or communion between sinful human beings and Himself." *(Missions, 3)*. Through Christ God reconciled all things unto Himself "making peace through the blood of His cross" so that "we might be called sons of God and truly be such." *(Message to Humanity)*.

84. Since Jesus Christ "is God, all divine fullness dwells bodily in Him. According to His human nature, He is the new Adam, made head of a renewed humanity and full of grace and truth. Therefore the Son of God walked the ways of a true incarnation that He might make men sharers in the divine nature." *(Missions, 3)*.

85. Christ did indeed come to reconcile sinful men to God but His purpose was also to reconcile men to each other and to bring light and comfort to them for their journey on earth. "By suffering for us He not only provided us with an example for our imitation. He blazed a trail and if we follow it, life and death are made holy and take on a new meaning." *(Modern World, 22)*.

86. While the immediate aim of mediation is reconciliation between God and man, the ultimate goal is that union with God for which man was created. In view of man's rational nature, the first step towards such union must be made by the mind as it accepts the truths of revelation. Vatican II tells us that "in His goodness and wisdom, God chose to reveal Himself and to make known to us the hidden purposes of His will by which through Christ, the Word made flesh, man has access in the Holy Spirit and comes to share in the divine nature. Through this revelation, therefore, the invisible God, out of the abundance of His love, speaks to men as friends and lives among them so that He may invite them and take them into fellowship with Himself." *(Revelation, 2)*.

87. In the same document, Vatican II tells us that the Father "sent His Son, the eternal Word, Who enlightens all men so that He might dwell among men and tell them the innermost realities about God." *(Revelation, 4)*.

88. Christ "manifested His Father and Himself by deeds and words, and completed His work by His death, resurrection and glorious ascension and by sending the Holy Spirit. Having been lifted up from the earth He draws all men to Himself." *(Revelation, 17)*.

89. When Vatican II tells us that the invisible God speaks to men as friends and invites them into fellowship with Him, or when it says that Christ draws all men to Himself, the Council is not referring merely to a meeting of minds between God and men but points rather to that union of hearts and wills for which man was created. Echoing Christ's attitude in this respect, the Council quotes Christ's own words as follows: "Greater love than this no one has that one lay down his life for his friends." In the same paragraph, the Council reminds us that Christ "commanded His apostles to preach to all peoples the gospel message so that the human race might become the family of God in which the fullness of the law would be love." (*Modern World,* 32).

90. It has been said that there are three things that Christ wants of us more than anything else, viz., understanding, confidence and love. He wants us first of all to understand His attitude and the attitude of His Father towards us. The reason for this is that if we really understand that attitude, we will find it easy to have great confidence in God and in the Son Whom He sent to save us. With this understanding and confidence it will also be easy to deepen our love for God and thereby solve all of our spiritual problems.

91. In this view, one important reason why God revealed Himself and one of the basic reasons for Bethlehem, Calvary, the tabernacle, etc., is to enable us to understand God's attitude towards us and thus set in motion that chain reaction which leads to confidence and boundless love.

CHRIST THE REDEEMER

92. Man's "call to grandeur" (*Modern World,* 13) is shown for the first time in the destiny chosen for him when God created him to His own image and likeness in order that man should have a share in God's own nature, His life, His love and His happiness. Humanly speaking, it seems hard to find a greater proof of God's love for man than in this destiny and in the fact that God used, and still uses, His omnipotence to create each individual soul. And yet, to human eyes, it would seem that God gave a still greater proof of His love when He sought reconciliation with rebellious man by sending His Son as a Mediator to remove the obstacles to union with God by means of His supreme act of redemption. This is why the Church for centuries sang out in the *Exultet* on Holy Saturday: *O Felix Culpa.* It would almost seem as if God wished to add a new title of nobility to man by reason of man's sin. By imprinting on man's soul the sign of his incorporation in Christ's Mystical Body, God provided a proof visible to all the choirs of Heaven that He

had paid an infinite price for man's ransom from wretchedness and slavery.

93. By sin man had "disrupted his proper relationship to his own ultimate goal." . . . He was "out of harmony with himself, with others and with all created things." . . . He was "split within himself. As a result, all of human life, whether individual or collective, shows itself to be a dramatic struggle between good and evil, between light and darkness. Indeed, man finds that by himself he is incapable of battling the assaults of evil successfully so that everyone feels as though he is bound by chains. But the Lord Himself came to free and strengthen man, renewing him inwardly and casting out that prince of this world who held him in the bondage of sin" which blocks "his path to fulfillment." (*Modern World*, 13).

94. As an innocent lamb, Christ, by shedding His own Blood delivered us "from bondage to the devil and sin." (*Modern World*, 22). He came "to heal the contrite of heart" and "to be a bodily and spiritual medicine" for us. (*Liturgy*, 5). With His divine testimony, He confirmed "what revelation proclaimed: that God is with us to free us from the darkness of sin and death and to raise us up to eternal life." (*Revelation*, 4).

95. In obedience to His Father's will, Christ achieved His work by giving "Himself for us that He might redeem us from all iniquity and cleanse for Himself an acceptable people." (*Priests*, 12). He gave His life "as a ransom for many." (*Religious*, 14).

96. Men engaged in social or educational work in our day often speak of the "redemptive" value of knowledge, object lessons, example, etc., for those who have not had the advantage of an adequate education. Even from this view, the example of Christ and His teaching are of immense supplementary importance to His entire work of redemption.

97. The real tragedy of the human race is due mainly to man's disobedience towards his Creator and Vatican II tells us again that Christ by His obedience "brought about redemption." (*Church*, 3).

98. Another cause of much of man's misery in this life is due to avarice and all the sins resulting therefrom. In this connection, Vatican II tells us that Jesus Christ "carried out the work of redemption in poverty and oppression." Christ Jesus, "though He was by nature God . . . emptied Himself taking the nature of a slave, and being rich, He became poor for our sakes." (*Church*, 8).

99. Men love to lord it over their fellow men but "the Son of Man came not that He might be served, but that He might be a servant and give His life as a ransom for the many — that is for all of us." (*Missions*, 3).

100. Theologians tell us that the first of all sins was a sin of pride and

that this was the reason for the fall of the angels who would "not serve." According to Sacred Scripture, it was the tempter's lying promise that they would be "as gods" that induced our first parents to commit their first sin. Christ did indeed establish the Eucharistic Sacrifice to "perpetuate the sacrifice of the Cross" (*Liturgy,* 47) but at the same time He gave us the supreme example of humility by reducing Himself to Food and Drink so as to give life to all of us.

MINISTERIAL MEDIATORSHIP — CO-REDEEMERS

101. Theologians tell us that fallen man would never have been able to make adequate atonement for his sin by his own unaided efforts. It was for this reason that the Son of God became Man in order that His action as Mediator and Redeemer would be of infinite value. He came to do for men what men could not do for themselves, but He did not thereby exempt men from the obligation of doing what they can do with divine help. That He might be truly a man, representative and brother of all men, infinite Wisdom dictated that the Son of God should be born of a woman. This Wisdom also dictated that as Eve by a free act of disobedience brought spiritual death and disaster to mankind, so Mary, the Mother of the God-Man, should be a free instrument in the hand of God for bringing spiritual life and salvation. For this reason, "the Father of Mercies willed that the consent of the predestined Mother should precede the Incarnation." (*Church,* 56). The graciousness and sublimity of God's plan is revealed in the fact that Mary is not only the "Mother of the Son of God" but also "the favorite daughter of the Father and the temple of the Holy Spirit" (*Church,* 53), thus revealing once again the intimacy God wishes men to have with all three Persons of the Blessed Trinity. Because of these gifts of sublime grace, Mary "surpasses all other creatures both in heaven and on earth." (*Church,* 53).

MARY AS MEDIATRIX

102. Though the Church does insist that Jesus Christ is the *one* Mediator between God and man, she also speaks openly of Mary, the Mother of Christ as a "Mediatrix." Vatican II in defending this title for the Blessed Mother explains that "just as the priesthood of Christ is shared in various ways both by sacred ministers and the faithful, and as the one goodness of God is in reality communicated diversely to His creatures, so also the unique mediation of the Redeemer does not ex-

clude, but rather gives rise among creatures to a manifold cooperation which is but a sharing in this unique source." (*Church,* 62).

103. In another place, Vatican II also explains that the "maternal duty of Mary towards men in no way obscures this unique mediation of Christ, but rather shows its power. For all the saving influences of the Blessed Virgin on men originate not from some inner necessity but from the divine pleasure. They flow forth from the superabundance of the merits of Christ, rest on His mediation, depend entirely on it and draw all their power from it. In no way do they impede the immediate union of the faithful with Christ. Rather, they foster this union." (*Church,* 60). It is in this context that we are to understand the title of "mediatrix of all grace" conferred upon Mary.

MARY AS CO-REDEMPTRIX

104. Though some have disputed Mary's right to be called "Co-Redemptrix," St. Pius X himself gave an indulgence for the recitation of a prayer in which this title is given to the Blessed Mother. Vatican II tells us that Mary at the foot of the cross "united herself with a maternal heart to His sacrifice and lovingly consented to the immolation of this Victim which she herself had brought forth." (*Church,* 58).

105. Insofar as it can be said that Christ's obedience, humility, etc., were contributing factors in His redemptive work, one can surely say that Mary's virtues were also factors in her work as Co-Redemptrix. Vatican II tells us that "rightly the holy Fathers see her (Mary) as used by God not merely in a passive way, but as cooperating in the work of human salvation through free faith and obedience. For, as St. Irenaeus says, she 'being obedient, became the cause of salvation for herself and for the whole human race.' Hence, in their preaching, not a few of the early Fathers gladly assert with him: 'the knot of Eve's disobedience was untied by Mary's obedience. What the virgin Eve bound through her unbelief, Mary loosed by her faith.' Comparing Mary with Eve, they call her 'the mother of the living' and still more often they say: 'death through Eve, life through Mary.' " (*Church,* 56). The Council again says that Mary was "after her Son, exalted by divine grace above all angels and men." (*Church,* 66).

MARY'S WORK IN SOULS

106. While this may not be the place to discuss devotion to the Blessed Mother which is dealt with in many other conciliar texts, it is

well to note that Vatican II in its Dogmatic Constitution on the Church says that Mary cooperates with a maternal love in the "birth and development" of the many brethren of Christ, "namely the faithful." (*Church,* 63). The Council furthermore declares that "from the most ancient times, the Blessed Virgin has been venerated under the title of 'God-bearer.' In all perils and needs, the faithful have fled prayerfully to her protection." (*Church,* 66).

OUR ROLE AS SAVIORS, MEDIATORS AND CO-REDEEMERS

107. In a prayer recited publicly by Pope Paul VI immediately after he had ordained a large number of priests during the Eucharistic Congress in Bogota, the Holy Father begged Our Divine Lord to help us understand "how we have been made ministers of Your efficacious mediation." He went on to say that this "ministerial mediation . . . tends to assimilate the sentiment of our personal consciousness to that which filled Your Divine Heart, O Christ, for we too, as though living with You and in You, have become both priests and victims."

108. Vatican II in the text already quoted in connection with the Blessed Virgin, tells us that "just as the priesthood of Christ is shared in various ways both by the sacred ministers and by the faithful . . . the unique mediation of the Redeemer does not exclude but rather gives rise among creatures to a manifold cooperation which is but a sharing of this unique source." (*Church,* 62).

109. Concerning priests, the Council also tells us that "for the penitent or ailing among the faithful, priests exercise fully the ministry of reconciliation and alleviation, and they present the needs and the prayers of the faithful to God the Father. Exercising within the limits of their authority the function of Christ as Shepherd and Head, they gather together God's family as a brotherhood all of one mind and lead them in the Spirit, through Christ to God the Father." (*Church,* 28).

110. Even the laity have their part in Christ's work of Redemption since Vatican II tells us that the People of God, "established by Christ as a fellowship of life, charity and truth is also used by Him as an instrument for the redemption of all." (*Church,* 9).

111. It must be admitted that some people doubt or even deny what has been said about priests as "mediators" and "co-redeemers" but it would seem that they do not grasp the full significance of our doctrine concerning the Mystical Body of Christ and of the Communion of Saints. It was not necessary for God to create such an organism as the Mystical Body of Christ but in His love for mankind He wanted to give

all of us a chance to share to some extent at least in the entire redemptive work of Christ. It is for this same reason that He accepts the spiritual offerings of all the members of His family for inclusion in that treasury which is one of the foundation stones of the Communion of Saints.

JESUS' WORK FOR OUR SANCTIFICATION

112. Christ came into this world not only to save men from their sins but especially also "that all men might be made holy." (*Bishops,* 1). Vatican II tells us that "since human nature as He assumed it was not annulled, by that very fact it has been raised to a divine dignity in our respect too. The process of sanctification is not automatic, however," (*Modern World,* 22), for "all stand in need of Christ, their Model, their Mentor, their Liberator, their Savior, their Source of Life." (*Missions,* 8). Men are "justified in the Lord Jesus and through baptism sought in faith they truly become sons of God and sharers in the divine nature. In this way they are really made holy. Then, too, by God's gifts they must hold on to and complete in their lives this holiness which they have received. They are warned by the Apostle to 'live as becomes saints' and to put on 'as God's chosen ones, holy and beloved, a heart of mercy, kindness, humility, meekness, patience and to possess the fruits of the Spirit unto holiness.' " (*Church,* 10).

113. Vatican II thus enumerates many virtues as factors in man's sanctification but the simplest summary of this process is provided, perhaps, by those ascetic theologians who identify perfection with the so-called love of conformity. Moral as well as ascetic theologians distinguish many kinds of love such as the love of gratitude, desire, benevolence, friendship, complacency, etc., all of which have rich meaning for our relationship with God also. The highest form of love is the love of conformity whereby man conforms his mind to Christ's Mind, his heart to the Heart of Christ and his will to the Will of Christ.

114. It is especially through grace and this kind of love that He who is "the image of the invisible God" . . . restores to the sons of Adam "the divine likeness which had been disfigured from the first sin onward." (*Modern World,* 22).

It is with regard to this love of conformity that these other words of Vatican II have their finest application: "All the elect, before time began, the Father 'foreknew and predestined to become conformed to the image of His Son that He should be the firstborn among many brethren.' " (*Church,* 2). Conforming men's minds to the Mind of God is a prime purpose of all divine revelation while the example of Christ is the greatest challenge to us to conform our hearts and wills to the Heart and Will of Christ as He was conformed in all things to His Father. Vatican II also gives us a practical application of this principle when it tells us that "the world which is entrusted to the loving ministry of the pastors of the Church is that world which God so loved that He gave His only Son for it." (*Priests,* 22).

115. Addressing itself to the world in general, Vatican II gives us the widest application of this principle when it tells us that Christ "revealed to us that 'God is love' . . . and taught us that the new command of love was the basic law of human perfection and hence of the world's transformation. . . . The way of love lies open to all men . . . and is not something that is reserved for important matters but must be pursued chiefly in the ordinary circumstances of life." (*Modern World,* 38).

116. Man, as Vatican II reminds us in many of its documents, was created for the purpose of sharing God's nature, His Life, His Love and His Happiness. Christ, as an innocent lamb, merited that "life for us by the free shedding of His Blood." (*Modern World,* 22). Man, however, is still faced with "a monumental struggle with the powers of darkness" in a battle which "was joined from the very origins of the world and will continue until the last day, as the Lord has attested. Caught in this conflict, man is obliged to wrestle constantly if he is to cling to what is good. Nor can he achieve his own integrity without valiant efforts and the help of God's grace." (*Modern World,* 37).

117. All of the graces needed by fallen man not only to survive in this struggle but also to attain to holiness, were merited by Christ on the Cross. According to God's plan for man, it is a principal function of the Holy Spirit, the mutual love of Father and Son, to distribute the graces merited by the Son of God to the souls of men. Though the Holy Spirit "was already at work in the world before Christ was glorified" (*Missions,* 4), the graces He then bestowed on men were granted as a result of Christ's Passion which is always present to the Trinity in that eternal vision which sees past, present and future as one.

118. For the further unfolding of that saving work which was actualized by the Passion, Death and Resurrection of Christ, the Holy Spirit "came down" on the day of Pentecost "upon the disciples to remain with them forever. On that day the Church was publicly revealed to the multitude and the gospel began to spread among the nations by means of preaching." (*Missions,* 4).

4. The Church

PARTNERSHIP WITH CHRIST

119. Saints and Doctors of the Church remind us that God did indeed create our souls without our cooperation but that He will not save us without such cooperation on our part.

120. One of our greatest glories is to be found in the fact that we can cooperate with God in working out our salvation and this can be said to have been God's real reason for giving us free will. Our own unaided efforts, however, would never have sufficed to remove the obstacles created by sin. Happily for us, our merciful God sent His own Son to do for us what we could never have been able to do for ourselves.

121. Christ's work was sufficient by itself to bring about the salvation of all men but, as the loving Father of a great family, God wanted His children to do what they could do with the help of our Savior to save our brothers and sisters in this family. It was really for this reason that God planned such an organism as the Mystical Body of Christ and the Communion of Saints. It was part of His plan also that those who become members of the Mystical Body of Christ should serve in some slight measure as co-redeemers and co-mediators with Christ.

122. Perhaps the most grandiose part of God's plan was the establishment of the Church not only as the Mystical Body of His Son but as a real partner in the whole work of man's salvation. As the Second Council of the Vatican tells us: "Christ the Lord, Son of the living God, came that He might save His people from their sins and that all men might become holy. Just as He Himself had been sent by the Father, so He also sent His apostles. Therefore He sanctified them, conferring on them the Holy Spirit so that they too might glorify the Father on earth and save men." (*Bishops,* 1).

123. "Before freely giving His life for the world, the Lord Jesus so arranged the ministry of the apostles and so promised to send the Holy

Spirit, that both they and the Spirit were to be associated in effecting the work of salvation always and everywhere. Throughout all ages, the Holy Spirit gives the entire Church 'unity in fellowship and in service; He furnishes her with various gifts, both hierarchical and charismatic.' He vivifies ecclesiastical institutions as a kind of soul and instills into the hearts of the faithful the same mission spirit which animated Christ Himself.'' (*Missions,* 4). As someone has observed: "The Holy Spirit is as necessary for the life of the Church as oxygen is for the life of the human body."

124. Concerning Christ's own action in the Church, Vatican II tells us that "He continually distributes in His Body, that is in the Church, gifts of ministries through which by His own power, we serve each other unto salvation." (*Church,* 7).

125. Stressing the supreme importance of the Church established by Christ, Vatican II tells us that "it is through Christ's Catholic Church alone, which is the all-embracing means of salvation, that the fullness of the means of salvation can be obtained. It was to the apostolic college alone, of which Peter is the head, that we believe our Lord entrusted all the blessings of the new covenant, in order to establish on earth the one Body of Christ into which all those should be incorporated who already belong in any way to God's People." (*Ecumenism,* 3).

THE CHURCH AND HER CHARACTERISTICS

126. Ever since the Second Council of the Vatican, people have often spoken of the Church as the universal sacrament of salvation. In the second paragraph of its Dogmatic Constitution on the Church, the Council tells us that "by her relationship with Christ, the Church is a kind of sacrament or sign of intimate union with God and of the unity of all mankind. She is also an instrument for the achievement of such union and unity." (*Church,* 1). It is her task to bring "all men to full union with Christ" (*Church,* 1) and it is through her that Christ "communicates truth and grace to all." (*Church,* 8).

127. In the same paragraph, Vatican II tells us that the Church is "one interlocked reality which is composed of a divine and a human element. For this reason, by an excellent analogy, this reality is compared to the mystery of the Incarnate Word. Just as the assumed nature inseparably united to the Divine Word serves Him as a living instrument of salvation, so in a similar way, does the communal structure of the Church serve Christ's Spirit Who vivifies it by way of building up the Body." (*Church,* 8).

128. In the Constitution on the Liturgy, Vatican II tells us also that

"It is of the essence of the Church that she is both human and divine, visible and yet invisibly endowed, eager to act yet devoted to contemplation, present in this world yet not at home in it. She is all these things in such a way that in her the human is directed and subordinated to the divine, the visible likewise to the invisible, action to contemplation and this present world to that city yet to come which we seek." (*Liturgy*, 2).

129. The Council also tells us that "Christ, the one Mediator, established and ceaselessly sustains here on earth His Holy Church, the community of faith, hope and charity, as a visible structure." (*Church*, 8).

130. In further describing and analyzing the Church and her functions, the Council tells us that "the Church has been cultivated by the heavenly Vine-dresser as His choice vineyard" and adds that the "true Vine is Christ Who gives life and fruitfulness to the branches, that is, to us. Through the Church we abide in Christ, without Whom we can do nothing." (*Church*, 6).

131. Other ways in which the Council describes the Church are to say that she is "a sheepfold whose one and necessary door is Christ. She is a flock of which God Himself foretold that He would be the Shepherd. Although guided by human shepherds, her sheep are nevertheless ceaselessly led and nourished by Christ Himself, the Good Shepherd, and the Prince of Shepherds Who gave His life for the sheep." (*Church*, 6).

132. Again the Council tells us that the Church is an edifice which "is adorned by various names: the house of God in which dwells His family; the household of God in the Spirit; the dwelling place of God among men and especially the holy temple." (*Church*, 6). Finally we are told that the Church of God "is called the Church of Christ. For He has bought it for Himself with His Blood, has filled it with His Spirit and provided it with those means which befit it as a visible and social unity." (*Church*, 9).

133. Through the gift of His Spirit, Christ after His resurrection founded the Church "as a new brotherly community composed of all who receive Him in faith and love." (*Modern World*, 32). He filled the Church "with heavenly gifts for all eternity in order that we might know the love of God and of Christ for us, a love which surpasses all knowledge." (*Church*, 6). "Joined with Christ in the Church and signed with the Holy Spirit 'Who is the pledge of our inheritance' (Eph. 1:14) we are truly called sons of God and such we are (1 John 3:1). But we have not yet appeared with Christ in the state of glory (Col. 3:4), in which we shall be like to God, since we shall see Him as He is (1 John 3:2). Therefore 'while we are in the body, we are exiled from the Lord' (2 Cor. 5:6) and having the first fruits of the Spirit we groan within our-

selves (Rom. 8:23) and desire to be with Christ (Phil. 1:23). A common love urges us to live more for Him Who died for us and rose again (2 Cor. 5:15). We strive therefore to please the Lord in all things (2 Cor. 5:9). We put on the armor of God that we may be able to stand against ... the devil and resist on the evil day (Eph. 6:11-13)." (*Church,* 48).

134. In His preaching Christ "clearly taught the sons of God to treat one another as brothers. In His prayers He pleaded that all of His disciples should be 'one.' Indeed, as the Redeemer of all He offered Himself for all even to the point of death. 'Greater love than this no one has that one lay down his life for his friends.' He commanded His apostles to preach to all peoples the gospel message so that the human race should become the family of God in which the fullness of the law would be love." (*Modern World,* 32).

135. "While helping the world and receiving many benefits from it, the Church has but a single intention: that God's Kingdom may come and that the salvation of the whole human race may come to pass." (*Modern World,* 45).

136. What the Kingdom of God is, is explained by the Council in its Dogmatic Constitution on the Church as follows: "To carry out the will of the Father, Christ inaugurated the Kingdom of heaven on earth and revealed to us the mystery of the Father. By His obedience, He brought about redemption. The Church, or, in other words, the Kingdom of Christ now present in mystery, grows visibly in the world through the power of God." (*Church,* 3).

137. Lest the faithful, victimized by an unhealthy humanism, should forget what they are in themselves and what they owe to God, the Council tells them that "all the sons of the Church should remember that their exalted status is to be attributed not to their own merits, but to the special grace of Christ. If they fail moreover to respond to that grace in thought, word and deed, not only will they not be saved, but they will be the more severely judged." (*Church,* 14).

138. In order to explain more clearly the function of the Church in God's plan of salvation and to show what it means for the faithful to be "sons of God," the Council tells us that the Church, "contemplating Mary's mysterious sanctity, imitating her charity, and faithfully fulfilling the Father's will, becomes herself a mother by accepting God's word in faith. For by her preaching and by baptism she brings forth to a new and immortal life, children who are conceived of the Holy Spirit and born of God. The Church herself is a virgin who keeps whole and pure the fidelity she has pledged to her Spouse. Imitating the Mother of her Lord, and by the power of the Holy Spirit, she preserves with virginal purity, an integral faith, a firm hope and sincere charity." (*Church,* 64).

THE CHURCH A MYSTERY

139. The title of Chapter I of the Dogmatic Constitution on the Church is: "The Mystery of the Church." In a footnote we read: "The term 'mystery' indicates that the Church, as a divine reality inserted into history, cannot be fully captured by human thought or language." As Paul VI said in his opening allocution at the second session of the Council on September 29, 1963, "The Church is a mystery. It is a reality imbued with the hidden presence of God. It lies, therefore, within the very nature of the Church to be always open to new and greater exploration." (*Church*, 1).

140. How great this mystery of the Church really is can be seen from what Vatican II says about her origin: "Coming forth from the eternal Father's love, founded in time by Christ the Redeemer, and made one in the Holy Spirit, the Church has a saving and eschatological purpose which can be fully attained only in the future world. But she is already present in this world and is composed of men, that is, of members of the earthly city who have a call to form the family of God's children during the present history of the human race, and to keep increasing it until the Lord returns. . . . She serves as a leaven and as a kind of soul for human society as it is to be renewed in Christ and transformed into God's family." (*Modern World*, 40).

141. Again the Council tells us that God "planned to assemble in the holy Church all those who would believe in Christ. Already from the beginning of the world the foreshadowing of the Church took place. She was prepared for it in a remarkable way through the history of the people of Israel and by means of the Old Covenant. Established in the present era of time, the Church was made manifest by the outpouring of the Spirit. At the end of time she will achieve her glorious fulfillment. Then, as may be read in the Holy Fathers, all just men from the time of Adam, 'from Abel, the just one, to the last of the elect,' will be gathered together with the Father in the universal Church." (*Church*, 2).

142. Concerning the function, destiny and unity of the Church, the Council again says: "The Church, then, God's only flock, like a standard lifted high for the nations to see (Is. 11:10-12), ministers the gospel of peace to all mankind (Eph. 2:17-18 in connection with Mk. 16:15), as she makes her pilgrim way in hope towards her goal, the fatherland above (1 Pet. 1:3-9).

"This is the sacred mystery of the unity of the Church, in Christ and through Christ, with the Holy Spirit energizing a variety of functions. The highest exemplar and source of this mystery is the unity, in the Trinity of Persons, of one God, the Father and the Son and the Holy Spirit." (*Ecumenism*, 2).

COMING OF CHRIST AND MISSION OF THE HOLY SPIRIT

143. "Christ the Lord, Son of the living God, came that He might save His people from their sins and that all men might be made holy." (*Bishops*, 1). "What was once preached by the Lord, what was once wrought by Him for the saving of the human race must be proclaimed and spread abroad to the ends of the earth, beginning from Jerusalem. Thus, what He once accomplished for the salvation of all, may in the course of time come to achieve its effect in all." (*Missions*, 3).

144. "To accomplish this goal, Christ sent the Holy Spirit from the Father. The Spirit was to carry out His saving work inwardly and to impel the Church toward her proper expansion." (*Missions*, 4).

145. It is through the Holy Spirit that Christ "has called and gathered together the people of the New Covenant who comprise the Church." (*Ecumenism*, 2). The task of the Holy Spirit is to "forever sanctify the Church" so that all believers may "have access to the Father through Christ in one Spirit. He is the Spirit of life, a fountain of water springing up to eternal life. Through Him, the Father gives life to men who are dead from sin till at last He revives in Christ even their mortal bodies." (*Church*, 4).

146. It is by the seeds of the Word and the preaching of the gospel that the Spirit "calls all men to Christ . . . stirs up in their hearts the obedience of faith," and "in the baptismal font begets to a new life those who believe in Christ." (*Missions*, 15).

147. Referring to the personal relationship existing between the Holy Spirit and each one of the faithful, Vatican II tells us that the Holy Spirit "dwells in the Church and in the hearts of the faithful as in a temple. In them He prays and bears witness to the fact that they are adopted sons." (*Church*, 4). "Allotting His gifts 'to everyone as He will,' He distributes special graces among the faithful of every rank. By these gifts He makes them fit and ready to undertake the tasks or offices advantageous for the renewal and up-building of the Church." (*Church*, 12).

148. One of the most consoling features of the Church as a Mystery is the partnership between the Holy Spirit, the apostles and the faithful which was referred to by Vatican II in the following words:

149. "Before freely giving His life for the world, the Lord Jesus so arranged the ministry of the apostles and so promised to send the Holy Spirit that both they and the Spirit were to be associated in effecting the work of salvation always and everywhere. Throughout all ages, the Holy Spirit gives the entire Church 'unity in fellowship and in service'; He furnishes her with various gifts, both hierarchical and charismatic.

He vivifies ecclesiastical institutions as a kind of soul and instills into the hearts of the faithful the same mission spirit which motivated Christ Himself. Sometimes He visibly anticipates the Apostles' action, just as He unceasingly accompanies and directs it in different ways." (*Missions*, 4).

MISSION OF THE CHURCH

150. "The pilgrim Church is missionary by her very nature. For it is from the mission of the Son and the mission of the Holy Spirit that she takes her origin, in accordance with the decree of God the Father. This decree flows from the 'fountain of love' or charity within God the Father. From Him, Who is 'the origin without origin,' the Son is begotten and the Holy Spirit proceeds through the Son." (*Missions*, 2).

151. A main function of the Church as led by the Holy Spirit is "to make God the Father and His Incarnate Son present and in a sense visible." (*Modern World*, 21).

152. The missionary activity of the Church "is nothing else and nothing less than a manifestation or epiphany of God's will and the fulfillment of that will in the world and in world history. In the course of this history God plainly works out the history of salvation by means of mission." (*Missions*, 9).

153. Vatican II speaks of the Church as "the universal sacrament of salvation" (*Missions*, 1) and tells us that she "has been commissioned by the Lord Christ to bring salvation to every man." (*Communications*, 3). This salvation "is to be achieved by belief in Christ and by His grace. Hence the apostolate of the Church and of all her members is primarily designed to manifest Christ's message by words and deeds and to communicate His grace to the world." (*Laity*, 6).

154. "By means of this missionary activity, God is fully glorified provided that men consciously and fully accept His work of salvation, which He has accomplished in Christ. Through this activity that plan of God is thus fulfilled to which Christ was obediently and lovingly devoted for the glory of the Father Who sent Him." (*Missions*, 7).

155. "Since it has been entrusted to the Church to reveal the mystery of God, Who is the ultimate goal of man, she opens up to man at the same time the meaning of his own existence, that is, the innermost truth about himself." (*Modern World*, 41).

CHURCH TO LEAD MEN TO CHRIST, THE SOURCE OF SALVATION

156. When God sent His Son into this world it was in order that that

Son should become the "source of salvation for all men." (*Church*, 17). "Just as the Son was sent by the Father, so He too sent the apostles (John 20:21) saying: 'Go, therefore, and make disciples of all nations, baptizing them in the name of the Father and of the Son and of the Holy Spirit, teaching them to observe all that I have commanded you; and behold, I am with you all days even unto the consummation of the world.'" (*Church*, 17).

157. The Church is therefore "compelled by the Holy Spirit to do her part towards the full realization of" God's will. (*Church*, 17). Her task is to bring "all men to full union with Christ." (*Church*, 1). Christ had "proclaimed the kingdom of His Father by the testimony of His life and the power of His words." (*Church*, 35). The Church was founded in order that "by spreading the Kingdom of Christ everywhere for the glory of God the Father, she might bring all men to share in Christ's saving redemption; and that through them the whole world might in fact be brought into relationship with Him." (*Laity*, 2). Christ is the King "to whom the nations were given for an inheritance." (*Church*, 13). He is also the Head of that Body which is the Church and the Catholic Church therefore "strives energetically and constantly to bring all humanity with all its riches back to Christ the Head in the unity of the Spirit." (*Church*, 13).

ACTION OF THE HOLY SPIRIT FOR THE CHURCH'S MISSION

158. Few points are emphasized in the Vatican II documents as is the action of the Holy Spirit in the Church. In its decree on the missions, the Council reminds us that "Christ was conceived when the Spirit came upon the Virgin Mary. Thus, too, Christ was impelled to the work of His ministry when the Holy Spirit descended upon Him at prayer. (*Missions*, 4). The Council reminds us also that "doubtless the Holy Spirit was already at work in the world before Christ was glorified" (*Missions*, 4), but it tells us also that Christ had promised to send the Holy Spirit down upon the apostles when He said: "You shall receive power when the Holy Spirit comes upon you, and you shall be witnesses for me in Jerusalem and in Samaria and even to the very ends of the earth." (*Church*, 19).

159. "The apostles were fully confirmed in this mission on the day of Pentecost. . . . By everywhere preaching the gospel which was accepted by their hearers under the influence of the Holy Spirit, the apostles gathered together the universal Church which the Lord established on the apostles and built upon blessed Peter, their chief, Christ Jesus Himself remaining the supreme cornerstone." (*Church*, 19).

45

160. Referring to this same "partnership" between the Holy Spirit and the missioners in our day Vatican II again tells us that "when the Holy Spirit opens their heart, non-Christians may believe and be freely converted to the Lord, and may sincerely cling to Him Who, as 'the way, the truth and the life' fulfills their spiritual expectations and even infinitely surpasses them." (*Missions,* 13).

NECESSITY OF THE CHURCH AND OF MISSION

161. Perhaps never before has the necessity of the Church and of mission work been called into question by priests and missioners as it is being questioned in our day. The reason for this questioning is evidently to be found in the declaration made by Vatican II in its Dogmatic Constitution on the Church concerning the salvation of sincere and well-meaning non-Christians who know nothing about the gospel of Christ or the Church. The declaration reads as follows:

162. "Those also can attain to everlasting salvation who through no fault of their own do not know the gospel of Christ or His Church, yet sincerely seek God, and, moved by grace, strive by their deeds to do His will as it is known to them through the dictates of conscience. Nor does divine Providence deny the help necessary for salvation to those who, without blame on their part, have not yet arrived at an explicit knowledge of God, but who strive to live a good life, thanks to His grace." (*Church,* 16).

163. This teaching is not new. It has long been propounded by certain theologians but seems never to have been stated so clearly by any other ecumenical Council. Those who think that the Church or its missionary work is no longer necessary have simply misinterpreted the mind of Vatican II. This is clear from many other statements contained in the conciliar documents. Concerning the Church's duty to carry on its mission work, the Council tells us that "this duty exists not only in virtue of the express command which was inherited from the apostles. . . . It exists also in virtue of that life which flows from Christ into His members." (*Missions,* 5).

164. The Council itself quotes both texts of the great mission command as given in the gospels of St. Matthew and St. Mark as follows: "Go, therefore, and make disciples of all nations, baptizing them in the name of the Father and of the Son and of the Holy Spirit, teaching them to observe all that I have commanded you" (Mt. 28:19 f); "Go into the whole world; preach the gospel to every creature. He who believes and is baptized shall be saved, but he who does not believe shall be condemned." (Mk. 15:1, 15 f).

46

165. Commenting on Christ's missionary command, Vatican II itself declares that "all must be converted to Him as He is made known by the Church's preaching. All must be incorporated into Him by baptism, and into the Church which is His body. For Christ Himself in explicit terms . . . affirmed the necessity of faith and baptism (Mk. 16:16; John 3:5) and thereby affirmed also the necessity of the Church, for through baptism as through a door men enter the Church. Whosoever, therefore, knowing that the Catholic Church was made necessary by God through Jesus Christ, would refuse to enter her or to remain in her could not be saved." (*Missions, 7*).

166. Commenting on the question of conversion, the Council adds that "this conversion, to be sure, must be regarded as a beginning. Yet it is sufficient that a man realize that he has been snatched away from sin and led into the mystery of the love of God, Who has called him to enter into a personal relationship with Him." (*Missions, 13*).

167. Again the Council speaks of the "Church to which we are all called and in which we acquire sanctity through the grace of God" (*Church, 48*), and says in another context that "it is through Christ's Catholic Church alone, which is the all-embracing means of salvation, that the fullness of the means of salvation can be obtained." (*Ecumenism, 3*).

168. Concerning the way in which men with no knowledge of gospel or Church can be saved, the Council merely says: "God in ways known to Himself can lead those inculpably ignorant of the gospel to that faith without which it is impossible to please Him (Heb. 11:6)." (*Missions, 7*).

169. The necessity of the Church is proven also by the Vatican II statement that "all must be incorporated into Him by baptism" (cf. par. 165 above). The words "incorporated into Him" clearly refer to the fact that the Church is the Mystical Body of Christ — a fact which seems to be ignored by practically all of the so-called dissenters and a high percentage of those who challenge the traditional doctrine concerning the Church. Pertinent to this erratic attitude towards the Church is the statement of Vatican II that "loyalty toward Christ can never be divorced from loyalty toward His Church." (*Priests, 14*).

WHY CHRIST GAVE HIS MISSION COMMAND

170. Since people who know nothing about the gospel of Christ or the Church can, under certain circumstances, be saved, the question may legitimately be asked why Christ imposed such a strong missionary command upon the Church. Down through the centuries most theologians and missiologists were satisfied merely to quote that command

without asking themselves why Christ gave it. This seems to be the reason why people were so pessimistic about the salvation of the countless millions of unbaptized people who lived before the time of Christ and about the salvation of the billions who have died since then or are still alive today.

171. Christ was fully aware that all men from the first that came forth from the creative hands of God down to the last that will ever be born, depend for their salvation on Christ's own redemptive work. He also knew that the Holy Spirit was at work in the hearts of all men to bestow on them the graces they needed and which Christ merited for them. He knew that souls were being saved in "ways known to God" and to Himself as the Son of God. Christ had come to do for men what they *could not do for themselves,* but it was not a part of His Father's plan to dispense men from doing what they *could do with God's help* both for their own salvation and for the salvation of others.

172. Here, surely, was ample reason for issuing His command so as to promote active cooperation on the part of all in His glorious work of redemption. If there is something surprising in the command it is that such a command should have been deemed necessary for Vatican II tells us that working to make the divine message of salvation known and accepted by all men throughout the world" is a "splendid burden." (*Laity,* 3). As members of the Mystical Body of Christ and of the Communion of Saints, all of the faithful have a splendid opportunity to contribute in some small measure to the entire redemptive work of Christ.

EVERY ONE A MISSIONER

173. Such cooperation in the mission work of the Church is heavily emphasized by Vatican II in several of its documents. Thus the Council tells us that "the holy People of God shares also in Christ's prophetic office. It spreads abroad a living witness to Him, especially by means of a life of faith and charity and by offering to God a sacrifice of praise." (*Church,* 12). In its decree on the Apostolate of the Laity, the Council says that "by its very nature, the Christian vocation is also a vocation to the apostolate. No part of the structure of a living body is merely passive but each has a share in the functions as well as in the life of the body. So too, in the Body of Christ, which is the Church, the whole body 'according to the functioning in due measure of each single part, derives its increase' (Eph. 4:16). Indeed, so intimately are the parts linked and inter-related in the body (cf. Eph. 4:16) that the member who fails to make his proper contribution to the development of the Church must be said to be useful neither to the Church nor to himself." (*Laity,* 2).

174. The Council also tells us that not only individuals but communities are involved in the work. For "by the living witness of each one of the faithful and of the whole community, let the particular Church be a sign which points out Christ to others." (*Missions*, 20).

175. The goal in all of this work is that "the entire world may become the People of God, the Body of the Lord, and the Temple of the Holy Spirit and that in Christ, the Head of all, there may be rendered to the Creator and Father of the universe all honor and glory." (*Church*, 17).

176. The driving force which impels the faithful to take part in this work is "the love with which they love God and by which they desire to share with all men in the spiritual goods of both this life and the life to come." (*Missions*, 7). It is "the law of love which is the Lord's greatest commandment" which "impels all the faithful to promote God's glory through the spread of His Kingdom and to obtain for all men that eternal life which consists in knowing the one true God and Him Whom He has sent, Jesus Christ." (*Laity*, 3).

177. It is the Holy Spirit Who "instills into the hearts of the faithful the same mission spirit which motivated Christ Himself." (*Missions*, 4). Apostolic workers are also warned that "in the exercise of their apostolate they must depend on the power of God Who very often reveals the might of the gospel through the weakness of the witnesses." (*Modern World*, 76).

MISSION TO ALL MEN

178. "The Catholic Church has been commissioned by the Lord Christ to bring salvation to all men." (*Communications*, 3). In the Christian community itself, especially among those who seem to understand or believe little of what they practice (*Priests*, 4), "the Church must ever preach faith and repentance. She must prepare them for the sacraments and teach them to observe all that Christ has commanded." (*Liturgy*, 9).

179. Among non-Christians, the "universal design of God for the salvation of the human race is not carried out exclusively in the soul of a man, with a kind of secrecy. Nor is it achieved merely through those multiple endeavors, including religious ones, by which men search for God, groping for Him that they may by chance find Him (though He is not far from any one of us) (Acts 17:27). For these attempts need to be enlightened and purified, even though, through the kindly workings of Divine Providence, they may sometimes serve as a guidance course toward the true God, or as a preparation for the gospel." (*Missions*, 3).

180. "Whatever truth and grace are to be found among the nations as

a sort of secret presence of God," missionary activity "frees from all taint of evil and restores to Christ its maker, Who over-throws the devil's domain and wards off the manifold malice of vice." (*Missions,* 9). In this way, "whatever good is in the minds and hearts of men, whatever good lies latent in the religious practices and cultures of diverse peoples, is not only saved from destruction but is also healed, ennobled and perfected unto the glory of God, the confusion of the devil and the happiness of man." (*Church,* 17).

181. In order that these results may be achieved, Vatican II urges that missioners "profoundly penetrated by the Spirit of Christ, should know the people among whom they live, and should establish contact with them. Thus they themselves can learn by sincere and patient dialogue what treasures a bountiful God has distributed among the nations of the earth. But at the same time, let them try to illumine these treasures with the light of the gospel, to set them free, and to bring them under the dominion of God their Savior." (*Missions,* 11).

182. For the accomplishment of their work among Christians and non-Christians alike, "Christ conferred upon the apostles and their successors the duty of teaching, sanctifying and ruling in His name and power. But the laity, too, share in this priestly, prophetic and royal office of Christ and therefore have their own role to play in the mission of the whole People of God in the Church and in the world." (*Laity,* 2).

MEANS USED BY THE CHURCH IN HER MISSION

183. Among the principal means to be used by the Church in fulfilling her mission is the proclamation of the gospel by which "she prepares her hearers to receive and profess the faith, disposes them for baptism, snatches them from the slavery of error and incorporates them into Christ so that through charity they may grow up into the full maturity of Christ." (*Church,* 17).

184. This preaching "must be nourished and ruled by Sacred Scripture. For in the sacred books, the Father Who is in heaven meets His children with great love and speaks with them; and the force and power in the word of God is so great that it remains the support and energy of the Church, the strength of faith for her sons, the food of the soul, the pure and perennial source of spiritual life. Consequently, these words are perfectly applicable to sacred Scripture: 'For the word of God is living and efficient' (Heb. 4:12) and is able to build up and give the inheritance among all the sanctified (Acts 20:32)." (*Revelation,* 21).

185. By her preaching and by baptism, the Church "brings forth to a new and immortal life children who are conceived by the Holy Spirit and born of God." (*Church,* 64).

186. By such preaching "and by the celebration of the sacraments, whose center and summit is the Eucharist, missionary activity brings about the presence of Christ, the author of salvation." (*Missions*, 9).

187. "The Eucharist shows itself to be the source and apex of the whole work of preaching the gospel. Those under instruction are introduced by stages to a sharing in the Eucharist. The faithful, already marked with the sacred seal of baptism and confirmation, are through the reception of the Eucharist fully joined to the Body of Christ." (*Priests*, 5).

188. The sacraments "are entrusted in a special way to the clergy but the laity, too, have their very important roles to play if they are to be 'fellow-workers for the truth.' It is especially on this level that the apostolate of the laity and the pastoral ministry complement one another." (*Laity*, 6).

189. Let all realize that their first and most important obligation toward the spread of the faith is this: to lead a profoundly Christian life. For their fervor in the service of God and their charity toward others will cause new spiritual inspiration to sweep over the whole Church. Then she will appear as a sign lifted up among the nations (Is. 11:12)." (*Missions*, 36).

SUFFERING AND MISSION

190. "On behalf of Christ's Body which is the Church, they (the apostles) supplied what was wanting of the sufferings of Christ by their own many trials and sufferings (Col. 1:24). Often, too, the blood of Christians was like a seed." (*Missions*, 5).

191. In the same document, Vatican II tells us that "prompted by the Holy Spirit, the Church must walk the same road which Christ walked, a road of poverty and obedience, of service and self-sacrifice to the death, from which death He came forth a victor by His resurrection." (*Missions*, 5).

192. Stressing the value of suffering for mission work, Vatican II tells us again that "it will be the bishop's task to raise up from among his own people, especially the sick and those oppressed by hardship, souls who will offer prayers and penance to God with a generous heart for the evangelization of the world." (*Missions*, 36).

193. Referring to the duration of the Church and her work, Vatican II tells us furthermore that "that divine mission, entrusted by Christ to the apostles, will last until the end of the world (Mt. 28:20) since the gospel which was to be handed down by them is for all time the source of all life for the Church. For this reason, the apostles took care to appoint successors in this hierarchically structured society." (*Church*, 20).

5. The Church as the People of God, the Mystical Body of Christ, and the Communion of Saints

THE CHURCH AS THE PEOPLE OF GOD

194. "It has not pleased God to call men to share His life merely as individuals without any mutual bonds. Rather, He wills to mold them into a people in which His sons, once scattered abroad, can be gathered together (John 11:52)." (*Missions*, 2).

195. "All men are called to belong to the new People of God. Wherefore this People, while remaining one and unique is to be spread throughout the whole world and must exist in all ages so that the purpose of God's will may be fulfilled. In the beginning God made human nature one. After His children were scattered He decreed that they should at length be unified again (John 11:52). It was for this reason that God sent His Son, Whom He appointed heir of all things (Heb. 1:2) that He might be Teacher, King and Priest of all, the Head of the new and universal people of the sons of God. For this God finally sent His Son's Spirit as Lord and Lifegiver. He it is Who, on behalf of the whole Church and each and every one of those who believe, is the principle of their coming together and remaining together in the teaching of the apostles and in fellowship, in the breaking of bread and in prayers (Acts 2:42, Greek text)." (*Church*, 13).

196. "Thus, the Church shines forth 'as a people made one with the unity of the Father, the Son and the Holy Spirit.' " (*Church*, 4).

197. This "messianic people has for its Head, Jesus Christ 'Who was delivered up for our sins, and rose again for our justification' and Who now . . . reigns in glory in Heaven. The heritage of this people are the dignity and freedom of the sons of God in whose hearts the Holy Spirit dwells as in His temple." (*Church*, 9).

198. "After being lifted up on the cross and glorified, the Lord Jesus

poured forth the Spirit Whom He had promised and through Whom He has called and gathered together the people of the New Covenant, who comprise the Church, into a unity of faith, hope and charity. For, as the apostle teaches, the Church is: 'one Body and one Spirit, even as you are called in one hope of your calling; one Lord, one faith, one baptism.' " (*Ecumenism*, 2).

199. The members of this people "share a common dignity from their rebirth in Christ. They have the same filial grace and the same vocation to perfection. They possess in common one salvation, one hope and one undivided charity. Hence, there is in Christ and in the Church no inequality on the basis of race or nationality, social condition or sex because 'there is neither Jew nor Greek; there is neither slave nor freeman; there is neither male nor female. For you are all "one" in Christ Jesus.' " (*Church*, 32).

200. "Those who believe in Christ, who are reborn not from a perishable but from an imperishable seed through the Word of the living God (1 Pet. 1:23), not from the flesh but from water and the Holy Spirit (John 3:5-6) are finally established as 'a chosen race, a royal priesthood, a holy nation, a purchased people. . . . You who in times past were not a people but are now the People of God (1 Pet. 2:9-10)." (*Church*, 9).

201. "Established by Christ as a fellowship of life, charity and truth," the People of God is also "used as an instrument for the redemption of all and is sent forth into the whole world as the light of the world and the salt of the earth." (*Church*, 9).

202. "The People of God finds its unity first of all in the Word of the living God" . . . through which "the spark of faith is struck in the hearts of unbelievers and fed in the hearts of the faithful." (*Priests*, 4).

203. This holy people also shares "in Christ's prophetic office. It spreads abroad a living witness to Him, especially by means of a life of faith and charity and by offering to God a sacrifice of praise, the tribute of lips that give honor to His name (Heb. 13:15). The body of the faithful as a whole, anointed as they are by the Holy One (John 2:20, 27) cannot err in the matters of belief. Thanks to a supernatural sense of the faith which characterizes the People as a whole it manifests this unerring quality when 'from the bishops down to the last member of the laity' (Augustine) it shows universal agreement in matters of faith and morals." (*Church*, 12).

204. The law of the People of God is "the new commandment to love as Christ loved us. Its goal is the kingdom of God which has been begun by God Himself on earth and which is to be further extended until it is brought to perfection by Him at the end of time." (*Church*, 9).

205. For achieving this goal, one important condition is that the people should undertake "the narrow way of the Cross." (*Missions*, 1).

Another condition is that the people "taking part in the Eucharistic Sacrifice which is the fount and apex of the whole Christian life . . . offer the divine Victim to God and offer themselves along with it. . . . Strengthened anew at the holy table by the Body of Christ, they manifest in a practical way that unity of God's people which is suitably signified and wondrously brought about by this most awesome sacrament." (*Church,* 11).

THE CHURCH AS THE MYSTICAL BODY OF CHRIST

206. Perhaps the most tragic symptom in the life of the Church today is the tendency among many Catholics to ignore the description of the Church as "the Body of Christ," while emphasizing the term "People of God." The use of the term "People of God" is eminently justified not only by Vatican II but also by Holy Scripture. In the Dogmatic Constitution on the Church the term "People of God" is used 50 times while the term "Body of Christ" occurs only 40 times. In the Decree on the Missions, the corresponding figures are 13 and 12. The importance of the two terms can be appreciated especially in the light of the Vatican II statement that "before giving His life for the world, the Lord Jesus so arranged the ministry of the apostles and so promised to send the Holy Spirit that both they and the Spirit were to be associated in effecting the work of salvation always and everywhere." (*Missions,* 4).

207. The term "People of God" leads one to think mainly of the human contribution to the work of salvation while the term "Body of Christ" seems to stress the action of Christ and of the Holy Spirit. Yet the Vatican documents repeatedly remind us of Christ's own words at the Last Supper: "Without Me you can do nothing."

208. In this democratic age it is not surprising that many like to stress the rights and the works of the people, but it is utterly disastrous for the whole Church if the action of Christ and the Holy Spirit is underestimated. In this connection, it is highly significant that in many of the statements made against the "institutional Church" the term "Body of Christ" is rarely if ever used, while the words "People of God" are often used in defense of the "democratic" rights of priests and laity.

WORK OF CHRIST AND THE HOLY SPIRIT IN THE MYSTICAL BODY

209. In describing the origin of the Church as the Mystical Body of Christ, Vatican II tells us that Our Savior "having been lifted up from the earth, is drawing all men to Himself. Rising from the dead He sent His life-giving Spirit upon His disciples and through this Spirit es-

tablished His body, the Church, as the universal sacrament of salvation. Sitting at the right hand of the Father, He is continually active in the world, leading men to the Church and through her joining them more closely to Himself." (*Church*, 48).

210. The Head of this body is Christ Himself. "He is the image of the invisible God and in Him all things came into being. He has priority over everyone and in Him all things hold together. He is the Head of that body which is the Church. He is the beginning, the firstborn from the dead, so that in all things He might have the first place (Col. 1:15-18). By the greatness of His power He rules the things of heaven and the things of earth, and with His all-surpassing perfection and activity He fills the whole body with the riches of His glory." (*Church*, 7).

211. To equip His Body, the Church, to do what it was established to do, Christ made "His whole Mystical Body share in the anointing by the Holy Spirit with which He Himself had been anointed." (*Priests*, 2).

212. The Church is subject to her Head. "For in Him dwells all the fullness of the Godhead bodily (Col. 2:9). He fills the Church, which is His Body and His fullness, with divine gifts (Eph. 1:22-23) so that she may grow and reach all the fullness of God." (*Church*, 7).

213. In another context the Council tells us that "by divine institution, Holy Church is structured and governed with a wonderful diversity. 'For just as in one body we have many members, yet all the members have not the same function, so we, being many, are one body in Christ, but severally members of one another.' " (*Church*, 32). The Council also quotes St. Paul to the effect that " 'the whole body, supplied and built up by joints and ligaments, attains a growth that is of God.' He continually distributes in His Body, that is, in the Church, gifts and ministries through which, by His own power, we serve each other unto salvation so that, carrying out the truth in love, we may through all things grow up into Him Who is our Head." (*Church*, 7).

214. Referring specifically to the action of the Holy Spirit in the Mystical Body of Christ, the Council says that the Holy Spirit, "existing as one and the same Being in the Head and in the members, vivifies, unifies, and moves the whole body. This He does in such a way that His work could be compared by the holy Fathers with the functioning which the soul fulfills in the human body, whose principle of life the soul is." (*Church*, 7). "The Holy Spirit does in the whole Church what the soul does in all the members of one body (St. Augustine)." (*Missions*, 5).

215. "It is the Holy Spirit, dwelling in those who believe, pervading and ruling over the entire Church, Who brings about that marvelous communion of the faithful and joins them together so intimately in Christ that He is the principle of the Church's unity. By distributing

various kinds of spiritual gifts and ministries (1 Cor. 12:4-11) He enriches the Church of Jesus Christ with different functions 'in order to perfect the saints for a work of ministry for building up the body of Christ.' " (*Ecumenism*, 2).

216. Concerning Christ's own action in His Mystical Body, the Church, Vatican II says that "Christ, the Son of God, Who with the Father and the Holy Spirit is praised as being 'alone holy,' loved the Church as His Bride, delivering Himself up for her. This He did that He might sanctify her. He united her to Himself as His own body and crowned her with the Holy Spirit for God's glory. Therefore, every one in the Church . . . is called to holiness." (*Church*, 39). In that Mystical Body, "the life of Christ is poured into believers who, through the sacraments are united in a hidden and real way to Christ Who suffered and was glorified. Through baptism we are formed in the likeness of Christ, 'for in one Spirit we were baptized into one body.' " (*Church*, 7).

217. "As members of the living Christ, all the faithful have been incorporated into Him and made like unto Him through baptism, confirmation and the Eucharist. Hence all are duty-bound to cooperate in the expansion and growth of His Body, so that they can bring it to fullness as swiftly as possible." (*Missions*, 36).

218. "That Church, Holy and Catholic, which is the Mystical Body of Christ, is made up of the faithful who are organically united in the Holy Spirit through the same faith, the same sacraments and the same government and who, combining into various groups held together by a hierarchy, form separate Churches or rites. Between these, there flourishes such an admirable brotherhood that this variety within the Church in no way harms her unity, but rather manifests it. For it is the mind of the Catholic Church that each individual Church or rite retain its traditions whole and entire, while adjusting its way of life to the various needs of time and place." (*Eastern Churches*, 2).

219. "All the faithful scattered throughout the world are in communion with each other in the Holy Spirit, so that 'he who occupies the See of Rome knows the people of India are his members.' " (*Church*, 13).

220. As members of Christ's Body, all are also "members one of the other" and are to "render mutual service according to the different gifts bestowed on each." (*Modern World*, 32).

221. All members of this Body also "have a part in the mission of the whole Body" . . . and "ought to hallow Jesus in his heart and bear witness to Jesus in the spirit of prophecy." (*Priests*, 2).

222. "All the members ought to be molded into Christ's image until He is formed in them (Gal. 4:19). For this reason we who have been made like unto Him, who have died with Him and have been raised up in Him, are taken up into the mysteries of His life, until we reign to-

gether with Him (Phil. 3:21; 2 Tim. 2:11; Eph. 2:6; Col. 2:12). Still in pilgrimage upon the earth, we trace in trial and under oppression the paths He trod. Made one with His sufferings as the body is one with the head, we endure with Him, that with Him we may be glorified." (*Church*, 7).

223. "Truly partaking of the body of the Lord in the breaking of the Eucharistic bread, we are taken up into communion with Him and with one another. 'Because the bread is one, we though many, are one body, all of us who partake of the one bread' (1 Cor. 10:17). In this way all of us are made members of His body (1 Cor. 12:27) 'but severally members of one another' (Rom. 12:5)." (*Church*, 7).

THE COMMUNION OF SAINTS

224. Concerning the traditional belief in the triumphant, militant and suffering branches of the one, holy, Catholic Church, Vatican II declares that it "accepts with great devotion the venerable faith of our ancestors regarding this vital fellowship with our brothers who are in heavenly glory or who are still being purified after death." (*Church*, 51).

225. "The Church has always believed that the apostles, and Christ's martyrs who had given the supreme witness of faith and charity by the shedding of their blood, are quite closely joined with us in Christ. She has always venerated them with special devotion, together with the Blessed Virgin Mary and the holy angels. The Church too has devoutly implored the aid of their intercession. To these were soon added those who had imitated Christ's virginity and poverty more exactly, and finally others whom the outstanding practice of the Christian virtues and the divine charisma recommended to the pious devotion and imitation of the faithful." (*Church*, 50).

226. "As long as all of us, who are sons of God and comprise one family in Christ (Heb. 3:6), remain in communion with one another in mutual charity and in one praise of the Most Holy Trinity, we are responding to the deepest vocation of the Church and partaking in a foretaste of the liturgy of consummate glory. For when Christ shall appear and the glorious resurrection of the dead takes place, the splendor of God will brighten the heavenly city and the Lamb will be the lamp thereof (Apoc. 21:24). Then in the supreme happiness of charity the whole Church of the saints will adore God and 'the Lamb Who was slain' (Apoc. 5:12), proclaiming with one voice: 'To Him Who sits upon the throne, and to the Lamb, blessing and honor and glory and dominion forever and ever' (Apoc. 5:13-14)." (*Church*, 51).

227. "It is not only by the title of example that we cherish the memory of those in heaven. We do so still more in order that the union of the whole Church may be strengthened in the Spirit by the practice of fra-

ternal charity (Eph. 4:1-6). For just as the communion among wayfarers brings us closer to Christ, so companionship with the saints joins us to Christ, from Whom as from their fountain and head issue every grace and the life of God's People itself." (*Church,* 50).

228. "It is supremely fitting, therefore, that we love those friends and fellow-heirs of Jesus Christ, who are also our brothers and extraordinary benefactors, that we render due thanks to God for them and 'suppliantly invoke them and have recourse to their prayers, their power and help in obtaining benefits from God through His Son, Jesus Christ Our Lord Who is our sole Redeemer and Savior *(Trent).*' For by its very nature every genuine testimony of love which we show to those in heaven tends towards and terminates in Christ, Who is the 'crown of all saints.' Through Him it tends towards and terminates in God, Who is wonderful in His saints and is magnified in them." (*Church,* 50).

229. "By reason of the fact that those in Heaven are more closely united with Christ, they establish the whole Church more firmly in holiness, lend nobility to the worship which the Church offers on earth to God, and in many ways contribute to its greater upbuilding (1 Cor. 12:12-27). For after they have been received into their heavenly home and are present to the Lord (2 Cor. 5:8), through Him and with Him and in Him, they do not cease to intercede with the Father for us. Rather, they show forth the merits which they won on earth through the one Mediator between God and man, Christ Jesus (1 Tim. 2:5). There they served God in all things and filled up in their flesh whatever was lacking of the sufferings of Christ on behalf of His Body which is the Church (Col. 1:24). Thus by their brotherly interest our weakness is very greatly strengthened." (*Church,* 49).

230. Referring to all of those members of the Church who are still "exiles on earth," who are "being purified" in Purgatory or are already "in glory," Vatican II stresses the point that "in various ways and degrees, we all partake in the same love for God and neighbor and all sing the same hymn of glory to our God. For all who belong to Christ, having His Spirit, form one Church and cleave together in Him (Eph. 4:16). Therefore the union of the wayfarers with the brethren who have gone to sleep in the peace of Christ is not in the least interrupted. On the contrary, according to the perennial faith of the Church, it is strengthened through the exchanging of spiritual goods." (*Church,* 49).

231. "Very much aware of the bonds linking the whole Mystical Body of Christ, the pilgrim Church from the very first ages of the Christian religion has cultivated with great piety the memory of the dead. Because it is 'a holy and wholesome thought to pray for the dead that they may be loosed from sins' (2 Mach. 12:46), she has also offered prayers for them." (*Church,* 50).

58

232. Stressing the consoling aspects of this doctrine, Vatican II also says that "to every thoughtful man a solidly established faith provides the answer to his anxiety about what the future holds for him. At the same time faith gives him the power to be united in Christ with his beloved ones who have already been snatched away by death. Faith arouses the hope that they have found true life with God." (*Modern World*, 18).

233. "Our union with the Church in Heaven is put into effect in its noblest manner when with common rejoicing we celebrate together the praise of the divine Majesty. Then all those from every tribe and tongue and people and nation (Apoc. 5:9) who have been redeemed by the Blood of Christ and gathered together into one Church, with one song of praise magnify the one and triune God. Such is especially the case in the sacred liturgy, where the power of the Holy Spirit acts upon us through sacramental signs. Celebrating the Eucharistic Sacrifice, therefore, we are most closely united to the worshipping Church in Heaven as we join with and venerate the memory first of all of the glorious ever-Virgin Mary, of Blessed Joseph and the blessed apostles and martyrs and of all the saints." (*Church*, 50).

234. "The Church has also included in the annual cycle, days devoted to the memory of the martyrs and other saints. Raised up to perfection by the manifold grace of God and already in possession of eternal salvation, they sing God's perfect praise in heaven and offer prayers for us. By celebrating the passage of these saints from earth to heaven, the Church proclaims the paschal mystery as achieved in the saints who have suffered and been glorified with Christ; she proposes them to the faithful as examples who draw all to the Father through Christ, and through their merits she pleads for God's favors." (*Liturgy*, 104).

235. Among all of the saints — and even among the angels — no one could even approximate the holiness or glory of her who is acclaimed as the Queen of the Universe. "Indeed she is 'clearly the mother of the members of Christ . . . since she cooperated out of love so that there might be born in the Church the faithful, who are members of Christ, their Head' (Augustine). Therefore she is also hailed as a pre-eminent and altogether singular member of the Church, and as the Church's model and exemplar in faith and charity. Taught by the Holy Spirit, the Catholic Church honors her with filial affection and piety as a most beloved mother." (*Church*, 53).

236. Since Mary was chosen by God to be the Mother of His Son — the Mother, therefore, of God — it is not surprising that in the words of Vatican II, she was "exalted by divine grace above all angels and men." (*Church*, 66).

6. The Institutional Church

THE HIERARCHY

237. It seems safe to say that most of the troubles that have been plaguing the Catholic Church since the Second Council of the Vatican are due to the fact that many Catholics have come to think of the Church only as an "institution" and practically ignore the fact that the Church is the Mystical Body of Christ.

238. The problem has been vastly complicated in our democratic age by the notion that since the Church is also the "People of God," this people should be ruled in a "democratic" way. That, in itself of course, is not a bad viewpoint and it is well to recall that in modern times, apologists for the Church have often stressed the "democratic" idea that even a poor country boy can become a priest, a bishop or even a pope.

239. Vatican II did lay stress on the Church as an institution and on the importance and the rights of all of the members of the Church. Unfortunately, many of the texts in the Council documents have been taken out of their context and interpreted from an anthropocentric viewpoint. The unhappy result has been that what the Council actually did say has been grossly misinterpreted and the Church itself deplorably betrayed.

240. Volumes written by solid and competent theologians will be needed to provide a really adequate analysis of the problem and to correct the mass of confused, misleading and completely false conclusions that have been drawn by contemporary writers from distorted Vatican II texts. Meanwhile, however, it seems imperative to assemble at least enough of the conciliar declarations to warn those who are being victimized by a whole horde of erratic commentators and to persuade those victims to make a deeper study of the conciliar documents themselves.

241. Vatican II in its Dogmatic Constitution on the Church tells us that Christ chose His apostles, formed them into a group over which He placed Peter, shared with them His power to make all peoples into His disciples and gave them governing powers over those disciples.

242. "The Lord Jesus, after praying to the Father and calling to Himself those whom He desired, appointed twelve men who would stay in His company and whom He would send to preach the kingdom of God" (Mk. 3:13-19; Mt. 10:1-42).

"These apostles (Lk. 6:13) He formed after the manner of a college or fixed group, over which He placed Peter, chosen from among them (John 21:15-17). He sent them first to the children of Israel and then also to all nations (Rom. 1:16) so that as sharers in His power they might make all men His disciples, sanctifying and governing them (Mt. 28:16-20). Thus they would spread His Church and by ministering to it under the guidance of the Lord, would shepherd it all days even to the consummation of the world (Mt. 28:20)." (*Church*, 19).

243. The Council also tells us that "Christ, the one Mediator, established and ceaselessly sustains here on earth His holy Church, the community of faith, hope and charity, as a visible structure. Through her He communicates truth and grace to all. But the society furnished with hierarchical agencies and the Mystical Body of Christ are not to be considered as two realities, nor are the visible assembly and the spiritual community, nor the earthly Church and the Church enriched with heavenly things. Rather, they form one interlocked reality which is comprised of a divine and a human element. For this reason by an excellent analogy, this reality is compared to the mystery of the Incarnate Word. Just as the assumed nature inseparably united to the divine Word serves Him as a living instrument of salvation, so, in a similar way, does the communal structure of the Church serve Christ's Spirit, Who vivifies it by way of building up the Body (Eph. 4:16)." (*Church*, 8).

244. Through the apostles, Christ also "made their successors, the bishops, partakers of His consecration and His mission. These in turn, have legitimately handed on to different individuals in the Church, various degrees of participation in this ministry. Thus the divinely established ecclesiastical ministry is exercised in different levels by those who from antiquity have been called bishops, priests and deacons." (*Church*, 27).

245. "Christ, the great Prophet Who proclaimed the kingdom of His Father by the testimony of His life and the power of His words, continually fulfills His prophetic office until His full glory is revealed. He does this not only through the hierarchy who teach in His name and

with His authority, but also through the laity. For that very purpose He made them His witnesses and gave them understanding of the faith and the grace of speech (Acts 2:17-18; Apoc. 19:10) so that the power of the gospel might shine forth in their daily social and family life." (*Church*, 35).

246. How theocentric the view of Vatican II is concerning clerics who are not yet deacons and concerning the laity is also brought out by the Council in the following texts of the same document. Of these clerics, the Council says that they are "called by the Lord and set aside as His portion. . . . They are bound to bring their hearts and minds into accord with the splendid calling which is theirs, and will do so by constancy in prayer, burning love, and attention to whatever is true, just and of good repute, all for the glory of God." (*Church,* 41).

247. The members of the clergy referred to in the preceding paragraph belong to the 'institutional Church' in a very special way since tonsure and the lower orders were instituted by the Church herself for the exercise of various functions in the Church as an organization. With regard to the clergy as well as the laity in their dealings with those whom Christ has put in positions of authority in the Church Vatican II again declares: "With ready Christian obedience, laymen as well as all disciples of Christ should accept whatever their sacred pastors, as representatives of Christ, decree in their role as teachers and rulers in the Church. Let laymen follow the example of Christ Who, by His obedience, even at the cost of death, opened to all men the blessed way to the liberty of the children of God. Nor should they omit to pray to God for those placed over them, who keep watch as having to render an account of their souls, so that they may render this account with joy and not with grief (Heb. 13:17)." (*Church,* 37).

ACTION OF THE HOLY SPIRIT IN THE INSTITUTIONAL CHURCH

248. It was "by communicating His Spirit to his brothers called together from all peoples" that "Christ made them mystically into His body." (*Church,* 7). It is the Holy Spirit also Who constantly strengthens "the organic structure and inner harmony of the Church" (*Church,* 27) and "unfailingly preserves the form of government established by Christ in His Church." (*Church,* 27).

249. In a text that deserves to be constantly repeated, Vatican II tells us that "before freely giving His life for the world, the Lord Jesus so arranged the ministry of the apostles and so promised to send the Holy Spirit that both they and the Spirit were to be associated in effecting the

work of salvation always and everywhere. Throughout the ages, the Holy Spirit gives the entire Church 'unity in fellowship and in service; He furnishes her with various gifts, both hierarchical and charismatic.' He vivifies ecclesiastical institutions as a kind of soul and instills into the hearts of the faithful the same mission spirit which motivated Christ Himself. Sometimes He visibly anticipates the apostles' action, just as He unceasingly accompanies and directs it in different ways." (*Missions*, 4).

250. "Allotting His gifts 'to everyone as He will' (1 Cor. 12:11)" the Holy Spirit "distributes special graces among the faithful of every rank. By these gifts He makes them fit and ready to undertake the various tasks or offices advantageous for the renewal and upbuilding of the Church according to the words of the apostle: 'the manifestation of the Spirit is given to everyone for profit' (1 Cor. 12:7). These charismatic gifts, whether they be the most outstanding or the more simple and widely diffused, are to be received with thanksgiving and consolation, for they are exceedingly suitable and useful for the needs of the Church." (*Church*, 12).

251. "Still, extraordinary gifts are not to be readily sought after nor are the fruits of apostolic labor to be presumptuously expected from them. In any case, judgment as to their genuineness and proper use belongs to those who preside over the Church, and to whose special competence it belongs, not, indeed, to extinguish the Spirit, but to test all things and hold fast to that which is good (1 Th. 5:12, 19-21)." (*Church*, 12).

STRUCTURE OF THE CHURCH

252. "By divine institution, Holy Church is structured and governed with a wonderful diversity. 'For just as in one body we have many members, yet all members have not the same function, so we, the many, are one body in Christ, but severally members of one another' (Rom. 12:4-5)." (*Church*, 32).

253. "If therefore everyone in the Church does not proceed by the same path, nevertheless all are called to sanctity and have received an equal privilege of faith through the justice of God (2 Pet. 1:1). And if by the will of Christ some are made teachers, dispensers of mysteries, and shepherds on behalf of others, yet all share a true equality with regard to the dignity and to the activity common to all the faithful for the building up of the Body of Christ.

254. "For the distinction which the Lord made between sacred ministers and the rest of the People of God entails a unifying purpose, since

pastors and the other faithful are bound to each other by a mutual need. Pastors of the Church, following the example of the Lord, should minister to one another and to the other faithful. The faithful in their turn should enthusiastically lend their cooperative assistance to their pastors and teachers. Thus in their diversity all bear witness to the admirable unity of the Body of Christ. This very diversity of graces, ministries and works gathers the children of God into one, because 'all these things are the work of one and the same Spirit' (1 Cor. 12:11)." (*Church, 32*).

255. Referring to the origin of authority in the Church along with its nature and function, Vatican II reminds priests of the "necessary unity with their brothers in the ministry, most of all those whom the Lord has appointed the visible rulers in the Church." (*Priests, 15*). It is Christ Himself Who "instituted in His Church a variety of ministries which work for the good of the whole body. For those ministers who are endowed with sacred power are servants of their brethren, so that all who are of the People of God, and therefore enjoy a true Christian dignity, can work towards a common goal freely and in an orderly way and can arrive at salvation." (*Church, 18*).

256. Again the Council tells us that the Church, "which is the Mystical Body of Christ, is made up of the faithful who are organically united in the Holy Spirit through the same faith, the same sacraments and the same government, and who, combining into various groups held together by a hierarchy, form separate Churches and rites." (*Eastern Churches, 2*).

257. The existence of "ranks . . . even in the inner structure" of the People of God is explained by Vatican II when it says that "this diversity among the members arises either by reason of their duties, as in the case of those who exercise the sacred ministry for the good of their brethren, or by reason of their situation and way of life, as is the case of those many who enter the religious state and, tending towards holiness by a narrower path, stimulate their brethren by their example." (*Church, 13*).

THE POPE, THE BISHOPS AND THE MAGISTERIUM

258. "To the Lord was given all power in heaven and on earth." (*Church, 24*). As the Father had sent Him, so He also sent the apostles, conferring on them "and their successors the duty of teaching, sanctifying and ruling in His name and power." (*Laity, 2*). The Holy Spirit, sent by Christ, gives the Church "unity of fellowship and service. He furnishes and directs her with various gifts, both hierarchical and charismatic and adorns her with the fruits of His grace." (*Church, 4*).

259. "In this Church of Christ the Roman Pontiff is the successor of St. Peter, to whom Christ entrusted the feeding of his sheep and lambs. Hence, by divine institution, he (the Roman Pontiff) enjoys full, immediate and universal authority over the care of souls. Since he is pastor of all the faithful, his mission is to provide for the common good of the universal Church and . . . individual churches. He holds, therefore, a primacy of ordinary power over all the Churches." (*Bishops*, 2).

260. The bishops as successors of the apostles, "faithfully recognizing the primacy and pre-eminence of their head (the Pope), exercise their own authority for the good of their own faithful and indeed of the whole Church, with the Holy Spirit constantly strengthening its organic structure and inner harmony." (*Church*, 22).

261. "The Church is, by the will of Christ, the teacher of the truth. It is her duty to give utterance to, and authoritatively to teach that truth which is Christ Himself and also to declare and confirm by her authority those principles of the moral order which have their origin in human nature itself." (*Religious Freedom*, 4).

262. The "infallibility with which the divine Redeemer willed His Church to be endowed in defining a doctrine of faith and morals extends as far as extends the deposit of divine revelation, which must be religiously guarded and faithfully expounded. This is the infallibility which the Roman Pontiff, the head of the college of bishops, enjoys in virtue of his office, when, as the supreme shepherd and teacher of all the faithful who confirms his brethren in their faith (Lk. 22:32) he proclaims by a definitive act some doctrine of faith or morals. Therefore, his definitions, of themselves, and not from the consent of the Church, are justly styled irreformable, for they are pronounced with the assistance of the Holy Spirit, an assistance promised to him in blessed Peter. Therefore, they need no approval of others, nor do they allow an appeal to any other judgment. For then the Roman Pontiff is not pronouncing judgment as a private person. Rather, as the supreme teacher of the universal Church, as one in whom the charism of the infallibility of the Church herself is individually present, he is expounding or defending a doctrine of the Catholic faith." (*Church*, 25).

263. "The Church is concerned to move ahead daily toward a deeper understanding of the sacred Scriptures so that she may unceasingly feed her sons with the divine words. Therefore she also rightly encourages the study of the holy Fathers of both East and West and of sacred liturgies. Catholic exegetes then and other students of sacred theology, working diligently together and using appropriate means, should devote their energies, under the watchful care of the sacred teaching office of the Church, to an exploration and exposition of the divine writings." (*Revelation*, 23).

264. "Sacred tradition and sacred Scripture form one sacred deposit of the word of God, which is committed to the Church. . . . The task of authentically interpreting the word of God, whether written or handed on, has been entrusted exclusively to the living teaching office of the Church, whose authority is exercised in the name of Jesus Christ. This teaching office is not above the word of God, but serves it, teaching only what has been handed on, listening to it devoutly, guarding it . . . and explaining it faithfully by divine commission and with the help of the Holy Spirit; it draws from this one deposit of faith everything which it presents for belief as divinely revealed." (*Revelation,* 10).

265. "It is clear, therefore, that sacred tradition, sacred Scripture and the teaching authority of the Church, in accord with God's most wise design, are so linked and joined together that one cannot stand without the others, and that all together and each in its own way under the action of one Holy Spirit contribute effectively to the salvation of souls." (*Revelation,* 10).

266. "The Spirit guides the Church into the fullness of truth" (*Church,* 4), and under His guiding light "revelation is thus religiously preserved and faithfully expounded in the Church. The Roman Pontiff and the bishops, in view of their office and of the importance of the matter, strive painstakingly and by appropriate means to inquire properly into that revelation and to give apt expression to its contents. But they do not allow that there could be any new public revelation pertaining to the divine deposit of faith." (*Church,* 25).

267. "When either the Roman Pontiff or the body of bishops together with him defines a judgment, they pronounce it in accord with revelation itself. All are obliged to maintain and be ruled by this revelation, which, as written or preserved by tradition, is transmitted in its entirety through the legitimate succession of bishops and especially through the care of the Roman Pontiff himself." (*Church,* 25).

268. "Bishops, teaching in communion with the Roman Pontiff, are to be respected by all as witnesses to divine and Catholic truth. In matters of faith and morals, the bishops speak in the name of Christ and the faithful are to accept their teaching and adhere to it with religious assent of soul. This religious submission of will and of mind must be shown in a special way to the authentic teaching authority of the Roman Pontiff, even when he is not speaking ex cathedra. That is, it must be shown in such a way that his supreme magisterium is acknowledged with reverence, the judgments made by him are sincerely adhered to, according to his manifest mind and will. His mind and will in the matter may be known chiefly either from the character of the documents, from his frequent repetition of the same doctrine, or from his manner of speaking." (*Church,* 25).

BISHOPS

269. Since a bishop "is sent by the Father to govern His family, the bishop must keep before his eyes the example of the Good Shepherd Who came not to be ministered unto, but to minister, and to lay down his life for His sheep." (*Church*, 27).

270. "Bishops too have been appointed by the Holy Spirit and are the successors of the apostles as pastors of souls. Together with the Supreme Pontiff and under his authority, they have been sent to continue throughout the ages, the work of Christ, the eternal Pastor." (*Bishops*, 2).

271. "Episcopal consecration, together with the office of sanctifying, also confers the offices of teaching and governing. (These, however, by their very nature, can be exercised only in hierarchical communion with the head and the members of the college.) For from tradition, which is expressed especially in the liturgical rites and the practice of the Church both of the East and the West, it is clear that, by means of the imposition of hands and the words of consecration, the grace of the Holy Spirit is so conferred, and the sacred character so impressed, that bishops in an eminent and visible way undertake Christ's own role as Teacher, Shepherd and High Priest, and that they act in His Person." (*Church*, 21).

272. "In the bishops, for whom priests are assistants, our Lord Jesus Christ, the supreme High Priest, is present in the midst of those who believe. For, sitting at the right hand of God the Father, He is not absent from the gathering of His high priests, but above all through their excellent service He is preaching the Word of God to all nations, and constantly administering the sacraments of faith to those who believe. By their paternal role (1 Cor. 4:15) He incorporates new members into His Body by a heavenly regeneration, and finally by their wisdom and prudence He directs and guides the people of the New Testament in its pilgrimage toward eternal happiness." (*Church*, 21).

BISHOPS AS TEACHERS

273. Bishops are "authentic teachers, that is, teachers endowed with the authority of Christ, who preach to the people committed to them the faith they must believe and put into practice. By the light of the Holy Spirit they make that faith clear, bringing forth from the treasury of revelation new things and old, making faith bear fruit and vigilantly warding off any errors that threaten their flock." (*Church*, 25).

274. The ultimate goal of "bishops is that all men may walk 'in all

goodness and justice and truth' (Eph. 5:9)" and that all may know "the whole mystery of Christ," namely, "those truths the ignorance of which is ignorance of Christ." (*Bishops,* 11, 12).

BISHOPS AS SANCTIFIERS

275. "A bishop, marked with the fullness of Orders is the 'steward of the grace of the supreme priesthood,' especially in the Eucharist, which he offers or causes to be offered, and by which the Church constantly lives and grows." (*Church,* 26). Selected to shepherd the Lord's flock, bishops are also "servants of Christ and stewards of the mysteries of God. To them has been assigned the bearing of witness to the gospel of God's grace and to the ministration of the Spirit and of God's glorious power to make men just." (*Church,* 21).

276. "In fulfilling their duty to sanctify, bishops . . . should constantly exert themselves to have the faithful know and live the paschal mystery more deeply through the Eucharist and thus become a firmly knit body in the solidarity of Christ's love. 'Intent upon prayer and the ministry of the word' (Acts 6:4) they should devote their labor to this end, that all those committed to their care may be of one mind in prayer and through the reception of the sacraments may grow in grace and be faithful witnesses to the Lord." (*Bishops,* 15).

277. "By thus praying and laboring for the people, bishops channel the fullness of Christ's holiness in many ways and abundantly. By the ministry of the word they communicate God's power to those who believe unto salvation (Rom. 1:16). Through the sacraments, the regular and fruitful distribution of which they direct by their authority, they sanctify the faithful. . . . They earnestly exhort and instruct their people to carry out with faith and reverence their part in the liturgy and especially in the holy Sacrifice of the Mass." (*Church,* 26).

278. A bishop should be a good shepherd and true father who "excels in the spirit of love and solicitude for all and to whose divinely conferred authority all gratefully submit themselves. Let him so gather and mold the whole family of his flock that everyone, conscious of his own duties, may live and work in the communion of love." (*Bishops,* 16).

279. "Above all, upon the bishop rests the heavy responsibility for the sanctity of his priests. Hence he should exercise the greatest care on behalf of the continual formation of his priests. He should gladly listen to them, indeed, consult them, and have discussions with them about those matters which concern the necessities of pastoral work and the welfare of the diocese." (*Priests,* 7).

280. "Bishops govern the particular churches entrusted to them as the vicars and ambassadors of Christ. This they do by their counsel, exhortations and example, as well, indeed, as by their authority and sacred power. This power they use only for the edification of their flock in truth and holiness, remembering that he who is greater should become as the lesser and he who is the more distinguished, as the servant (Lk. 22:26-27). This power, which they personally exercise in Christ's name, is proper, ordinary and immediate, although its exercise is ultimately regulated by the supreme authority of the Church and can be circumscribed by certain limits for the advantage of the Church or of the faithful." (*Church*, 27).

281. "The pastoral office or the habitual and daily care of their sheep is entrusted to them (the bishops) completely. Nor are they to be regarded as vicars of the Roman Pontiff, for they exercise an authority which is proper to them and are quite correctly called 'prelates,' heads of the people whom they govern. Their power, therefore, is not destroyed by the supreme and universal power. On the contrary, it is affirmed, strengthened and vindicated thereby, since the Holy Spirit unfailingly preserves the form of government established by Christ the Lord in His Church." (*Church*, 27).

282. "With their helpers, the priests and deacons, bishops have therefore taken up the service of the community, presiding in place of God over the flock whose shepherds they are, as teachers of doctrine, priests of sacred worship and officers of good order. Just as the role that the Lord gave individually to Peter, the first of the apostles, is permanent and was meant to be transmitted to his successors, so also the apostles' office of nurturing the Church is permanent and was meant to be exercised without interruption by the sacred order of bishops. Therefore, this sacred Synod teaches that by divine institution bishops have succeeded to the place of the apostles as shepherds of the Church, and that he who hears them, hears Christ, while he who rejects them, rejects Christ and Him who sent Christ (Lk. 10:16)." (*Church*, 20).

VIRTUES AND ATTITUDES OF A BISHOP

283. "In the first place, the shepherds of Christ's flock ought to carry out their ministry with holiness, eagerness, humility and courage in imitation of the eternal High Priest, the Shepherd and Guardian of our souls. They will thereby make this ministry the principal means of their own sanctification. Those chosen for the fullness of the priesthood are

gifted with sacramental grace enabling them to exercise a perfect role of pastoral charity through prayer, sacrifice and preaching as through every form of a bishop's care and service. They are enabled to lay down their life for their sheep fearlessly, and, made a model for their flock (1 Pet. 5:3), can lead the Church to ever-increasing holiness through their own example." (*Church*, 41).

284. "By reason of the gift of the Holy Spirit which is given to priests in sacred ordination, bishops should regard them as necessary helpers and counsellors in the ministry and in the task of teaching, sanctifying and nourishing the People of God." (*Priests*, 7).

285. "Keeping in mind the fullness of the sacrament of orders which the bishop enjoys, priests must respect in him the authority of Christ, the Chief Shepherd." (*Priests*, 7).

286. "By divine condescension the laity have Christ for their brother Who, though He is the Lord of all, came not to be served but to serve (Mt. 20:28). They also have for their brothers those in the sacred ministry who by teaching, by sanctifying and by ruling with the authority of Christ so feed the family of God that the new commandment of charity may be fulfilled by all. St. Augustine puts this very beautifully when he says: 'What I am for you terrifies me; what I am with you consoles me. For you I am a bishop; but with you I am a Christian. The former is a title of duty; the latter, one of grace. The former is a danger; the latter, salvation." (*Church*, 32).

287. Commenting on the pastoral spirit of the Second Council of the Vatican in his Christmas message for 1965, shortly after the end of the Council, Pope Paul VI declared: "The dominant mood of the Council was inspired by the gospel image of the shepherd setting out in pursuit of the lost sheep, allowing himself no peace until he has found it. The awareness that mankind, represented with touching simplicity by the straying sheep, belongs to the Church was the guiding principle of the Council. For mankind, by a universally valid decree, does belong to the Church. . . . Mankind belongs to her by right of love, since the Church, no matter how distant or un-cooperative or hostile mankind may be, can never be excused from loving the human race for which Christ shed His Blood." (*Message to Humanity*).

7. Priests

PRIESTS AND THE TRINITY

288. Of all of the misrepresentations now current concerning the teachings of Vatican II, the most disastrous, perhaps, are those which deal with the priesthood. Defections from the ranks of Christ's chosen ones have always occurred since the days of Judas who was an apostle though probably not a priest. Clerical scandals were common at certain periods and in certain areas down through the centuries. Rarely, however, has the Church's teaching concerning the priesthood been under such a systematic attack as in our anthropocentric and ultra-democratic age. The problem existed long before Vatican II, of course, but it has become so serious in recent years that a lay convert, Professor Dietrich von Hildebrand, could declare publicly a few years ago that the condition of the Catholic clergy today is very similar to the condition of the European clergy just before the outbreak of the so-called Protestant Reformation. It was to restore the true theocentric and Christo-centric concept of the priesthood that Vatican II made so many declarations concerning what priests are and should be.

289. Thus, in its decree on the Ministry and Life of Priests, the Council declares that "God, Who alone is holy and bestows holiness, willed to raise up for Himself as companions and helpers men who would humbly dedicate themselves to the work of sanctification. Hence, through the ministry of the bishop, God consecrates priests so that they can share by a special title in the priesthood of Christ. Thus, in performing sacred functions they can act as the ministers of Him Who in the liturgy continually exercises His priestly office on our behalf by the action of the Holy Spirit." (*Priests*, 5).

290. Stressing the theocentric outlook demanded of priests and the fact that it was the Holy Spirit that called them, the Council says in the same decree that "among the virtues most necessary for the priestly

ministry must be named that disposition of soul by which priests are always ready to seek not their own will but the will of Him Who sent them. For the divine work which the Holy Spirit has raised them to fulfill transcends all human energies and human wisdom: '. . . the foolish things of the world has God chosen to put to shame the wise' (1 Cor. 1:27)." (*Priests*, 15).

291. After stating that priests are "consecrated by the anointing of the Spirit and sent by Christ," the Council tells us that "they are grounded in the life of the Spirit while they exercise the ministry of the Spirit and of justice as long as they are docile to Christ's Spirit, Who vivifies and leads them." (*Priests*, 12).

CHRIST AND THE PRIEST

292. "Christ sent the apostles just as He Himself had been sent by the Father. Through these same apostles He made their successors, the bishops, sharers in His consecration and mission. Their ministerial role has been handed down to priests in a limited degree." (*Priests*, 2). "All priests, together with the bishops, so share the same priesthood and ministry of Christ that the very unity of their consecration and mission requires their hierarchical communion with the order of bishops." (*Priests*, 7).

293. "The sacerdotal office of priests is conferred by that special sacrament through which priests by the anointing of the Holy Spirit, are marked with a special character and are so configured to Christ the Priest that they can act in the Person of Christ the Head." (*Priests*, 2).

294. "Since every priest in his own way represents the Person of Christ Himself, he is also enriched with special grace. Thus, serving the people committed to him and the entire People of God, he can more properly imitate the perfection of Him Whose part he takes." (*Priests*, 12).

295. "Though they differ from one another in essence and not only in degree, the common priesthood of the faithful and the ministerial or hierarchical priesthood are nonetheless interrelated. Each of them in its own special way is a participation in the one priesthood of Christ. The ministerial priest, by the sacred powers he enjoys, molds and rules the priestly people. Acting in the Person of Christ, he brings about the Eucharistic Sacrifice, and offers it to God in the name of all the people. For their part, the faithful join in the offering of the Eucharist by virtue of their royal priesthood. They likewise exercise that priesthood by receiving the sacraments, by prayer and thanksgiving, by the witness of a holy life, and by self-denial and active charity." (*Priests*, 10).

296. "By the sacrament of orders, priests are configured to Christ the Priest so that as ministers of the Head and co-workers of the episcopal order, they can build up and establish His whole Body which is the Church." (*Priests*, 12).

297. By this same sacrament of orders and "by the mission they receive from their bishops, priests are promoted to the service of Christ the Teacher, the Priest and the King. They share in His ministry of unceasingly building up of the Church on earth into the People of God, the Body of Christ and the Temple of the Holy Spirit." (*Priests*, 1).

298. Christ Himself works through His priests "to achieve unceasingly in the world that same will of the Father by means of the Church. Hence Christ remains the source and origin of their unity of life. Therefore priests attain to the unity of their lives by uniting themselves with Christ in acknowledging the Father's will and in the gift of themselves on behalf of the flock committed to them." (*Priests*, 14).

WORK OF THE PRIEST

299. "Priests are taken from among men and appointed for men in the things which pertain to God, in order to offer gifts and sacrifices for sins. Hence they deal with other men as with brothers. This was the way that the Lord Jesus, the Son of God, a man sent by the Father to men, dwelt among us and willed to become like His brothers in all things except sin. The holy apostles imitated Him; and blessed Paul, the teacher of the gentiles, who was 'set apart for the gospel of God' (Rom. 1:1), declares that he has become all things to all men that he might save all." (*Priests*, 3).

300. "The purpose which priests pursue by their ministry and life is the glory of God the Father as it is to be achieved in Christ. That glory consists in this: that men knowingly, freely and gratefully accept what God has achieved perfectly through Christ and manifest it in their whole lives. Hence, whether engaged in prayer and adoration, preaching the word, offering the Eucharistic Sacrifice, ministering the other sacraments, or performing any of the other works of the ministry for men, priests are contributing to the extension of God's glory as well as to the development of divine life in men. Since all of these activities result from Christ's Passover, they will be crowned in the glorious return of the same Lord when He Himself hands over the kingdom to His God and Father." (*Priests*, 2).

301. "To the degree of their authority and in the name of their bishop, priests exercise the office of Christ the Head and Shepherd. Thus they gather God's family together as a brotherhood of living unity, and

lead it through Christ and in the Spirit to God the Father. For the exercise of this ministry, as for other priestly duties, spiritual power is conferred upon them for the upbuilding of the Church." (*Priests,* 6).

302. Priests "have become living instruments of Christ the eternal Priest so that through the ages they can accomplish His wonderful work of re-uniting the whole society of men with heavenly power." (*Priests,* 12).

303. Priests "are united in the single goal of building up Christ's Body. . . . Each and every priest, therefore, is joined to his brother priests by a bond of charity, prayer and every kind of cooperation. In this manner, they manifest that unity with which Christ willed His own to be one, so that the world might know that the Son had been sent by the Father." (*Priests,* 8).

STATUS OF THE PRIEST

304. "Inasmuch as it is connected with the episcopal order, the priestly office shares in the authority by which Christ Himself builds up, sanctifies, and rules His Body." (*Priests,* 2).

305. "Although priests do not possess the highest degree of the priesthood, and although they are dependent on bishops in the exercise of their power, they are nevertheless united with the bishops in sacerdotal dignity. By the power of the sacrament of orders, and in the image of Christ, the eternal High Priest (Heb. 5:1-10; 7:24; 9:11-28), they are consecrated to preach the gospel, shepherd the faithful, and celebrate divine worship as true priests of the New Testament. Partakers of the function of Christ, the sole Mediator (1 Tim. 2:5) on their level of ministry, they announce the divine word to all. They exercise this sacred function of Christ most of all in the Eucharistic liturgy or synaxis. There, acting in the Person of Christ, and proclaiming His mystery, they join the offering of the faithful to the sacrifice of their Head. Until the coming of the Lord (1 Cor. 11:26) they re-present and apply the Sacrifice of the Mass, the one sacrifice of the New Testament, namely the sacrifice of Christ offering Himself once and for all to His Father as a spotless victim (Heb. 9:11-28)." (*Church,* 28).

306. "By reason of the gift of the Holy Spirit which is given to priests in sacred ordination, bishops should regard them as necessary helpers and counsellors in the ministry and in the task of teaching, sanctifying and nourishing the People of God." (*Priests,* 7).

307. "In virtue of the sacrament of orders, priests of the New Testament exercise the most excellent and necessary office of father and teacher among the People of God, and for them. They are, nevertheless,

together with all of Christ's faithful, disciples of the Lord, made sharers in His kingdom by the grace of God Who calls them. For priests are brothers among brothers with all those who have been reborn at the baptismal font. They are all members of one and the same Body of Christ, whose upbuilding is entrusted to all." (*Priests, 9*).

308. "Having become from the heart a pattern to the flock," let priests "so lead and serve their local community that it may worthily be called by that name by which the one and entire People of God is distinguished, namely, the Church of God (1 Cor. 1:2; 2 Cor. 1:1 and passim). They should remember that by their daily life and interests they are showing the face of a truly priestly and pastoral ministry to the faithful and the unbeliever, to Catholics and non-Catholics, and that to all men they should bear witness about truth and life, and, as good shepherds, go after those also (Lk. 15:4-7) who, though baptized in the Catholic Church, have fallen away from the sacraments or even from the faith." (*Church, 28*).

MINISTRY OF THE WORD

309. "The mission of the Church concerns the salvation of men, which is to be achieved by belief in Christ and by His grace. Hence the apostolate of the Church and of all her members is primarily designed to manifest Christ's message by words and deeds and to communicate His grace to the world. This work is done mainly through the ministry of the Word and of the sacraments, which are entrusted in a special way to the clergy. But the laity, too, have their very important roles to play if they are to be 'fellow-workers for the truth' (3 John 8). It is especially on this level that the apostolate of the laity and the pastoral ministry complement one another." (*Laity, 6*).

310. "Since in their own measure priests participate in the office of the apostles, God gives them the grace to be ministers of Christ Jesus among the people. They shoulder the sacred task of the gospel, so that the offering of the people can be made acceptable through the sanctifying power of the Holy Spirit. For, through the apostolic proclamation of the gospel, the People of God is called together and assembled so that when all who belong to this people have been sanctified by the Holy Spirit, they can offer themselves as a 'sacrifice, living, holy, pleasing to God' (Rom. 12:1)." (*Priests, 2*).

311. "The ministry of priests . . . derives its power and force from the Sacrifice of Christ. Its aim is that 'the entire commonwealth of the redeemed, that is, the community and society of the saints, be offered as a universal sacrifice to God through the High Priest Who in His Passion

offered His very self for us that we might be the body of so exalted a Head' (St. Augustine)." (*Priests,* 2).

312. "The People of God finds its unity first of all through the Word of the living God, which is quite properly sought from the lips of priests. Since no one can be saved who has not first believed, priests as co-workers with their bishops, have as their primary duty the proclamation of the gospel of God to all. In this way they fulfill the Lord's command: 'Go into the whole world and preach the gospel to every creature' (Mark 16:15). Thus they establish and build up the People of God."

313. "For through the saving Word, the spark of faith is struck in the hearts of unbelievers, and fed in the hearts of the faithful. By this faith the community of the faithful begins and grows. As the apostle says: 'Faith depends on hearing and hearing on the word of Christ' (Rom. 10:17).

314. "Towards all men, therefore, priests have the duty of sharing the gospel truth in which they themselves rejoice in the Lord. And so, whether by honorable behavior among the nations they lead them to glorify God, whether by openly preaching they proclaim the mystery of Christ to unbelievers, whether they hand on the Christian faith or explain the Church's teaching, or whether in the light of Christ they strive to deal with contemporary problems, the task of priests is not to teach their own wisdom but God's Word and to summon all men urgently to conversion and to holiness." (*Priests,* 4).

315. "In the exercise of their teaching office" pastors must "preach God's Word to all the Christian people so that, rooted in faith, hope and charity, they may grow in Christ and that the Christian community may bear witness to that charity which the Lord commanded." (*Bishops,* 30). "As educators in the faith, priests must see to it, either by themselves or through others, that the faithful are led individually in the Holy Spirit to a development of their own vocation as required by the gospel." (*Priests,* 6).

316. "All the clergy must hold fast to the sacred Scriptures through diligent sacred reading and careful study. . . . This cultivation of Scripture is required lest any of them become an 'empty preacher of the Word of God outwardly who is not a listener to it inwardly' (St. Augustine." (*Revelation,* 25). "As St. Paul wrote to Timothy: 'Meditate on these things, give thyself entirely to them, that thy progress may be manifest to all. Take heed to thyself and to thy teaching, be earnest in them. For in doing so thou wilt save both thyself and those who hear thee' (1 Tim. 4:15-16)." (*Priests,* 13).

317. "Remembering that it is the Lord Who opens hearts and that sublime utterance comes not from themselves but from God's power, in

the very act of preaching His word priests will be united more closely with Christ the Teacher and be led by His Spirit. Thus joined to Christ, they will share in God's love, whose mystery, hidden for ages, has been revealed in Christ." (*Priests*, 13).

318. "As priests search for a better way to share with others the fruits of their own contemplation, they will win a deeper understanding of 'the unfathomable riches of Christ' (Eph. 3:8) as well as the manifold wisdom of God." (*Priests*, 13).

319. To further Christian maturity "priests should help men see what is required and what is God's will in the great and small events of life. Christians should also be taught that they do not live for themselves alone but, according to the demands of the new law of charity, every man must administer to others the grace he has received. In this way all will discharge in a Christian manner their duties within the community of men." (*Priests*, 6).

320. "Announcing the gospel among the nations he (the missioner) confidently makes known the mystery of Christ whose ambassador he is. Thus, in Christ he dares to speak as he ought (Eph. 6:19 f; Acts 4:31) and is not ashamed of the scandal of the cross. Following in his Master's footsteps, meek and humble of heart, he shows that His yoke is easy and His burden light (Mt. 11:29 f). By a truly evangelical life, in much patience, in long-suffering, in kindness, in unaffected love (2 Cor. 6:4 f) he bears witness to his Lord, if need be, to the shedding of his blood." (*Missions*, 24).

SACRAMENTAL MINISTRY

321. When referring to the sacrament of baptism, the Second Council of the Vatican usually stressed the action of the Holy Spirit in conferring supernatural life on those who are baptized and said little about the human minister of the sacrament. More is said about our priestly power to forgive sins and to offer up the Holy Sacrifice of the Mass.

EUCHARIST

322. "As ministers of sacred realities, especially in the Sacrifice of the Mass, priests represent the Person of Christ in a special way. He gave Himself as a victim to make men holy. Hence, priests are invited to imitate the realities they deal with. Since they celebrate the mystery of the Lord's death, they should see to it that every part of their being is dead to evil habits and desires." (*Priests*, 13).

77

323. The Council reminds us also that it is "in the name of the whole Church" that "the Lord's Sacrifice is offered in the Eucharist in an unbloody and sacramental manner until He returns." (*Priests,* 2).

324. "Priests fulfill their chief duty in the mystery of the Eucharistic Sacrifice. In it the work of our redemption continues to be carried out. For this reason, priests are strongly urged to celebrate Mass every day, for even if the faithful are unable to be present, it is an act of Christ and the Church." (*Priests,* 13).

325. In the same section, Vatican II tells us that "while priests are uniting themselves with the act of Christ the Priest, they are offering their whole selves every day to God. While being nourished by the Body of Christ, their hearts are sharing in the love of Him Who gives Himself as food for His faithful ones." (*Priests,* 13).

326. Again in its Decree on the Missionary Activity of the Church, the Council says that "by means of their own ministry, which deals principally with the Eucharist as the source of perfecting the Church they (priests) are in communion with Christ the Head and are leading others to this communion. Hence they cannot help realizing how much is yet wanting to the fullness of that Body, and how much therefore must be done if it is to grow from day to day. They will consequently organize their pastoral activity in such a way that it will serve to spread the gospel among non-Christians." (*Missions,* 39).

327. "In discharging their duty to sanctify their people, pastors should arrange for the celebration of the Eucharistic Sacrifice to be the center and culmination of the whole life of the Christian community. They should labor to see that the faithful are nourished with spiritual food through the devout and frequent reception of the sacraments and through intelligent and active participation in the liturgy." (*Bishops,* 30).

328. Priests "must lead the faithful along to an ever-improved spirit of prayer offered throughout the whole of life according to the graces and needs of each. They must persuade everyone to the discharge of the duties of his proper state of life and bring the saintlier ones to an appropriate exercise of the evangelical counsels." (*Priests,* 5). Thus "through the ministry of priests, the spiritual sacrifice of the faithful is made perfect in union with the Sacrifice of Christ, the sole Mediator." (*Priests,* 2).

THE SACRAMENT OF PENANCE

329. "For the penitent or ailing among the faithful, priests exercise fully the ministry of reconciliation and alleviation and they present the needs and prayers of the faithful to God the Father." (*Church,* 28).

330. "In the spirit of Christ the Shepherd, priests should train the faithful to submit their sins with a contrite heart to the Church in the sacrament of penance. Thus, mindful of the Lord's words: 'Repent, for the kingdom of God is at hand' (Mt. 4:17) the people will be drawn closer to Him each day." (*Priests*, 5).

331. "In a similar way, priests are joined with the intention and love of Christ . . . when they show themselves entirely and always ready to perform the office of the sacrament of penance as often as the faithful reasonably request it." (*Priests*, 13).

THE PRIEST AS RULER

332. Those pastors who were "selected to shepherd the Lord's flock, are servants of Christ and stewards of the mysteries of God. To them has been assigned the bearing of witness . . . to the ministration of the Spirit and of God's glorious power to make men just." (*Church*, 21)

333. "Priests, therefore, should preside in such a way that they seek the things of Jesus Christ, not the things which are their own. They must work together with the lay faithful and conduct themselves in their midst after the example of their Master, Who among men 'has not come to be served but to serve, and to give His life as a ransom for many.' " (*Priests*, 9).

334. "Guiding and nourishing God's people, priests are inspired by the love of the Good Shepherd to give their lives for their sheep. They are ready to make the supreme sacrifice, following the example of those priests who even in our time have not refused to lay down their lives." (*Priests*, 13).

335. "As rulers of the community, priests ideally cultivate the asceticism proper to a pastor of souls, renouncing their own conveniences, seeking what is profitable for the many and not for themselves, so that the many may be saved. They are always going to greater lengths to fulfill their pastoral duties more adequately. Where there is need, they are ready to undertake new pastoral approaches under the lead of the loving Spirit Who breathes where He will." (*Priests*, 13).

336. "By assuming the role of the Good Shepherd, priests will find in the very exercise of pastoral love the bond of priestly perfection which will unify their lives and activities." (*Priests*, 14).

337. "Let the clergy highly esteem the arduous apostolate of the laity. Let them train the laity to become conscious of the responsibility which as members of Christ they bear for all men. Let them instruct them deeply in the mystery of Christ, introduce them to practical methods, and be at their side in difficulties, according to the tenor of the Coun-

cil's Constitution on the Church *(Lumen Gentium)* and its Decree on the Apostolate of the Laity *(Apostolicam Actuositatem)*." *(Missions,* 21).

THE PRIEST'S SPIRITUAL LIFE

338. "The shepherds of Christ's flock ought to carry out their ministry with holiness, eagerness, humility and courage in imitation of the eternal High Priest, the Shepherd and Guardian of souls. They will thereby make this ministry the principal means of their own sanctification. Those chosen for the fullness of the priesthood are gifted with sacramental grace enabling them to exercise a perfect role of pastoral charity through prayer, sacrifice and preaching as through every form of a bishop's care and service. They are enabled to lay down their life for their sheep fearlessly, and, made a model for their flock (1 Pet. 5:3), can lead the Church to ever-increasing holiness through their own example." *(Church,* 41).

339. "Priests will attain sanctity in a manner proper to them if they exercise their offices sincerely and tirelessly in the Spirit of Christ. Since they are ministers of God's Word, they should every day read and listen to that Word which they are required to teach to others. If they are at the same time preoccupied with welcoming this message into their own hearts, they will become ever more perfect disciples of the Lord." *(Priests,* 52).

RELATIONS BETWEEN BISHOPS AND PRIESTS

340. "Thanks to Christ, the eternal and sole Mediator, priests share in the grace of the bishop's rank and form his spiritual crown. Like bishops, priests should grow in love for God and neighbor through the daily exercise of their duty. They should preserve the bond of priestly fraternity, abound in every spiritual good, and give living evidence of God to all men. Let their heroes be those priests who have lived during the course of centuries, often in lowly and hidden service, and have left behind them a bright pattern of holiness. Their praise lives on in the Church.

"A priest's task is to pray and offer sacrifice for his own people and indeed for the entire People of God, realizing what he does and reproducing in himself the holiness of the things he handles. Let him not be undone by his apostolic cares, dangers and toils, but rather led by them to higher sanctity. His activities should be fed and fostered by a wealth of meditation, to the delight of the whole Church of God. All priests,

80

especially those who are called diocesan, in view of the particular title of their ordination, should bear in mind how much their sanctity profits from loyal attachment to the bishop and generous collaboration with him." (*Church*, 41).

341. "The relationships between the bishop and his diocesan priests should rest above all upon the bonds of supernatural charity so that the harmony of the will of the priests with that of their bishop will render their pastoral activity more fruitful." (*Bishops*, 28).

342. "Above all, upon the bishop rests the heavy responsibility for the sanctity of his priests. Hence he should exercise the greatest care on behalf of the continual formation of his priests. He should gladly listen to them, indeed, consult them, and have discussions with them about those matters which concern the necessities of pastoral work and the welfare of the diocese." (*Priests*, 7).

343. "Pastoral love requires that a priest always work in the bond of communion with the bishop and with his brother priests, lest his efforts be in vain. If he acts in this way, a priest will find the unity of his own life in the very unity of the Church's mission. Thus he will be joined with the Lord and through Him with the Father in the Holy Spirit. Thus he will be able to be full of consolation and to overflow with joy." (*Priests*, 14).

344. "Keeping in mind the fullness of the sacrament of orders which the bishop enjoys, priests must respect in him the authority of Christ, the chief Shepherd. They must therefore stand by their bishop in sincere charity and obedience. This priestly obedience, animated with a spirit of cooperation, is based on the very sharing in the episcopal ministry which is conferred on priests both through the sacrament of orders and the canonical mission." (*Priests*, 7).

PRIESTS AND THE WORLD

345. Conscious of how important priests are for the fulfillment of the Church's pastoral aims and her dialogue with the world, Vatican II fervently exhorted "all priests to use the appropriate means endorsed by the Church as they ever strive for the greater sanctity which will make them increasingly useful instruments in the service of God's people." (*Priests*, 12).

346. "By their vocation and ordination, priests of the New Testament are indeed set apart in a certain sense within the midst of God's People. But this is so, not that they may be separated from this people or from any man, but that they may be totally dedicated to the work for which the Lord has raised them up. They cannot be ministers of Christ unless

they are witnesses and dispensers of a life other than this earthly one. But they cannot be of service to men if they remain strangers to the life and condition of men. Their ministry itself by a special title forbids them to be conformed to this world. Yet at the same time this ministry requires that they live in this world among men." (*Priests*, 3).

347. "The world which is entrusted today to the loving ministry of the pastors of the Church is that world which God so loved that He gave His only Son for it. The truth is that though entangled indeed in many sins, this world is also endowed with great talents and provides the Church with the living stones to be built up into the dwelling place of God in the Spirit. Impelling the Church to open new avenues of approach to the world today, this same Holy Spirit is suggesting and fostering fitting adaptations in the ministry of priests." (*Priests*, 22).

348. The words of Vatican II quoted in the preceding paragraph can provide almost unlimited consolation, encouragement and inspiration for every thoughtful priest. God so loved the world as to give not only His Son but also his priests to save the world. It was for this that God called them that they too might share in the priestly, redemptive and mediatorial work of His Son, the Priest of priests.

349. Though their ministry forbids priests to be conformed to this world it demands they they "live in this world among men and that as good shepherds they know their sheep. It requires that they seek to lead those who are not of this sheepfold so that they too may hear the voice of Christ and that there may be one fold and one shepherd." (*Priests*, 3).

350. "The Lord is 'the portion and the inheritance' (Num. 18:20) of priests. Hence they should use temporal goods for those purposes to which it is permissible to direct them according to the teaching of Christ the Lord and the regulations of the Church. . . ." (*Priests*, 17).

"Indeed, they are invited to embrace voluntary poverty. By it they will be more clearly likened to Christ and will become more devoted to the sacred ministry. For Christ became poor for our sakes whereas He had been rich, so that we might be enriched by His poverty. By their own example the apostles gave witness that God's free gift must be freely given. They knew how to abound and how to suffer want. . . . Led, therefore, by the Lord's Spirit Who anointed the Savior and sent Him to preach the gospel to the poor, priests as well as bishops will avoid all things which can offend the poor in any way. More than other followers of Christ, priests and bishops should spurn any type of vanity in their affairs. Finally, let them have the kind of dwelling which will appear closed to no one and which no one will fear to visit, even the humblest." (*Priests*, 17).

351. "Using the world as though they used it not" priests will attain

"to that liberty which will free them from all excessive concern and make them docile to the divine voice which makes itself heard in every-day life. From this freedom and docility will grow a spiritual discernment through which a proper relationship to the world and its goods will be worked out." (*Priests,* 17).

PRIESTLY OBEDIENCE AND HUMILITY

352. "Among the virtues most necessary for the priestly ministry may be named that disposition of soul by which priests are always ready to seek not their own will, but the will of Him Who sent them. For the divine work which the Holy Spirit has raised them up to fulfill transcends all human energies and human wisdom: '. . . the foolish things of the world has God chosen to put to shame the wise' (1 Cor. 1:27). Therefore, conscious of his own weakness, the minister of Christ labors in humility, testing what is God's will." (*Priests,* 15).

353. "Priests, who are already involved in and distracted by the very numerous duties of their office, cannot without anxiety seek for a way which will enable them to unify their interior lives with their program of external activities. No merely external arrangement of the works of the ministry, no mere practice of religious exercises can bring about this unity of life, however much these things can help foster it. But priests can truly build up this unity by imitating Christ the Lord in the fulfillment of their ministry. His food was to do the will of Him Who sent Him to accomplish His work." (*Priests,* 14).

354. "That they may be able to verify the unity of their lives in concrete situations too, priests should subject all their undertakings to the test of God's will, which requires that projects conform to the laws of the Church's evangelical mission. For loyalty toward Christ can never be divorced from loyalty towards the Church." (*Priests,* 14).

355. By "responsible and voluntary humility and obedience, priests make themselves like Christ, having in themselves the attitude which was in Christ Jesus, Who 'emptied Himself, taking the nature of a slave . . . becoming obedient to death' (Phil 2:7-9). By such obedience Christ overcame and redeemed the disobedience of Adam. For, as the apostle gave witness: 'By the disobedience of one man the many were constituted sinners, so also by the obedience of the one, the many will be constituted just.' (Rom. 5:19)." (*Priests,* 15).

356. "This obedience leads to the more mature freedom of God's sons. Of its nature it demands that in the fulfillment of their duty, priests lovingly and prudently look for new avenues for the greater good of the Church. At the same time, it demands that they confidently

propose their plans and urgently expose the needs of the flock committed to them, while remaining ready to submit to the judgment of those who exercise the chief responsibility for governing the Church of God." (*Priests*, 15).

357. "Conscious of his own weakness, the true minister of Christ labors in humility, testing what is God's will. In a kind of captivity to the Spirit (Acts 20:22) he is led in all things by the will of Him Who wishes all men to be saved. He can detect and pursue this will in the circumstances of daily life by humbly serving all those who are entrusted to him by God through the office assigned to him and through the various happenings of his life." (*Priests*, 15).

358. Let priests "very gladly spend themselves and be spent in any task assigned to them, even the more lowly and poor ones. For in this way they will preserve and strengthen the necessary unity with their brothers in the ministry, most of all with those whom the Lord has appointed the visible rulers of His Church. Thus, too, they will work to build up Christ's Body, which grows 'through every joint in the system.' " (*Priests*, 15).

PRIESTS CALLED TO HOLINESS

359. Like all other Christians, priests have been called in the consecration of baptism to strive for perfection in accordance with the words of Christ: "You therefore are to be perfect as your heavenly Father is perfect" (Mt. 5:48). "To the acquisition of this perfection priests are bound by a special claim, since they have been consecrated to God in a new way by the reception of orders. They have become living instruments of Christ, the eternal Priest so that through the ages they can accomplish His wonderful work of reuniting the whole society of men with heavenly power. Therefore, since every priest in his own way represents the Person of Christ Himself, he is also enriched with special grace." (*Priests*, 12).

360. "Priestly holiness itself contributes very greatly to a fruitful fulfillment of the priestly ministry. True, the grace of God can complete the work of salvation even through unworthy ministers. Yet, ordinarily God desires to manifest His wonders through those who have been made particularly docile to the impulse and guidance of the Holy Spirit. Because of their intimate union with Christ and their holiness of life, these men can say with the apostle: 'It is now no longer I that live, but Christ lives in me' (Gal. 2:20)." (*Priests*, 12).

361. "Priests should remember that in performing their tasks, they are never alone. Relying on the power of Almighty God and believing

in Christ Who called them to share in His priesthood, they should devote themselves to their ministry with complete trust, knowing that God can intensify in them the ability to love." (*Priests*, 22).

362. "By assuming the role of the Good Shepherd" priests "will find in the very exercise of pastoral love the bond of priestly perfection which will unify their lives and activities. This pastoral love flows mainly from the Eucharistic Sacrifice, which is therefore the center and root of the whole priestly life. The priestly soul strives thereby to apply to itself the action which takes place on the altar of sacrifice. But this goal cannot be achieved unless priests themselves penetrate ever more deeply through prayer into the mystery of Christ." (*Priests*, 13).

PRIESTS AND CELIBACY

363. "With respect to the priestly life, the Church has always held in especially high regard perfect and perpetual continence on behalf of the kingdom of heaven. Such continence was recommended by Christ the Lord and has been gladly embraced and praiseworthily observed down through the years and in our own day, too, by many Christians. For it simultaneously signifies and stimulates pastoral charity and is a special fountain of spiritual fruitfulness on earth. It is not, indeed, demanded by the very nature of the priesthood as is evident from the practice of the primitive Church and from the tradition of the Eastern Churches. . . .

"Celibacy accords with the priesthood on many scores. For the whole priestly mission is dedicated to that new humanity which Christ, the conqueror of death, raises up in the world through His Spirit. This humanity takes its origin 'not of blood, nor of the will of the flesh, nor of the will of man, but of God.' (John 1:13). Through virginity or celibacy, observed for the sake of the kingdom of heaven, priests are consecrated to Christ in a new and distinguished way. They more easily hold fast to Him with undivided heart. They more freely devote themselves in Him and through Him to the service of God and men. They more readily minister to His kingdom and to the work of heavenly regeneration, and thus become more apt to exercise paternity in Christ, and do so to a greater extent." (*Priests*, 16).

364. "For these reasons, which are based on the mystery of the Church and her mission, celibacy was at first recommended to priests. Then, in the Latin Church, it was imposed by law on all those who were promoted to sacred orders. This legislation, to the extent that it concerns those who are destined for the priesthood, this holy Synod again approves and confirms. It trusts in the Spirit that the gift of celibacy,

which so befits the priesthood of the New Testament, will be generously bestowed by the Father, as long as those who share in Christ's priesthood through the sacrament of holy orders, and indeed the whole Church humbly and earnestly pray for it." (*Priests,* 16).

365. "Many men today call perfect continence impossible. The more they do so, the more humbly and perseveringly priests should join with the Church in praying for the grace of fidelity. It is never denied to those who ask. At the same time let priests make use of all the supernatural and natural helps which are available to all. Let them not neglect to follow the norms, especially the ascetical ones, which have been tested by the experience of the Church and which are by no means less necessary in today's world. And so this most holy Synod beseeches not only priests, but all the faithful to have at heart this precious gift of priestly celibacy. Let all beg of God that He may always lavish this gift on His Church abundantly." (*Priests,* 16).

PRIESTLY VIRTUES

366. "The Apostle of the Gentiles says: 'I, therefore, the prisoner in the Lord, exhort you to walk in a manner worthy of the calling with which you were called, with all humility and meekness, with patience, bearing with one another in love, careful to preserve the unity of the Spirit in the bond of peace' (Eph. 4:1-3). This exhortation applies especially to those who have been raised to sacred orders so that the mission of Christ may be carried on. He came among us 'not to be served but to serve' (Mt. 20:28)." (*Ecumenism,* 7).

367. "The leaders of the People of God must walk in faith, following the example of the faithful Abraham, who in faith 'obeyed by going out into a place which he was to receive for an inheritance; and he went out, not knowing where he was going' (Heb. 11:8)." (*Priests,* 22).

368. Though preoccupied mainly with the supernatural virtues with special emphasis on faith, hope and charity, the Council Fathers also urged the practice of the natural social virtues. Thus they tell us that for the achievement of their goals, "priests will find great help in the possession of those virtues which are deservedly esteemed in human affairs, such as goodness of heart, sincerity, strength and constancy of character, zealous pursuit of justice, civility, and those other traits which the Apostle Paul commends saying: 'Whatever things are true, whatever honorable, whatever just, whatever holy, whatever lovable, whatever of good repute, if there be any other virtue, if anything worthy of praise, think upon these things' (Phil. 4:8)." (*Priests,* 3).

369. A missioner who is to work in a land that is foreign to him must

be "prepared by a special spiritual and moral training. For he must be ready to take initiatives, constant in the execution of projects, persevering in difficulties, patient and strong of heart in bearing with solitude, fatigue and fruitless labor.

370. "He must bring an open mind and heart to men, and gladly shoulder the duties entrusted to him. He needs a noble spirit for adapting himself to strange customs and changing circumstances. He needs a sympathetic mind and responsive heart for cooperating with his brethren and with all who dedicate themselves to a common task. Thus, together with the faithful, missioners will be of one heart and mind (Acts 2:42; 4:32) in imitation of the apostolic community."

371. "Even during a missioner's training period, these attitudes should be earnestly practiced and developed. For its part, his spiritual life should ennoble and nourish them. Imbued with a living faith and a hope that never fails, the missioner should be a man of prayer. He should glow with a spirit of strength and of love and of self-discipline (2 Tim. 1:7)." (*Missions*, 25).

372. "Out of zeal for souls" let the missioner "gladly spend all and be spent himself for souls (2 Cor. 12:15 f); so that 'by the daily exercise of his duty he may grow in the love of God and neighbor.' Thus, joined with Christ in obedience to the will of the Father, he will continue His mission under the hierarchical authority of the Church and cooperate in the mystery of salvation." (*Missions*, 25).

373. Let the missioner "in the spirit of sacrifice always bear about in himself the dying of Jesus, so that the life of Jesus may work in those to whom he is sent (2 Cor. 4:10 ff)." (*Missions*, 25).

374. "Christ, Whom the Father sanctified and consecrated, and sent into the world, 'gave Himself for us that He might redeem us from all iniquity and cleanse for himself an acceptable people, pursuing good works' (Tit. 2:14). And so He entered into His glory through His Passion. Likewise, consecrated by the anointing of the Holy Spirit and sent by Christ, priests mortify in themselves the deeds of the flesh and devote themselves entirely to the service of men." (*Priests*, 12).

DEVOTIONAL PRACTICES FOR PRIESTS

375. "A priest's task is to pray and offer sacrifice for his own people and indeed the entire People of God, realizing what he does and reproducing in himself the holiness of the things he handles. Let him not be undone by his apostolic cares, dangers and toils, but rather led by them to higher sanctity. His activities should be fed and fostered by a wealth of meditation, to the delight of the whole Church of God." (*Church*, 41).

376. "Priests should gladly undertake spiritual retreats and highly esteem spiritual direction. In manifold ways, especially through approved methods of mental prayer and various voluntary forms of prayer, priests should search for and earnestly beg of God that spirit of genuine adoration by which they themselves, along with the people entrusted to them can unite themselves with Christ, the Mediator of the New Testament." (*Priests, 18*).

377. Since priests "are ministers of God's Word, they should every day read and listen to that Word which they are required to teach to others. If they are at the same time preoccupied with welcoming this message into their own hearts, they will become ever more perfect disciples of the Lord. For as the apostle Paul wrote to Timothy: 'Meditate on these things, give thyself entirely to them, that thy progress may be manifest to all. Take heed to thyself and to thy teaching, be earnest in them. For in doing so thou wilt save both thyself and those who hear thee.' (1 Tim. 4:15-16)." (*Priests, 13*).

378. "With the light of faith nourished by spiritual reading, priests can carefully detect the signs of God's will and the impulses of His grace in the various happenings of life, and can become more docile day by day to the mission they have undertaken in the Holy Spirit." (*Priests, 18*).

379. "Priests engaged in the sacred pastoral ministry will offer the praises of the hours with fervor to the extent that they vividly realize that they must heed St. Paul's exhortation: 'Pray without ceasing' (Th. 5:17). For only the Lord can give fruitfulness and increase to the works in which they are engaged. 'Without me,' He said, 'you can do nothing' (John 15:5). That is why the apostles, appointing deacons, said: 'We will devote ourselves to prayer and to the ministry of the Word' (Acts 6:4)." (*Liturgy, 86*).

380. "Clerics not bound to Office in choir, if they are in major orders, are bound to pray the entire office every day, either in common or individually as laid down in Article 89 (of the Constitution on the Liturgy). In particular cases, and for just reasons, ordinaries can dispense their subjects wholly or in part from the obligation of reciting the Divine Office, or may commute the obligation." (*Liturgy, 96 and 97*).

EXAMEN AND CONFESSION

381. "To Christ the Savior and Shepherd, ministers of sacramental grace are intimately united through the fruitful reception of the sacraments, especially the repeated sacramental act of penance. For this sacrament, prepared for by a daily examination of conscience, greatly

fosters the necessary turning of the heart towards the love of the Father of mercies." (*Priests*, 18).

382. "The weakness of human flesh can be healed by the holiness of Him Who has become for our sake a High Priest, 'holy, innocent, undefiled, set apart from sinners' (Heb. 7:26)." (*Priests*, 12).

MASS

383. "As ministers of sacred realities, especially in the Sacrifice of the Mass, priests represent the Person of Christ in a special way. He gave Himself as a victim to make men holy. Hence priests are invited to imitate the realities they deal with. Since they celebrate the mystery of the Lord's death, they should see to it that every part of their being is dead to evil habits and desires.

384. "Priests fulfill their chief duty in the mystery of the Eucharistic Sacrifice. In it the work of our redemption continues to be carried out. For this reason, priests are strongly urged to celebrate Mass every day, for even if the faithful are unable to be present, it is an act of Christ and the Church.

385. "So it is that while priests are uniting themselves with the act of Christ the Priest, they are offering their whole selves every day to God. While being nourished by the Body of Christ, their hearts are sharing in the love of Him Who gives Himself as food for His faithful ones." (*Priests*, 13).

VISITS TO THE BLESSED SACRAMENT

386. In order that priests "may discharge their ministry with fidelity, they should prize daily conversations with Christ the Lord by visits of personal devotion to the Most Holy Eucharist." (*Priests*, 18).

DEVOTION TO MARY

387. Led by the Holy Spirit, Mary "devoted herself entirely to the mystery of man's redemption. With the devotion and veneration of sons, priests should lovingly honor this Mother of the supreme and eternal Priest, this Queen of the Apostles and protectress of their ministry." (*Priests*, 18).

8. Religious

388. "From the very infancy of the Church, there have existed men and women who strove to follow Christ more freely and imitate Him more nearly by the practice of the evangelical counsels. Each in his own way, these souls have led a life dedicated to God. Under the influence of the Holy Spirit, many of them pursued a solitary life, or founded religious families to which the Church . . . gave . . . approval. . . .

"And so it happened by divine plan that a wonderful variety of religious communities grew up. This variety contributed mightily towards making the Church experienced in every good deed (2 Tim. 3:17) and ready for a ministry of service in building up Christ's Body (Eph. 4:12)." (*Religious,* 1).

389. "The evangelical counsels of chastity dedicated to God, poverty, and obedience are based upon the words and example of the Lord. They were further commended by the apostles and the Fathers and other teachers and shepherds of the Church. The counsels are a divine gift, which the Church has received from her Lord and which she ever preserves with the help of His grace. Church authority has the duty, under the inspiration of the Holy Spirit, of interpreting these evangelical counsels, of regulating their practice, and finally of establishing stable forms of living according to them." (*Church,* 43).

390. "By the charity to which they lead, the evangelical counsels join their followers to the Church and her mystery in a special way. Since this is so, the spiritual life of these followers should be devoted to the welfare of the whole Church. Thence arises their duty of working to implant and strengthen the kingdom of Christ in souls and to extend that kingdom to every land. This duty is to be discharged to the extent of their capacities and in keeping with the form of their proper vocation. The chosen means may be prayer or active undertakings. It is for this reason that the Church preserves and fosters the special character of her various religious communities." (*Church,* 44).

391. "Whatever the diversity of their spiritual endowments, all who are called by God to practice the evangelical counsels and who do so faithfully, devote themselves in a special way to the Lord. They imitate Christ the virgin and the poor man (Mt. 8:20; Lk. 9:58), Who, by an obedience which carried Him even to death on the cross (Phil. 2:8) redeemed men and made them holy. As a consequence, impelled by a love which the Holy Spirit has poured into their hearts (Rom. 5:5), these Christians spend themselves ever increasingly for Christ and for His Body, the Church." (*Religious*, 1).

392. "The faithful of Christ can bind themselves to the three previously mentioned counsels either by vows or by other sacred bonds which are like vows in their purpose. Through such a bond a person is totally dedicated to God by an act of supreme love and is committed to the honor and service of God under a new and special title." (*Church*, 44).

393. "Since it is the duty of the hierarchy of the Church to nourish the People of God and lead them to the choicest pastures (Ezech. 34:14), it devolves on the same hierarchy to govern with wise legislation the practice of the evangelical counsels. For by that practice is uniquely fostered the perfection of love for God and neighbor.

"Submissively following the promptings of the Holy Spirit, the hierarchy also endorses rules formulated by eminent men and women, and authentically approves later modifications. Moreover, by its watchful and shielding authority, the hierarchy keeps close to communities established far and wide for the upbuilding of Christ's Body, so that they can grow and flourish in accord with the spirit of their founders." (*Church*, 45).

FOLLOWING THE EVANGELICAL COUNSELS

394. It is true that through baptism the Christian "has died to sin and has been consecrated to God. However, in order to derive more abundant fruit from baptismal grace, he intends by the profession of the evangelical counsels in the Church, to free himself from those obstacles which might draw him away from the fervor of charity and the perfection of divine worship. Thus he is more intimately consecrated to divine service. This consecration gains in perfection since by virtue of firmer and steadier bonds it serves as a better symbol of the unbreakable link between Christ and His Spouse, the Church." (*Church*, 44).

395. "The members of each community should recall above everything else that by their profession of the evangelical counsels they have given answer to a divine call to live for God alone not only by dying to

sin (Rom. 6:11) but also by renouncing the world. They have handed over their entire lives to God's service in an act of special consecration which is deeply rooted in their baptismal consecration and which provides an ampler manifestation of it." (*Religious*, 5).

396. "Those who profess the evangelical counsels love and seek before all else that God Who took the initiative in loving us (1 John 4:10); in every circumstance they aim to develope a life hidden with Christ in God (Col. 3:3). Such dedication gives rise and urgency to the love of one's neighbor for the world's salvation and the upbuilding of the Church. From this love the very practice of the evangelical counsels takes life and direction." (*Religious*, 6).

397. "In fidelity to their profession and in renunciation of all things for the sake of Christ (Mk. 10:28) let religious follow Him (Mt. 19:21) as their one necessity (Lk. 10:42). Let them listen to His words (Lk. 10:39) and be preoccupied with His work (1 Cor. 7:32)." (*Religious*, 5).

398. "Everyone should realize that the profession of the evangelical counsels, though entailing the renunciation of certain values which undoubtedly merit high esteem, does not detract from a genuine development of the human person. Rather, by its very nature it is most beneficial to that development. For the counsels, voluntarily undertaken according to each one's personal vocation, contribute greatly to purification of heart and spiritual liberty. They continually kindle the fervor of charity. As the example of so many saintly founders shows, the counsels are especially able to pattern the Christian man after that manner of virginal and humble life which Christ the Lord elected for Himself, and which His Virgin Mother also chose." (*Church*, 46).

399. "The profession of the evangelical counsels, then, appears as a sign which can and ought to attract all the members of the Church to an effective and prompt fulfillment of the duties of their Christian vocation. The People of God has no lasting city here below, but looks forward to one which is to come. This being so, the religious state by giving its members greater freedom from earthly cares, more adequately manifests to all believers the presence of heavenly goods already possessed here below." (*Church*, 44).

VOWS OF RELIGIOUS

400. "Since the disciples must always imitate and give witness to this charity and humility of Christ, Mother Church rejoices at finding within her bosom men and women who more closely follow and more clearly demonstrate the Savior's self-giving by embracing poverty with the free choice of God's sons, and by renouncing their own wills. They sub-

ject the latter to another person on God's behalf, in pursuit of an excellence surpassing what is commanded. Thus they liken themselves more thoroughly to Christ in His obedience." (*Church,* 42).

POVERTY

401. "Poverty voluntarily embraced in imitation of Christ provides a witness which is highly esteemed, especially today. Let religious painstakingly cultivate such poverty, and give it new expressions if need be. By it a man shares in the poverty of Christ, Who became poor for our sake when before He had been rich, that we might be enriched by His poverty (2 Cor. 8:9; Mt. 8:20).

"Religious poverty requires more than limiting the use of possessions to the consent of superiors; members of a community ought to be poor in both fact and spirit, and have their treasures in heaven (Mt. 6:20)." (*Religious,* 13).

CHASTITY

402. "That chastity which is practiced 'on behalf of the heavenly kingdom' (Mt. 19:12), and which religious profess, deserves to be esteemed as a surpassing gift of grace. For it liberates the human heart in a unique way (1 Cor. 7:32-35) and causes it to burn with greater love for God and all mankind. It is therefore an outstanding token of heavenly riches, and also a most suitable way for religious to spend themselves readily in God's service and in works of the apostolate. Religious thereby give witness to all Christ's faithful of that wondrous marriage between the Church and Christ, her only Spouse, a union which has been established by God and will be fully manifested in the world to come.

403. "As they strive to live their profession faithfully, religious do well to lodge their faith in the words of the Lord; trusting in God's help rather than presuming on their own resources, let them practice mortification and custody of the senses. They should take advantage of those natural helps which favor mental and bodily health. As a result they will not be influenced by those erroneous claims which present complete continence as impossible or as harmful to human development. In addition a certain spiritual instinct should lead them to spurn everything likely to imperil chastity. Above all, everyone should remember — superiors especially — that chastity has stronger safeguards in a community where true fraternal love thrives among its members." (*Religious,* 12).

OBEDIENCE

404. "Under the influence of the Holy Spirit, religious submit themselves to their superiors whom their faith presents as God's representatives and through whom they are guided into the service of all their brothers in Christ. Thus did Christ Himself out of submission to the Father minister to the brethren and surrender His life as a ransom for many (Mt. 20:28; John 10:14-18). In this way, too, religious assume a firmer commitment to the ministry of the Church and labor to achieve the mature measure of the fullness of Christ (Eph. 4:13)." (*Religious,* 14).

405. "Through the profession of obedience, religious offer to God a total dedication of their own wills as a sacrifice of themselves; they thereby unite themselves with greater steadfastness and security to the saving will of God. In this way they follow the pattern of Jesus Christ, Who came to do the Father's will (John 4:34; 5:30; Heb. 10:7; Ps. 40:9). 'Taking the nature of a slave' (Phil. 2:7), He learned obedience from His sufferings (Heb. 5:8)." (*Religious,* 14).

406. "In a spirit of faith and of love for God's will, let religious show humble obedience to their superiors in accord with the norms of rule and constitution. Realizing that they are giving service to the upbuilding of Christ's Body according to God's design, let them bring to the execution of commands and to the discharge of assignments entrusted to them the resources of their minds and wills, and their gifts of nature and grace. Lived in this manner, religious obedience will not diminish the dignity of the human person but will rather lead it to maturity in consequence of that enlarged freedom which belongs to the sons of God." (*Religious,* 14).

THE RELIGIOUS STATE

407. The religious state "not only witnesses to the fact of a new and eternal life acquired by the redemption of Christ. It foretells the resurrected state and the glory of the heavenly kingdom. Christ also proposed to His disciples that form of life which He, as the Son of God, accepted in entering this world to do the will of His Father. In the Church this same state of life is imitated with particular accuracy and perpetually exemplified. The religious state reveals in a unique way that the kingdom of God and its overmastering necessities are superior to all earthly considerations. Finally, to all men it shows wonderfully at work within the Church the surpassing greatness of the force of Christ, the King, and the boundless power of the Holy Spirit.

"Thus, although the religious state constituted by the profession of the evangelical counsels does not belong to the hierarchical structure of the Church, nevertheless it belongs inseparably to her life and holiness." (*Church*, 44).

408. "By their state in life, religious give splendid and striking testimony that the world cannot be transfigured and offered to God without the spirit of the Beatitudes." (*Church*, 31).

409. After telling us that religious communities are not midway between the laity and the clergy, Vatican II tells us that "the faithful of Christ are called by God from both these latter states of life so that they may enjoy this particular gift (religious life) in the life of the Church and thus, each in his own way, can forward the saving mission of the Church." (*Church*, 43).

410. "By her approval the Church not only raises the religious profession to the dignity of a canonical state. By the liturgical setting of that profession she also manifests that it is a state consecrated to God. The Church herself, by the authority given to her by God accepts the vows of those professing them. By her public prayer she begs aid and grace from God for them. She commends them to God, imparts a spiritual blessing to them, and accompanies their self-offering with the Eucharistic Sacrifice." (*Church*, 45).

KINDS OF RELIGIOUS

411. In its Dogmatic Constitution on the Church, Vatican II speaks of "various forms of solitary and community life" as well as of "different religious families." It goes on to say that "advancing the progress of their members and the welfare of the whole body of Christ, these groups have been like branches sprouting wondrously and abundantly from a tree growing in the field of the Lord from a seed divinely planted." (*Church*, 43).

MONASTICISM

412. Referring in particular to the monasticism of both the East and the West, the Council declares that "the venerable institution of monastic life should be faithfully preserved and should grow ever-increasingly radiant with its own authentic spirit. Through the long course of centuries, the institution has proved its merits splendidly to the Church and to human society. The main task of monks is to render to the Divine Majesty a service at once simple and noble, within the monastic con-

95

fines. This they do either by devoting themselves entirely to divine worship in a life that is hidden, or by lawfully taking up some apostolate or works of Christian charity. . . .

"There are religious communities which by rule or constitution closely join the apostolic life with choral prayer and monastic observances. Let these groups too, so harmonize their manner of life with the requirements of the apostolate belonging to them that they still faithfully preserve their form of life, for it is one which serves the highest welfare of the Church." (*Religious,* 9).

CONTEMPLATIVE COMMUNITIES

413. "Members of those communities which are totally dedicated to contemplation give themselves to God alone in solitude and silence and through constant prayer and ready penance. No matter how urgent may be the needs of the active apostolate, such communities will always have a distinguished part to play in Christ's Mystical Body where, 'all members have not the same function' (1 Rom. 12:4). For they offer God a choice sacrifice of praise. They brighten God's people with the richest splendors of sanctity. By their example they motivate this people; by imparting a hidden apostolic fruitfulness they make this people grow. Thus they are the glory of the Church and an overflowing fountain of heavenly graces. Nevertheless, their manner of living should be revised according to the aforementioned principles and standards of appropriate renewal, though their withdrawal from the world and the practices of their contemplative life should be maintained at their holiest." (*Religious,* 7).

414. In the Decree on the Missionary Work of the Church, Vatican II also tells us that "by their prayers, works of penance, and sufferings, contemplative communities have a very great importance in the conversion of souls. For it is God Who sends workers into His harvest when He is asked to do so (Mt. 9:38), Who opens the minds of non-Christians to hear the gospel (Acts 16:14) and Who makes the word of salvation fruitful in their hearts." (*Missions,* 40).

ACTIVE COMMUNITIES

415. In active communities "the very nature of the religious life requires apostolic action and services, since a sacred ministry and a special work of charity have been consigned to them by the Church and must be discharged in her name. Hence the entire religious life of the

96

members of these communities should be penetrated by an apostolic spirit, as their entire apostolic activity should be animated by a religious spirit. Therefore, in order that members may above all respond to their vocation of following Christ and may serve Christ Himself in His members, their apostolic activity should result from an intimate union with Him. In this way it will happen that love for God and neighbor will itself be nurtured." (*Religious*, 8).

EXEMPT RELIGIOUS

416. "Any institute of perfection and its individual members can be removed from the jurisdiction of the local ordinaries by the Supreme Pontiff and subjected to himself alone. This is possible by virtue of his primacy over the entire Church. He does so in order to provide more adequately for the necessities of the entire flock of the Lord and in consideration of the common good. In like manner, these communities can be left or committed to the charge of their proper patriarchal authorities. In fulfilling their duty towards the Church in accord with the special form of their life, the members of these communities should show towards bishops the reverence and obedience required by canonical laws. For bishops possess pastoral authority over individual churches and apostolic labor demands unity and harmony." (*Church*, 45).

RELIGIOUS AS A REVELATION OF CHRIST

417. "Religious should carefully consider that through them, to believers and non-believers alike, the Church truly wishes to give an increasingly clearer revelation of Christ. Through them, Christ should be shown contemplating on the mountain, announcing God's kingdom to the multitude, healing the sick and the maimed, turning sinners to wholesome fruit, blessing children, doing good to all and always obeying the will of the Father Who sent Him." (*Church*, 46).

418. The more ardently religious "unite themselves to Christ through a self-surrender involving their entire lives, the more vigorous becomes the life of the Church and the more abundantly her apostolate bears fruit. A life consecrated by a profession of the counsels is of surpassing value. Such a life has a necessary role to play in the circumstances of the present age." (*Religious*, 1).

419. "Since the fundamental norm of the religious life is a following of Christ as proposed by the gospel, such is to be regarded by all communities as their supreme law." (*Religious*, 2).

420. "Let all who have been called to the profession of the vows take painstaking care to persevere and excel increasingly in the vocation to which God has summoned them. Let their purpose be a more vigorous flowering of the Church's holiness and the greater glory of the one and undivided Trinity, which in Christ and through Christ is the fountain and the wellspring of all holiness." (*Church,* 17).

RELIGIOUS AND THE APOSTOLATE

421. "Fed at the table of the divine law and of the sacred altar, they (religious) can bring a brother's love to the members of Christ, and a son's love to their revered pastors; thus they can live and think with the Church to an ever-increasing degree and spend themselves completely on her mission." (*Religious,* 6).

422. "Let all religious therefore spread throughout the world the good news of Christ by the integrity of their faith, their love for God and neighbor, their devotion to the Cross, and their hope of future glory. Thus will their witness be seen by all, and our Father in heaven will be glorified. Thus, too, with the prayerful aid of that most loving Virgin Mary, God's Mother, 'whose life is a rule of life for all' (St. Ambrose), religious communities will experience a growth in numbers, and will yield a richer harvest of fruits of salvation." (*Religious,* 25).

423. "As they seek God before all things and only Him, the members of each community should combine contemplation with apostolic love. By the former they adhere to God in mind and heart; by the latter they strive to associate themselves with the work of redemption and to spread the kingdom of God." (*Religious,* 5).

RELIGIOUS AND THE MISSIONS

424. "Right from the planting stage of the Church, the religious life should be carefully fostered. This not only confers precious and absolutely necessary assistance on missionary activity. By a more inward consecration made to God in the Church, it also luminously manifests and signifies the inner nature of the Christian calling." (*Missions,* 18).

425. "Various forms of religious life should be cultivated in a young Church, so that they can display different aspects of Christ's mission and the Church's life, can devote themselves to various pastoral works, and prepare their members to exercise them rightly. . . .

"Worthy of special mention are the various projects aimed at helping the contemplative life take root. There are those who, while retaining the essential elements of monastic life, are bent on implanting the very rich traditions of their own Order. Others are returning to simpler forms of ancient monasticism. But all are striving to work out a genuine adaptation to local conditions. For the contemplative life belongs to the fullness of the Church's presence, and should therefore be everywhere established." (*Missions,* 18).

426. "Working to plant the Church, and thoroughly enriched with the treasures of mysticism adorning the Church's religious tradition, religious communities should strive to give expression to these treasures and to hand them on in a manner harmonious with the nature and the genius of each nation. Let them reflect attentively on how Christian religious life may be able to assimilate the ascetic and contemplative traditions whose seeds were sometimes already planted by God in ancient cultures prior to the preaching of the gospel." (*Missions,* 18).

RELIGIOUS LIFE IN COMMUNITY

427. "Thanks to God's love poured into hearts by the Holy Spirit (Rom. 5:5), a religious community is a true family gathered together in the Lord's name and rejoicing in His presence (Mt. 18:20). For love is the fulfillment of the law (Rom. 13:10) and the bond of perfection (Col. 3:14); where it exists we know that we have been taken from death to life (1 John 3:14). In fact, brotherly unity shows that Christ has come (John 13:35; 17:21); from it results great apostolic influence." (*Religious,* 15).

428. "Drawing on the authentic sources of Christian spirituality, let the members of communities energetically cultivate the spirit of prayer and the practice of it. In the first place they should take the sacred Scriptures in hand each day by way of attaining the excellent knowledge of Jesus Christ (Phil. 3:8) through reading these divine writings and meditating on them. They should enact the sacred liturgy, especially the most holy mystery of the Eucharist, with hearts and voices attuned to the Church; here is a most copious source of nourishment for the spiritual life." (*Religious,* 6).

429. "These religious families give their members the support of greater stability in their way of life, a proven method of acquiring perfection, fraternal association in the militia of Christ, and liberty strengthened by obedience. Thus these religious can securely fulfill and faithfully observe their religious profession, and rejoicing in spirit make progress on the road to charity." (*Church,* 43).

430. "The fact that they (religious) are in God's service should ignite and fan within them the exercise of virtues, especially humility, obe-

dience, courage and chastity. Through them they share spiritually in Christ's self-surrender (Phil. 2:7-8) and in His life (Rom. 8:1-13)." (*Religious*, 5).

431. "Let all religious therefore spread through the whole world the good news of Christ by the integrity of their faith, their love for God and neighbor, their devotion to the Cross and their hope of future glory. Thus will their witness be seen by all, and our Father in heaven will be glorified (Mt. 5:16). Thus, too, with the prayerful aid of that most loving Virgin Mary, God's Mother, 'whose life is a rule of life for all' (St. Ambrose), religious communities will experience a daily growth in numbers, and will yield a richer harvest of fruits that bring salvation." (*Religious*, 25).

DUTIES OF SUPERIORS

432. "For his part, as one who will render an account for the souls entrusted to him (Heb. 13:17) each superior should himself be docile to God's will in the exercise of his office. Let him use his authority in a spirit of service for the brethren and manifest thereby the charity with which God loves them. Governing his subjects as God's own sons, and with regard to their human personality, a superior will make it easier for them to obey gladly." (*Religious*, 14).

433. "Throughout their lives, religious should labor earnestly to perfect their spiritual, doctrinal and professional development. As far as possible, superiors should provide them with the opportunity, the resources and the time to do so.

"It also devolves upon superiors to see that the best persons are chosen for directors, spiritual guides and professors, and that they are carefully trained." (*Religious*, 18).

434. The superior "must make a special point of leaving" his subject "appropriately free with respect to the sacrament of penance and direction of conscience. Let him give the kind of leadership which will encourage religious to bring an active and responsible obedience to the offices they shoulder and the activities they undertake. Therefore a superior should listen willingly to his subjects and encourage them to make a personal contribution to the welfare of the community and of the Church. Not to be weakened, however, is the superior's authority to decide what must be done and to require the doing of it." (*Religious*, 14).

RENEWAL OF RELIGIOUS LIFE

435. "Since the religious life is intended above all else to lead those

who embrace it to an imitation of Christ and to union with God through the profession of the evangelical counsels, the fact must be honestly faced that even the most desirable changes made on behalf of contemporary needs will fail of their purpose unless a renewal of spirit gives life to them. Indeed, such an interior renewal must always be accorded the leading role even in the promotion of exterior works." (*Religious*, 2).

436. "Let all bear in mind that the hope of renewal must be lodged in a more diligent observance of rule and of constitutions rather than in a multiplication of individual laws." (*Religious*, 4).

437. "The appropriate renewal of religious life involves . . . a continuous return to the sources of all Christian life and to the original inspiration behind a given community. . . . It serves the best interest of the Church for communities to have their own special character and purpose. Therefore loyal recognition and safekeeping should be accorded to the spirit of the founders, as also to all the particular goals and wholesome traditions which constitute the heritage of each community." (*Religious*, 2).

9. Seminarians

BASIC PRINCIPLES

438. Seminarians "should be taught to look for Christ in many places: in faithful meditation on God's Word, in active communion with the most holy mysteries of the Church, especially in the Eucharist and the divine Office, in the bishop who sends them, and in the people to whom they are sent, especially the poor, the young, the sick, the sinful and the unbelieving." (*Priestly Formation,* 8).

439. "Spiritual formation should be closely linked with doctrinal and pastoral training. Especially with the help of the spiritual director such formation should help seminarians learn to live in familiar and constant companionship with the Father through Jesus Christ, in the Holy Spirit. By sacred ordination they will be molded in the likeness of Christ the Priest. As friends they should be used to loyal association with Him through a profound identification of their whole lives with His. They should live His paschal mystery in such a way that they know how to initiate into it the people entrusted to them." (*Priestly Formation,* 8).

440. "With the trust of a son, seminarians should love and honor the most Blessed Virgin Mary, who was given as a mother to His disciple by Christ Jesus as He hung dying on His cross.

"Let them earnestly practice those exercises of piety recommended by the venerable usage of the Church, though care should be taken to keep spiritual formation from consisting solely in these things, and from producing unsubstantial religious feelings. Seminarians should learn rather to live according to the gospel and to grow strong in faith, hope and charity. By exercising these virtues they will develop the spirit of prayer, secure strength and protection for their vocation, promote the vitality of the other virtues and grow in the desire to win all men for Christ." (*Priestly Formation,* 8).

441. "In minor seminaries, which are built to nurture the seeds of a

vocation, students can be conditioned to follow Christ the Redeemer with a generous and pure heart. The means should be a special religious formation which gives first place to spiritual direction." (*Priestly Formation,* 3).

442. "This most sacred Synod ... urgently entreats those who are readying themselves for the priestly ministry to realize clearly that the hope of the Church and the salvation of souls are being entrusted to them. Embracing the directives of this decree with a willing heart, let them bear most abundantly that fruit which remains forever." (*Priestly Formation,* Conclusion).

443. "Seminarians should be thoroughly penetrated by the mystery of the Church, especially as it has been presented with new clarity by this holy Synod. Bound even now to Christ's Vicar with humble and filial love, attached after ordination to their own bishop as loyal assistants, and working in concert with their brother priests, they will give witness to that unity by which men are attracted to Christ. Let them learn to share large-heartedly in the whole life of the Church according to the spirit of St. Augustine's saying: 'A man possesses the Holy Spirit to the measure of his love for Christ's Church.' " (*Priestly Formation,* 9).

SEMINARIANS TO BE TRAINED FOR MINISTRY

444. Let seminarians "be readied for the ministry of worship and sanctification, that by their prayers and participation in sacred liturgical ceremonies they may know how to exercise the work of salvation through the Eucharistic Sacrifice and other sacraments." (*Priestly Formation,* 4).

445. "In seminaries and houses of religious, clerics are to be given a liturgical formation in their spiritual life." (*Liturgy,* 17).

446. Let seminarians "be readied for the ministry of a shepherd. They should know how to represent Christ before men. He did not 'come to be served but to serve, and to give His life as a ransom for many' (Mk. 10:45; John 13:12-17). Becoming the servants of all, let them win over that many more (1 Cor. 9:19)." (*Priestly Formation,* 4).

447. "Major seminaries are necessary for priestly formation. In them the whole training of students ought to provide for the development of true shepherds of souls after the model of our Lord Jesus Christ, Who was Teacher, Priest and Shepherd." (*Priestly Formation,* 4).

448. Seminarians are to "be readied for the ministry of the Word, so that they may always grow in their understanding of God's revealed word, may know how to grasp it through meditation, and express it through word and conduct." (*Priestly Formation,* 4).

449. "Seminarians need to learn the art of exercising the apostolate not only in theory but also in practice. . . . Even during their course of studies, and also during holidays, they should be introduced into pastoral practice by appropriate undertakings. Depending on the age of the seminarians and the local conditions, and given the prudent approval of their bishops, such programs should be pursued in a methodical way and under the guidance of men experienced in pastoral matters. The surpassing value of supernatural helps should, however, be kept in mind." (*Priestly Formation,* 21).

DEACONS AND OTHER CLERICS

450. Since deacons "are servants of the mysteries of Christ and the Church, they should keep themselves free from every fault, be pleasing to God, and be a source of all goodness in the sight of men (1 Tim. 3:8-10; 12-13)."

"Called by the Lord and set aside as His portion, other clerics prepare themselves for various ministerial offices under the watchful eyes of pastors. They are bound to bring their hearts and minds into accord with the splendid calling which is theirs, and will do so by constancy in prayer, burning love, and attention to whatever is true, just and of good repute, all for the glory and honor of God." (*Church,* 41).

FORMATION OF CHARACTER — VIRTUES

451. Seminarians "should be trained in what strengthens character and, in general, they should learn to prize those qualities which are highly regarded among men and speak well of a minister of Christ. Such are sincerity of heart, a constant concern for justice, fidelity to one's word, courtesy of manner, restraint and kindliness in speech." (*Priestly Formation,* 11).

452. "The discipline required by seminary life should not be regarded merely as a strong support of community life and of charity. For it is a necessary part of the whole training program designed to provide self-mastery, to foster solid maturity of personality and to develop other traits of character which are extremely serviceable for the ordered and productive activity of the Church.

"Let discipline be exercised then, in a way which will develop in the students an internal attitude by which the authority of superiors will be accepted through an act of personal conviction, that is, conscientiously (Rom. 13:5) and for supernatural reasons . . . so that they can gradually learn to govern themselves and make wise use of their freedom." (*Priestly Formation,* 11).

453. "Seminarians should understand very plainly that they are not called to domination or to honors, but to give themselves over entirely to God's service and the pastoral ministry. With special care they must be trained in priestly obedience, in a program of humble living and in the spirit of self-denial. As a result, even in matters which are lawful, but not expedient, they will be accustomed to make prompt renunciation and to imitate Christ crucified." (*Priestly Formation,* 9).

454. "Seminarians should be informed about the obligations they must undertake, and no hardship of the priestly life should go unmentioned — not that they should see practically nothing but the elements of peril in the busy life which lies ahead, but rather that they may be confirmed in the spiritual life, which will be strengthened in the greatest measure by pastoral activity itself." (*Priestly Formation,* 9).

455. "Depending on the age of each seminarian and his state of progress, careful inquiry should be made concerning the rightness of his intention and the freedom of his choice, his spiritual, moral and intellectual fitness. . . .

"In all selection and testing of seminarians, necessary standards must always be firmly maintained, even when there exists a regrettable shortage of priests. For God will not allow His Church to lack ministers if worthy candidates are admitted while unsuited ones are speedily and paternally directed towards the assuming of other tasks and are encouraged to take up the lay apostolate readily, in a consciousness of their Christian vocation." (*Priestly Formation,* 6).

TRAINING SEMINARIANS FOR CELIBACY

456. "Students who, according to the holy and fixed laws of their own rite, follow the revered tradition of priestly celibacy, should be carefully trained for this state. By it they renounce the companionship of marriage for the sake of the kingdom of heaven (Mt. 19:12); they devote themselves to the Lord with an undivided love which is profoundly proper to the new covenant; they bear witness to the state which the resurrection will bring about in the world to come (Lk. 20:36); and they gain extremely appropriate help for exercising that perfect and unremitting love by which they can become all things to all men through their priestly ministration. May they deeply sense how gratefully this state deserves to be undertaken — not only as a requisite of Church law but as a precious gift which should be humbly sought of God and to which they should freely and generously hasten to respond

through the energizing and fortifying grace of the Holy Spirit." (*Priestly Formation,* 10).

457. Let seminarians "be warned of the very severe dangers with which their chastity will be confronted in present-day society. Aided by appropriate helps, both divine and human, may they learn so to integrate the renunciation of marriage into their life and activity that these will not suffer any detriment from celibacy; rather that they themselves may achieve a greater mastery of soul and body, and added growth in maturity; and may comprehend more profoundly the blessedness promised by the gospel." (*Priestly Formation,* 10).

STUDY OF SCRIPTURE, THEOLOGY AND PHILOSOPHY

458. "In the study of sacred Scripture, which ought to be the soul of all theology, students should be trained with special diligence. After a suitable introduction to it, they should be accurately initiated into exegetical method, grasp the pre-eminent themes of divine revelation, and take inspiration and nourishment from reading and meditating on the sacred books day by day." (*Priestly Formation,* 16).

459. "Under the light of faith and with the guidance of the Church's teaching authority, theology should be taught in such a way that the students will accurately draw Catholic doctrine from divine revelation, understand that doctrine profoundly, nourish their own spiritual lives with it and be able to proclaim it, unfold it, and defend it in their priestly ministry."

Fr. Walter M. Abbott's edition of the documents here contains a highly inspirational footnote from St. Bonaventure on how theology can be used to nourish one's spiritual life. It reads as follows: "Let no one believe that it is enough to read without unction, to speculate without devotion, to investigate without wonder, to observe without joy, to act without godly zeal, to know without love, to understand without humility, to study without divine grace or to reflect as a mirror without divinely inspired wisdom." (*Priestly Formation,* 16).

460. Let seminarians "learn to search for solutions to human problems with the light of revelation, to apply eternal truths to the changing conditions of human affairs, and to communicate such truths in a manner suited to contemporary man." (*Priestly Formation,* 16).

461. Philosophy and theology "should work together harmoniously to unfold ever increasingly to the minds of the seminarians the mystery of Christ, that mystery which affects the whole history of the human race, influences the Church continuously, and is mainly exercised by the priestly ministry. . . ."

In these studies, "the mystery of salvation should be presented in such a way that the students will see the meaning of ecclesiastical studies, their interrelationships, and their pastoral intent. They will be helped thereby to root their whole personal lives in faith and to permeate them with it. They will be strengthened to embrace their vocation with personal commitment and a joyful heart." (*Priestly Formation,* 14).

SEMINARY DIRECTORS AND PROFESSORS

462. "Since the training of seminarians hinges to a very large extent, on wise regulations and on suitable teachers, seminary directors and professors should be chosen from among the best, and be painstakingly prepared by solid doctrine, appropriate pastoral experience and special spiritual and pedagogical training." (*Priestly Formation,* 5).

In a footnote referring to the kind of professors to be chosen, Abbott's collection of the Vatican II documents contains the following excerpt from the Encyclical *Ad Catholici Sacerdotii* of Pope Pius XI, issued on December 20, 1935: "Be careful especially in the choice of moderators and teachers . . . and assign to sacred colleges of this type priests endowed with the greatest virtue; and do not hesitate to remove them from duties which, though in appearance of much greater import, can in no way be compared with this foremost duty, whose elements are supplied by nothing else." (*Priestly Formation,* 5).

The following is an excerpt from the circular letter sent out by the Sacred Congregation for the Clergy to the Presidents of the Episcopal Conferences concerning the permanent formation of the Clergy, and published in the English edition *L'Osservatore Romano* on February 19, 1970. "Those responsible for the training of priests should be selected for the task in view of their ecclesial sense *(sentire cum Ecclesia),* that is, they are supposed to be theologians with no doubt as to their integrity. A close link between their theological knowledge and their priestly spirituality will uphold their conviction in the priestly life.

"Suitable persons for this function are those who can solve problems that are laid before them and not those that raise and increase doubts. Reputation, research of novel ideas in the exposition and enunciation of arguments are not criteria to be chosen. Those that are accustomed to attack tradition, institutions and the authority of the Church are not suitable to fulfill such a task. Therefore, only priests that think with the Church and do not let themselves go astray from its tenets should be chosen. Mindful of the real values of our times and their needs, attached in their ways and teaching to the tradition of the Church, they should endeavor to reconcile both the legitimate requirements and present-day trends with the tradition of the Church." (*Circular Letter,* 12).

These same demands are put forth at greater length in the Basic Scheme for Priestly Training *(Ratio Fundamentalis Institutionis Sacerdotalis)* issued by the Sacred Congregation for Catholic Education on January 6, 1970, and published serially in the English edition *L'Osservatore Romano* on March 26, April 16, and April 23, 1970. This Decree was issued in response to a plea made by the Synod of Bishops, held in October 1967. This Decree goes one step farther by demanding that professors of theology must use "a basic and reliable text." (*Ratio Fundamentalis,* 88; April 23, 1970).

463. Seminary "directors and teachers need to be keenly aware of how greatly the outcome of seminary formation depends on their own manner of thinking and acting. Under their Rector's lead they should create the strictest harmony in spirit and behavior. Among themselves and with their students they should constitute the kind of family which answers the Lord's prayer 'that they may be one' (John 17:11) and which intensifies in each student the joy of his calling. With active and loving concern, the bishop ought to inspire those who work in the seminary and show himself to be a true father in Christ to his students. Finally, let every priest regard the seminary as the heart of the diocese, gladly offering the help of his own services." (*Priestly Formation,* 5).

10. Laity

DIGNITY OF THE LAITY

464. "The term laity is here understood to mean all the faithful except those in holy orders and those in a religious state sanctioned by the Church. These faithful are by baptism made one body with Christ and are established among the People of God. They are in their own way made sharers in the priestly, prophetic and kingly functions of Christ. They carry out their own part in the mission of the whole Christian people with respect to the Church and to the world." (*Church*, 31).

465. "By divine condescension the laity have Christ for their brother Who, though He is the Lord of all, came not to be served but to serve (Mt. 20:28). They also have for their brothers those in the sacred ministry who by teaching, by sanctifying and by ruling with the authority of Christ so feed the family of God that the new commandment of charity may be fulfilled by all. St. Augustine puts this very beautifully when he says: 'What I am for you terrifies me; what I am with you consoles me. For you I am a bishop; but with you I am a Christian. The former is a title of duty; the latter, one of grace. The former is a danger; the latter, salvation.' " (*Church*, 32).

466. "Since in their own measure priests participate in the office of the apostles, God gives them the grace to be ministers of Christ Jesus among the people. They shoulder the sacred task of the gospel, so that the offering of the people can be made acceptable through the sanctifying power of the Holy Spirit. For, through the apostolic proclamation of the gospel, the People of God is called together and assembled so that all who belong to this people have been sanctified by the Holy Spirit, they can offer themselves as 'a sacrifice, living, holy, pleasing to God' (Rom. 12:1)." (*Priests*, 2).

467. "Christ's faithful, though not of this world, are the light of the world and give glory to the Father in the sight of men." (*Liturgy*, 9).

468. "All artists who, in view of their talents, desire to serve God's glory in holy Church should ever bear in mind that they are engaged in a kind of sacred imitation of God, the Creator, and are concerned with works destined for use in Catholic worship, and for the edification, devotion and religious instruction of the faithful." (*Liturgy,* 127).

LAITY CALLED TO HOLINESS — TO SANCTIFY OTHERS

469. "Fortified by so many and such a powerful means of salvation (e.g., sacraments) all the faithful, whatever their condition or state, are called by the Lord, each in his own way, to that perfect holiness whereby the Father Himself is perfect." (*Church,* 11).

470. "Laborers, whose work is often toilsome, should by their human exertions try to perfect themselves, aid their fellow-citizens, and raise all of society, and even creation itself, to a better mode of existence. By their lively charity, joyous hope and sharing of one another's burdens, let them also truly imitate Christ, Who roughened His hands with carpenter's tools, and Who, in union with His Father is always at work for the salvation of all men. By their daily work itself, laborers can achieve greater apostolic sanctity." (*Church,* 41).

471. "By performing their work according to God's will, they (the laity) can grow in that union (with Christ). In this way must the laity make progress in holiness showing a ready and happy spirit, and trying prudently and patiently to overcome difficulties. Neither family concerns nor other secular affairs should be excluded from their religious program of life. For as the apostle states: 'Whatever you do in word or work, do all in the name of the Lord Jesus Christ, giving thanks to God the Father through Him' (Col. 3:17)." (*Laity,* 4).

472. "Following Jesus Who was poor they (the laity) are neither depressed by the lack of temporal goods nor puffed up by their abundance. Imitating Christ Who was humble, they have no obsession for empty honors (Gal. 5:26) but seek to please God rather than men, ever ready to leave all things for Christ's sake (Lk. 14:26) and to suffer persecution for justice' sake (Mt. 5:10). For they remember the words of the Lord, 'If any one wishes to come after me, let him deny himself and take up his cross and follow me' (Mt. 16:24). Promoting Christian friendship among themselves, they help one another in any kind of necessity." (*Laity,* 4).

473. The laity "show themselves to be children of the promise, if, strong in faith and in hope, they make the most of the present time (Eph. 5:16; Col. 4:5), and with patience await the glory that is to come

(Rom. 8:25). Let them not, then, hide this hope in the depths of their hearts, but even in the framework of secular life let them express it by a continual turning towards God and by wrestling 'against the world-rulers of this darkness, against the spiritual forces of wickedness' (Eph. 6:12)." (*Church,* 35).

474. "The laity have the right, as do all Christians, to receive in abundance from their sacred pastors, the spiritual goods of the Church, especially the assistance of the Word of God and the sacraments. Every layman should openly reveal to them his needs and desires with that freedom and confidence which befits a son of God and a brother in Christ. An individual layman, by reason of the knowledge, competence or outstanding ability which he may enjoy, is permitted and sometimes even obliged to express his opinion on things which concern the good of the Church. When occasions arise, let this be done through the agencies set up by the Church for this purpose. Let it always be done in truth, in courage and in prudence, with reverence and charity towards those who by reason of their sacred office represent the Person of Christ." (*Church,* 37).

475. "The faithful must learn the deepest meaning and the value of all creation, and how to relate it to the praise of God. They must assist one another to live holier lives even in their daily occupations. In this way the world is permeated by the spirit of Christ and more effectively achieves its purpose in justice, charity and peace. The laity have the principal role in the universal fulfillment of this purpose." (*Church,* 36).

476. "The Lord wishes to spread His kingdom by means of the laity also, a kingdom of truth and life, a kingdom of holiness and grace, a kingdom of justice, love and peace. In this kingdom, creation itself will be delivered out of its slavery to corruption and into the freedom of the glory of the sons of God (Rom. 8:21). Clearly then, a great promise and a great mandate are committed to the disciples: 'For all are yours, and you are Christ's, and Christ is God's' (1 Cor. 3:23)." (*Church,* 36).

477. "Impelled by divine charity, they (the laity) do good to all men, especially to those of the household of the faith (Gal. 6:10), laying aside 'all malice and all deceit and pretense, and envy and all slander' (1 Pet. 2:1) and thereby they draw men to Christ. This charity of God, which 'is poured forth in our hearts by the Holy Spirit Who has been given to us' (Rom. 5:5) enables the laity to express the true spirit of the beatitudes in their lives." (*Laity,* 4).

LAITY AND THE CHURCH AS THE PEOPLE OF GOD AND THE BODY OF CHRIST

478. "As members of the living Christ, all the faithful have been in-

corporated into Him and made like unto Him through baptism, confirmation and the Eucharist. Hence all are duty-bound to cooperate in the expansion and growth of His Body, so that they can bring it to fullness as swiftly as possible (Eph. 4:13)." (*Missions*, 36).

479. "The laity are gathered together in the People of God and make up the Body of Christ under one Head. Whoever they are, they are called upon, as living members, to expend all their energy for the growth of the Church and its continuous sanctification. For this very energy is a gift of the Creator and a blessing of the Redeemer." (*Church*, 33).

480. Rightly trained, the Christian "may grow into manhood according to the mature measure of Christ (Eph. 4:13), and devote himself to the upbuilding of the Mystical Body. Moreover, aware of his calling, he should grow accustomed to giving witness to the hope that is in him (1 Pet. 3:15)." (*Education*, 2).

481. "There is no member (of the Mystical Body) who does not have a part in the mission of the whole Body. Rather, each one ought to hallow Jesus in his heart and bear witness to Jesus in the Spirit of prophecy." (*Priests*, 2).

482. "The Church has not been truly established, and is not yet fully alive, nor is it a perfect sign of Christ among men, unless there exists a laity worthy of the name working along with the hierarchy. For the gospel cannot be deeply imprinted on the talents, life and work of any people without the active presence of laymen. Therefore, even in the very founding of a Church, the greatest attention is to be paid to raising up a mature Christian laity." (*Missions*, 21).

483. "Their sacred pastors know how much the laity contribute to the welfare of the entire Church. Pastors also know that they themselves were not meant by Christ to shoulder alone the entire saving mission of the Church toward the world. On the contrary, they understand that it is their noble duty so to shepherd the faithful and recognize their services and charismatic gifts that all according to their proper roles may cooperate in this common undertaking with one heart. For we must all 'practice the truth in love, and so grow up in all things in him Who is Head, Christ. For from Him the whole body (being closely joined and knit together through every joint of the system according to the functioning in due measure of each single part) derives its increase to the building up of itself in love' (Eph. 4:15-16)." (*Church*, 30).

484. "Let missionaries as God's co-workers (1 Cor. 3:9) raise up congregations of the faithful who will walk in a manner worthy of the vocation to which they have been called (Eph. 4:1) and will exercise the priestly, prophetic and royal office which God has entrusted to them. In this way the Christian community becomes a sign of God's presence in

the world. For by reason of the Eucharistic Sacrifice, this community is ceaselessly on the way with Christ to the Father." (*Missions*, 15).

485. "By the living witness of each one of the faithful and of the whole community, let the particular Church be a sign which points out Christ to others." (*Missions*, 20).

486. "No Christian community can be built up unless it has its basis and center in the celebration of the most Holy Eucharist. Here, therefore, all education in the spirit of community must originate. If this celebration is to be sincere and thorough, it must lead to various works of charity and mutual help, as well as to missionary activity and to different forms of Christian witness." (*Priests*, 6).

487. "The faithful are called upon to engage in the apostolate as individuals in the varying circumstances of their life. They should remember, nevertheless, that man is naturally social and that it has pleased God to unite those who believe in Christ in the People of God (1 Pet. 2:5-10) and into one body (1 Cor. 12:12)." (*Laity*, 18).

488. "For their part, the faithful must cling to their bishop, as the Church does to Christ, and Jesus Christ to the Father, so that everything may harmonize in unity, and abound to the glory of God (2 Cor. 4:15)." (*Church*, 27).

489. "With ready Christian obedience, laymen as well as all disciples of Christ should accept whatever their sacred pastors, as representatives of Christ, decree in their role as teachers and rulers in the Church. Let laymen follow the example of Christ, Who, by His obedience even at the cost of death, opened to all men the blessed way to the liberty of the children of God. Nor should they omit to pray to God for those placed over them, who keep watch as having to render an account of their souls, so that they may render this account with joy and not with grief (Heb. 13:17).

"Let sacred pastors recognize and promote the dignity as well as the responsibility of the layman in the Church. Let them willingly make use of his prudent advice. Let them confidently assign duties to him in the service of the Church, allowing him freedom and room for action. Further, let them encourage the layman so that he may undertake tasks on his own initiative. Attentively in Christ, let them consider with fatherly love the projects, suggestions, and desires proposed by the laity." (*Church*, 37).

490. "Although the Catholic Church has been endowed with all divinely revealed truth and with all means of grace, her members fail to live by them with all the fervor they should. As a result, the radiance of the Church's face shines less brightly in the eyes of our separated brethren and of the world at large, and the growth of God's kingdom is retarded. Every Catholic must therefore aim at Christian perfection

(Jas. 1:4; Rom. 12:1-2) and, each according to his station play his part so that the Church which bears in her own body the humility and dying of Jesus (2 Cor. 4:10; Phil. 2:5-8) may daily be more purified and renewed." (*Ecumenism,* 4).

PRIESTHOOD OF THE LAITY

491. In its Dogmatic Constitution on the Church, Vatican II gives us a clear-cut distinction between the hierarchical priesthood and the priesthood of the laity as follows: "Though they differ from one another in essence and not only in degree, the common priesthood of the faithful and the ministerial or hierarchical priesthood are nonetheless interrelated. Each of them in its own special way is a participation in the one priesthood of Christ. The ministerial priest by the sacred powers he enjoys, molds and rules the priestly people. Acting in the person of Christ, he brings about the Eucharistic Sacrifice, and offers it to God in the name of all the people. For their part, the faithful join in the offering of the Eucharist by virtue of their royal priesthood. They likewise exercise that priesthood by receiving the sacraments and by self-denial and active charity." (*Church,* 10).

492. "The baptized by regeneration and the anointing of the Holy Spirit are consecrated into a spiritual house and a holy priesthood. Thus, through all those works befitting Christian men they can offer spiritual sacrifices and proclaim the power of Him Who has called them out of darkness into His marvelous light (1 Pet. 2:4-10). Therefore all the disciples of Christ, persevering in prayer and praising God (Acts 2:42-47), should present themselves as a living sacrifice, holy and pleasing to God (Rom. 12:1). Everywhere on earth they must bear witness to Christ and give an answer to those who seek an account of that hope of eternal life which is in them (1 Pet. 3:15)." (*Church,* 10).

493. "Since the supreme and eternal Priest, Christ Jesus, wills to continue His witness and serve through the laity too, He vivifies them in His Spirit and unceasingly urges them on to every good and perfect work.

"For besides intimately associating them with His life and His mission, Christ also gives them a share in His priestly function of offering spiritual worship for the glory of God and the salvation of men. For this reason the laity, dedicated to Christ and anointed by the Holy Spirit, are marvelously called and equipped to produce in themselves ever more abundant fruits of the Spirit. For all their works, prayers and apostolic endeavors, their ordinary married and family life, their daily labor, their mental and physical relaxation, if carried out in the Spirit, and even the hardships of life, if patiently borne — all of these become spiritual sacrifices acceptable to God through Jesus Christ (1 Pet. 2:5). During the celebration of the Eucharist, these sacrifices are most lovingly offered to the Father along with the Lord's Body. Thus, as worshippers whose every deed is holy, the laity consecrate the world itself to God." (*Church*, 34).

494. The laity "are consecrated into a royal priesthood and a holy people (1 Pet. 2:4-10) in order that they may offer spiritual sacrifices through everything they do, and may witness to Christ throughout the world. For their part, the sacraments, especially the most Holy Eucharist, communicate and nourish that charity which is the soul of the entire apostolate." (*Laity*, 3).

495. In Christ "all the faithful are made a holy and royal priesthood. They offer spiritual sacrifices to God through Jesus Christ and they proclaim the perfections of Him Who has called them out of darkness into His marvelous light." (*Priests*, 2).

LAITY CALLED TO THE APOSTOLATE BY CHRIST HIMSELF

496. "The laity derive the right and duty with respect to the apostolate from their union with Christ their Head. Incorporated into Christ's Body through baptism and strengthened by the power of the Holy Spirit through confirmation, they are assigned to the apostolate by the Lord Himself." (*Laity*, 3).

497. "The lay apostolate is a participation in the saving mission of the Church itself. Through their baptism and confirmation, all are commissioned to that apostolate by the Lord Himself. Moreover, through the sacraments, especially the Holy Eucharist, there is communicated and nourished that charity towards God and man which is the soul of the entire apostolate. Now, the laity are called in a special way to make the Church present and operative in those places and circumstances where only through them can she become the salt of the earth. Thus every layman, by virtue of the very gifts bestowed upon him, is at the same time a witness and a living instrument of the mission of the Church herself, 'according to the measure of Christ's bestowal' (Eph. 4:7)." (*Church*, 33).

498. "For the exercise of the apostolate, the Holy Spirit Who sanctifies the People of God through the ministry and the sacraments gives to the faithful special gifts as well (1 Cor. 12:7) 'allotting to everyone according as He will' (1 Cor. 12:11). Thus may the individuals 'according to the gift that each has received, administer it to one another' and

become 'good stewards of the manifold grace of God' (1 Pet. 4:10), and build up thereby the whole body in charity (Eph. 16). From the reception of these charisms or gifts, including those which are less dramatic, there arise for each believer the right and duty to use them in the Church and in the world for the good of mankind and for the upbuilding of the Church. In so doing, believers need to enjoy the freedom of the Holy Spirit Who 'breathes where He wills' (John 3:8). At the same time they must act in communion with their brothers in Christ, especially with their pastors. The latter must make a judgment about the true nature and proper use of these gifts, not in order to extinguish but to test all things and hold fast to what is good (1 Th. 5:12, 19, 21)." (*Laity,* 3).

499. "Since Christ in His mission from the Father is the fountain and source of the whole apostolate of the Church, the success of the lay apostolate depends upon the laity's living union with Christ. For the Lord has said: "He who abides in me and I in him, he bears much fruit: for without me, you can do nothing' (John 15:5)." (*Laity,* 4).

500. "Christ, the great Prophet, Who proclaimed the kingdom of His Father by the testimony of His life and the power of His words, continually fulfills His prophetic office until His full glory is revealed. He does this not only through the hierarchy who teach in His name and with His authority, but also through the laity. For that very purpose He made them His witnesses and gave them understanding of the faith and the grace of speech (Acts 2:17-18; Apoc. 19:10) so that the power of the gospel might shine forth in their daily social and family life." (*Church,* 35).

501. "Above all, the lay person should learn to advance the mission of Christ and the Church by basing his life on belief in the divine mystery of creation and redemption, and by being sensitive to the movement of the Holy Spirit, Who gives life to the People of God and Who would impel all men to love God the Father as well as the world and mankind in Him. This formation should be deemed the basis and condition for every successful apostolate." (*Laity,* 29).

502. "As sharers in the role of Christ the Priest, the Prophet and the King, the laity have an active part to play in the life and activity of the Church. . . ." (*Laity,* 10).

"Strengthened by active participation in the liturgical life of community, they are eager to do their share in the apostolic works of that community. They lead to the Church people who are perhaps far removed from it, earnestly cooperate in presenting the word of God especially by means of catechetical instruction, and offer their special skills to make the care of souls and the administration of the temporalities of the Church more efficient . . ." (*Laity,* 10).

"They should above all make missionary activity their own by giving material or even personal assistance, for it is a duty of honor for Christians to return to God a part of the good things they receive from Him ..." (*Laity*, 10).

"Christian husbands and wives are cooperators in grace and witnesses of faith on behalf of each other, their children and all others in their household. They are the first to communicate the faith to their children and to educate them, by word and example they train their offspring for the Christian and apostolic life..." (*Laity*, 11).

"The family has received from God its mission to be the first and vital cell of society. It will fulfill this mission if it shows itself to be the domestic sanctuary of the Church through the mutual affection of its members and the common prayer they offer to God, if the whole family is caught up in the liturgical worship of the Church and if it provides active hospitality and promotes justice and other good works for the service of all the brethren in need." (*Laity*, 10 and 11).

503. "The perfect example of this type of spiritual and apostolic life is the most Blessed Virgin Mary, Queen of apostles. While leading on earth a life common to all men, one filled with family concerns and labors, she was always intimately united with her Son and cooperated in the work of the Savior in a manner altogether special. Now that she has been taken up into heaven 'with her maternal charity she cares for these brothers of her Son who are still on their earthly pilgrimage and are surrounded by dangers and difficulties; she will care until they are led into their blessed fatherland.' All should devoutly venerate her and commend their life and apostolate to her motherly concern." (*Laity*, 4).

NEED AND REASON FOR WITNESS

504. "Each individual layman must stand before the world as a witness to the resurrection and life of the Lord Jesus and as a sign that God lives. As a body and individually, the laity must do their part to nourish the world with spiritual fruits (Gal. 5:22), and to spread abroad in it that spirit by which are animated those poor, meek and peace-making men whom the Lord in the gospel calls blessed (Mt. 5:3-9). 'In a word, what the soul is to the body, let Christians be to the world' *(Epistle to Diognetus).*" (*Church*, 38).

505. "The apostolate is carried on through the faith, hope and charity which the Holy Spirit diffuses in the hearts of all members of the Church." (*Laity*, 3).

506. "The law of love, which is the Lord's greatest commandment, impels all the faithful to promote God's glory through the spread of His

kingdom and to obtain for all men that eternal life which consists in knowing the only true God and Him Whom He sent, Jesus Christ (John 17:3). On all Christians therefore is laid the splendid burden of working to make the divine message of salvation known and accepted by all men throughout the world." (*Laity*, 3).

APOSTOLATE OF EXAMPLE

507. "Let all realize that their first and most important obligation toward the spread of the faith is this: to lead a profoundly Christian life. For their fervor in the service of God and their charity toward others will cause new spiritual inspiration to sweep over the whole Church. Then she will appear as a sign lifted among the nations (Is. 11:12), 'the light of the world' (Mt. 5:14) and 'the salt of the earth' (Mt. 5:13)." (*Missions*, 36).

508. "There are innumerable opportunities open to the laity for the exercise of their apostolate of making the gospel known and men holy. The very testimony of their Christian life and good works done in a supernatural spirit, have the power to draw men to belief and to God; for the Lord says: 'Even so let your light shine before men, in order that they may see your good works and give glory to your Father in heaven' (Mt. 5:16).

"However, an apostolate of this kind does not consist only in the witness of one's way of life; a true apostle looks for opportunities to announce Christ by words. . . . The words of the apostle should echo in every Christian's heart: 'For woe is me if I do not preach the gospel' (1 Cor. 9:16)." (*Laity*, 6).

509. "The sacraments of the New Law, by which the life and the apostolate of the faithful are nourished, prefigure a new heaven and a new earth (Apoc. 21:1). So too the laity go forth as powerful heralds of a faith in things to be hoped for (Heb. 11:1) provided they steadfastly join to their profession of faith a life springing from faith. This evangelization, that is, this announcement of Christ by a living testimony as well as by the spoken word, takes on a specific quality and a special force in that it is carried out in the ordinary surroundings of the world." (*Church*, 35).

APOSTOLATE OF THE WORD

510. "A particular form of the individual apostolate, as well as a sign especially suited to our times, is the testimony of a layman's entire life

as it developes out of faith, hope and charity. This form manifests Christ living in those who believe in Him. Then by the apostolate of the word, which is utterly necessary under certain circumstances, lay people announce Christ, explain and spread His teaching according to their situation and ability, and faithfully profess it." (*Laity,* 16).

511. "There is a very urgent need for this individual apostolate in places where the freedom of the Church is seriously restricted. In exceedingly trying circumstances, the laity do what they can to take the place of priests, risking their freedom and sometimes their lives to teach Christian doctrine to those around them, to train them in a religious way of life and in a Catholic mentality, to lead them to receive the sacraments frequently and to develope their piety, especially toward the Eucharist. This most sacred Synod heartily thanks God for continuing in our times to raise up lay persons of heroic fortitude in the midst of persecutions, and it embraces them with fatherly affection and gratitude." (*Laity,* 17).

512. "Even when preoccupied with temporal cares, the laity can and must perform eminently valuable work on behalf of bringing the gospel to the world. Some of them do all they can to provide sacred services when sacred ministers are lacking or are blocked by a persecuting regime. Many devote themselves entirely to apostolic work. But all ought to cooperate in the spreading and intensifying of the kingdom of Christ in the world. Therefore, let the laity strive skillfully to acquire a more profound grasp of revealed truth, and insistently beg of God the gift of wisdom." (*Church,* 35).

APOSTOLATE OF THE SOCIAL MILIEU

513. "The apostolate of the social milieu, that is, the effort to infuse a Christian spirit into the mentality, customs, laws and structures of the community in which a person lives, is so much the duty and responsibility of the laity, that it can never be properly performed by others. In this area the laity can exercise the apostolate of like toward like. It is here that the laymen add to the testimony of life, the testimony of their speech; it is here in the arena of their labor, profession, studies, residence, leisure and companionship that laymen have a special opportunity to help their brothers. To fulfill the mission of the Church in the world, the laity need a life in harmony with their faith, so that they can become the light of the world. . . .

"This apostolate should reach out to all men wherever they can be found; it should not exclude any spiritual or temporal benefit which can possibly be conferred. True apostles, however, are not content with this activity alone, but look for the opportunity to announce Christ to their neighbors through the spoken word as well. For there are many persons who can hear the gospel and recognize Christ only through the laity who live near them." (*Laity,* 13).

514. "The laity by their very vocation, seek the kingdom of God by engaging in temporal affairs and by ordering them according to the plan of God. They live in the world, that is, in each and all of the secular professions and occupations. They live in the ordinary circumstances of family and social life, from which the very web of their existence is woven.

"They are called there by God so that by exercising their proper function and being led by the spirit of the gospel they can work for the sanctification of the world from within in the manner of leaven. In this way they can make Christ known to others, especially by the testimony of a life resplendent in faith, hope and charity. The layman is closely involved in temporal affairs of every sort. It is therefore his special task to illumine and organize these affairs in such a way that they may always start out, develope and persist according to Christ's mind, to the praise of the Creator and Redeemer." (*Church,* 31).

515. Let the laity "be one with their fellow countrymen in sincere charity, so that there may appear in their way of life a new bond of unity and of universal solidarity, drawn from the mystery of Christ. Let them also spread the faith of Christ among those with whom they live or have professional connections. This obligation is all the more urgent because very many men can hear of the gospel and recognize Christ only by means of the laity who are their neighbors. In fact, wherever possible, the laity should be prepared, in more immediate cooperation with the hierarchy, to fulfill a special mission of proclaiming the gospel and communicating Christian teachings. Thus they can add vigor to the developing Church." (*Missions,* 21).

516. The laity "also belong to Christ, because they were regenerated in the Church by faith and by baptism. Thus they are Christ's in newness of life and work (1 Cor. 15:23) so that in Christ, all things may be made subject to God, and finally God will be all in all (1 Cor. 15:28).

"Their main duty, whether they are men or women, is the witness which they are bound to bear to Christ by their life and works in the home, in their social group, and in their own professional circle. For in them there must appear the new man created according to God in justice and true holiness (Eph. 4:24). But they must give expression to this newness of life in the social and cultural framework of their own homeland, according to their own national traditions. They must be acquainted with this culture. They must heal it and preserve it. They must develope it in accordance with modern conditions, and finally perfect it in Christ. Thus the faith of Christ and the life of the Church will no longer be something extraneous to the society in which they live, but will begin to permeate and transform it." (*Missions*, 21).

517. "The presence of the Christian faithful in these human groups should be animated by that charity with which God has loved us, and with which He wills that we should love one another (1 John 4:11). Christian charity truly extends to all, without distinction of race, social condition, or religion. It looks for neither gain nor gratitude. For as God has loved us with a spontaneous love, so also the faithful should in their charity care for the human person himself by loving him with the same affection with which God sought out man." (*Missions*, 12).

CLERGY TO HELP LAY APOSTLES

518. "Let the clergy highly esteem the arduous apostolate of the laity. Let them train the laity to become conscious of the responsibility which as members of Christ they bear for all men. Let them instruct them deeply in the mystery of Christ, introduce them to practical methods, and be at their side in difficulties, according to the tenor of the Council's Constitution on the Church *(Lumen Gentium)* and its Decree on the Apostolate of the Laity *(Apostolicam Actuositatem)*." (*Missions*, 21).

519. "Upon all the laity, therefore, rests the noble duty of working to extend the divine plan of salvation ever increasingly to all men of each epoch and in every land. Consequently, let every opportunity be given them so that, according to their abilities and the needs of the times, they may zealously participate in the saving work of the Church." (*Church*, 33).

520. "It will be the bishop's task to raise up from among his own people, especially the sick and those oppressed by hardship, souls who will offer prayers and penance to God with a generous heart for the evangelization of the world." (*Missions*, 38).

ON FOSTERING VOCATIONS

521. "The task of fostering vocations devolves on the whole Christian community, which should do so in the first place by living in a fully Christian way. Outstanding contributions are made in this work by families which are alive with the spirit of faith, love and reverence and which serve as a kind of introductory seminary; and by parishes in whose pulsing vitality young people themselves have a part." (*Priestly Formation*, 2).

522. "By a truly Christian life, families must become nurseries . . . of vocations to the priesthood and the religious life." (*Missions,* 19).

523. After urging all to "lead a profoundly Christian life marked by prayer and works of penance," Vatican II gives assurance that "missionary vocations will be generated." (*Missions,* 36).

524. "To the greatest possible extent, every priest should manifest the zeal of an apostle in fostering vocations. Let him attract the hearts of young people to the priesthood by his own humble and energetic life, joyfully pursued, and by love for his fellow priests and brotherly collaboration with them." (*Priestly Formation,* 2).

"Pope Paul, prophesying that today's crisis in priestly vocations will be overcome, declared that it is 'up to priests themselves to make the priesthood shine with a light that renders it attractive' " *(NC News).*

"The Pope told national directors of vocations from twenty-five countries: 'Where the priest leads a really evangelical life, drawing love and courage and joy from a ministry carried out in deep union with Christ, this witness cannot long remain sterile of vocations.'

"And, he added: 'Every sagging of the priestly ideal, every hesitation about it, just as all mediocrity of life and all bickering among the clergy, inevitably dries up its source.'

"He urged the fifty participants in a congress of vocations directors May 13: 'It is up to you to study this situation deeply and objectively in order to initiate adequate spiritual and educational remedies.' " (*Idaho Register,* May 28, 1971).

11. Roads to Holiness for All

525. In dealing with the Church as a whole, the Second Council of the Vatican not only gave us a supremely inspirational interpretation of the Church as the People of God, the Mystical Body of Christ (*Chap. 5, 194*) and the temple of the Holy Spirit but also indicated the virtues as well as the duties of all of those groups that make up the Church as an organized institution. (*Chap. 6, 237*).

526. In addition to the ideals and virtues that are to characterize specific groups such as the bishops, priests, religious, laity, etc., however, the documents of Vatican II contain a wealth of spiritual teaching concerning topics common to the Christian community as a whole. Foremost among these are the conciliar teachings concerning the sacraments in which Christ Himself is the principal agent. Much is also contained in the conciliar documents concerning the Church's traditional asceticism, devotional practices, virtues, etc. If there is any one word that can be used to sum up the spiritual teaching of Vatican II, that word is *theocentric*.

THEOCENTRIC LIFE

527. The Church "knows that only God Whom she serves, meets the deepest longings of the human heart which is never fully satisfied by what this world has to offer." (*Modern World*, 41).

528. In the same document, Vatican II tells us that "God has called man and still calls him so that with his entire being he might be joined to Him in an endless sharing of a divine life beyond all corruption." (*Modern World*, 18).

529. "An outstanding cause of human dignity lies in man's call to communion with God. From the very circumstance of his origin, man is

already invited to converse with God. For man would not exist were he not created by God's love and constantly preserved by it." (*Modern World*, 19).

530. Emphasizing the personal relationship that should exist between each soul and God, Vatican II again speaks of the "mystery of the love of God Who has called" converts "to enter into personal relationship with Him in Christ" (*Missions*, 13), and urges missioners as God's co-workers to raise up congregations of the faithful who "will exercise the priestly, prophetic and royal office which God has entrusted to them. In this way the Christian community becomes a sign of God's presence in the world. For by reason of the Eucharistic sacrifice, this community is ceaselessly on the way with Christ to the Father." (*Missions*, 15).

531. All of these thoughts echo the words uttered by Pope John XXIII on Oct. 11, 1962, when His Holiness formally opened the Second Vatican Council. After saying that man is "a pilgrim on this earth," His Holiness declared that "all men, whether taken singly or as united in society, today have the duty of tending ceaselessly during their lifetime towards the attainment of heavenly things and to use for this purpose only the earthly goods, the employment of which must not prejudice their eternal happiness" (*Opening Speech to the Council*).

GOD, OUR FATHER AND OUR GOAL

532. "God, Who has fatherly concern for everyone, has willed that all men should constitute one family and treat one another in a spirit of brotherhood. For having been created in the image of God, Who 'from one man has created the whole human race and made them live all over the face of the earth' (Acts 17:26), all men are called to one and the same goal, namely God Himself." (*Modern World*, 24).

533. "The followers of Christ are called by God, not according to their accomplishments, but according to His own purposes and grace. They are justified in the Lord Jesus, and through baptism sought in faith they truly become sons of God and sharers in the divine nature. In this way they are really made holy. Then, too, by God's gifts they must hold on to and complete in their lives this holiness which they have received. They are warned by the apostle to live 'as becomes saints' (Eph. 5:3) and to put on 'as God's chosen ones, holy and beloved, a heart of mercy, kindness, humility, meekness, patience' (Col. 3:12) and to possess the fruits of the Spirit unto holiness (Gal. 5:22; Rom. 6:22). Since we all truly offend in many things (Jas. 3:2) we all need God's mercy continuously and must daily pray: 'Forgive us our debts.' " (*Church*, 40).

CHRIST CALLS ALL TO PERFECTION

534. "The Lord Jesus, the divine Teacher and Model of all perfection preached holiness of life to each and every one of His disciples, regardless of their situation. 'You therefore are to be perfect, even as your heavenly Father is perfect' (Mt. 5:48). He Himself stands as the Author and Finisher of this holiness of life. For He sent the Holy Spirit upon all men that He might inspire them from within to love God with their whole heart and their whole soul, with all their mind and all their strength (Mk. 12:30) and that they might love one another as Christ loved them (John 13:34; 15:12)." (*Church,* 40).

535. "Thus it is evident to everyone that all the faithful of Christ of whatever rank or status are called to the fullness of the Christian life and to the perfection of charity. By this holiness a more human way of life is promoted even in this earthly society. In order that the faithful may reach this perfection they must use their strength according as they have received it, as a gift from Christ. In this way they can follow in His footsteps and mold themselves in His image, seeking the will of the Father in all things, devoting themselves with all their being to the glory of God and the service of their neighbor. In this way, too, the holiness of the People of God will grow into an abundant harvest of good, as is brilliantly proved by the lives of so many saints in Church history." (*Church,* 40).

536. "All of Christ's faithful, therefore, whatever be the conditions, duties and circumstances of their lives, will grow in holiness day by day through these very situations, if they accept all of them with faith from the hand of their heavenly Father, and if they cooperate with the divine will by showing every man through their earthly activities the love with which God has loved the world." (*Church,* 41).

LOVING WHAT GOD LOVES

537. "Redeemed by Christ and made a new creature in the Holy Spirit, man is able to love the things themselves created by God, and ought to do so. He can receive them from God, and respect and reverence them as flowing constantly from the hand of God.

"Grateful to his Benefactor for these creatures, using and enjoying them in detachment and liberty of spirit, man is led forward into a true possession of the world, as having nothing, yet possessing all things. 'All are yours, and you are Christ's; and Christ is God's' (1 Cor. 3:22-23)." (*Modern World,* 37).

UNION WITH CHRIST

538. "Christ established the kingdom of God on earth, manifested His Father and Himself by deeds and words, and completed His work by His death, resurrection and glorious ascension and by the sending of the Holy Spirit. Having been lifted up from the earth, He draws all men to Himself (John 12:32, Greek text), He Who alone has the words of eternal life (John 6:68)." (*Revelation,* 17).

539. "All men are called to this union with Christ, Who is the light of the world, from Whom we go forth, through Whom we live, and toward Whom our journey leads us." (*Church,* 3).

540. "Christ, the Son of God, Who with the Father and the Spirit is praised as being 'alone holy,' loved the Church as His Bride, delivering Himself up for her. This He did that He might sanctify her (Eph. 5:25-26). He united her to Himself as His own Body and crowned her with the Holy Spirit, for God's glory. Therefore, in the Church, everyone belonging to the hierarchy, or being cared for by it, is called to holiness according to the saying of the apostle: 'For this is the will of God, your sanctification' (1 Th. 4:3; cf. Eph. 1:4)." (*Church,* 39).

541. "Joined with Christ in the Church and signed with the Holy Spirit 'Who is the pledge of our inheritance' (Eph. 1:14) we are truly called sons of God and such we are (1 John 3:1). But we have not yet appeared with Christ in the state of glory (Col. 3:4), in which we shall be like to God since we shall see Him as He is (1 John 3:2). Therefore, 'while we are in the body, we are exiled from the Lord' (2 Cor. 5:6) and having the first fruits of the Spirit we groan within ourselves (Rom. 8:23) and desire to be with Christ (Phil. 1:23). A common love urges us to live more for Him, Who died for us and rose again (2 Cor. 5:15). We put on the armor of God that we may be able to stand against the wiles of the devil and resist on the evil day (Eph. 6:11-13)." (*Church,* 48).

SANCTIFICATION THROUGH THE HOLY SPIRIT

542. "When the work which the Father had given the Son to do on earth (John 17:4) was accomplished, the Holy Spirit was sent on the day of Pentecost in order that He might forever sanctify the Church and thus all believers would have access to the Father through Christ in one Spirit (Eph. 2:18). He is the Spirit of life, a fountain of water springing up to eternal life (John 4:14; 7:38-39). Through Him the Father gives life to men who are dead from sin, till at last He revives in Christ even their mortal bodies (Rom. 8:10-11)." (*Church,* 4).

543. "The gifts of the Spirit are diverse. He calls some to give clear

witness to the desire for a heavenly home and to keep that desire green among the human family. He summons others to dedicate themselves to the earthly service of men and to make ready the material of the celestial realm by this ministry of theirs. Yet He frees all of them so that by putting aside love of self and bringing all earthly resources into the service of human life they can devote themselves to that future when humanity itself will become an offering accepted by God." (*Modern World*, 38).

544. "In the various types and duties of life, one and the same holiness is cultivated by all who are moved by the Spirit of God, and who obey the voice of the Father, worshipping God the Father in spirit and in truth. These souls follow the poor Christ, the humble and cross-bearing Christ, in order to be made worthy of being partakers in His glory. Every person should walk unhesitatingly according to his own personal gifts and duties in the path of a living faith which arouses hopes and works through charity." (*Church*, 41).

SPIRITUAL LIFE — MIXED LIFE — ASCETICISM — MYSTICISM

545. It is only by the light of faith and by meditation on the Word of God that we can "always and everywhere recognize God in Whom 'we live and move and have our being' (Acts 17:28), seek His will in every event, see Christ in all men whether they be close to us or strangers, and make correct judgments about the true meaning and value of temporal things, both in themselves and in relation to man's final goal." (*Laity*, 4).

546. The Council tells us that "it is through the gift of the Holy Spirit that man comes by faith to the contemplation and appreciation of the divine plan." (*Modern World*, 15).

547. The texts quoted above refer to the very heart of what has traditionally been referred to as "the spiritual life." Unfortunately some contemporary writers are inclined to reject this term on the pretense that it is redolent of the Cartesian split between body and soul. It seems worthwhile to recall therefore that the term "spiritual life" was used by Vatican II in several of its documents, notably the decrees on Missionary Activity of the Church, (*Missions*, 25), Religious Life, (*Religious Life*, 6), Priestly Formation (*Priestly Formation*, 9 and 16), and the Apostolate of the Laity (*Laity*, 4).

548. Another sad aspect of contemporary religious thinking is to be found in the ideas of those who ignore or downgrade the element of contemplation in the spiritual life and the whole idea of the contempla-

tive life itself. Vatican II, on the other hand urges the development of contemplative communities even in mission countries as a means for promoting vocations and conversions through prayer, penance, etc. (*Missions*, 40). The Council also stresses the importance of contemplation in the so-called active communities when it urges religious to "combine contemplation with apostolic love. By the former, they adhere to God in mind and heart; by the latter they strive to associate themselves with the work of redemption and to spread the kingdom of God" (*Religious Life*, 5). Of the Church herself, Vatican II says that she is "eager to act, and yet, devoted to contemplation" (*Liturgy*, 2). In the Modern World text quoted above, the Council tells us that "It is, finally, through the gift of the Holy Spirit that man comes by faith to the contemplation and appreciation of the divine plan." (*Modern World*, 15).

MIXED LIFE

549. Of all the statements made by Vatican II about contemplation, the most significant, perhaps, is that contained in the Decree on the Ministry and Life of Priests which reads as follows: "As priests search for a better way to share with others the fruit of their own contemplation, they will win a deeper understanding of the 'unfathomable riches of Christ' (Eph. 3:8) as well as the manifold wisdom of God" (*Priests*, 13). It is recalled that St. Thomas Aquinas was asked why Christ did not lead the contemplative life since, in the common opinion of His day, this was considered to be more exalted than the active life. His reply was that the "mixed life" in which men preach the fruit of their contemplation to others is the most perfect and that it was this life that Christ Himself led.

ASCETICAL AND MYSTICAL THEOLOGY

550. Even professors of theology have been heard to speak disparagingly of ascetical theology as if it were concerned only with a discussion of such virtues as prudence, fortitude, temperance, etc. Such men seem totally unaware of the fact that the very core of ascetical theology is its teaching concerning the so-called love of conformity by which men conform their minds to God's mind by a vivid and living faith, their hearts to God's heart by a love that is focussed primarily on God and secondarily on all that God loves and also conform their wills to God's will. Compared with this love which constitutes the very essence of holiness,

128

the cardinal virtues might well be described as being mere fringe benefits attached to this all-pervading love.

551. Since the aim of the Second Council of the Vatican was essentially pastoral, it did not intend to give a systematic treatise on asceticism, mysticism or the spiritual life in general. These subjects are so intimately intertwined with pastoral life and practice, however, that they are mentioned in almost every section of the conciliar documents and often constitute the very core and essence of many conciliar declarations. To cite but one example, the Council tells us that as rulers of the community, priests "ideally cultivate the asceticism proper to a pastor of souls renouncing their own convenience, seeking what is profitable for the many and not for themselves so that the many may be saved." (*Priests,* 13).

552. A separate book would be needed to explain all that is hinted at or explicitly stated by the Council concerning the Mystical Body of Christ and its meaning for both Christ and His members. The Council wishes that even the laity should reflect deeply on God's plan for man and the world and on the inner meaning of the whole of creation.

553. In the Pastoral Constitution on the Church in the Modern World which is addressed to mankind as a whole, the Council gives one of the deepest possible interpretations of man in his relationship with God and the universe as a whole:

554. "Though made up of body and soul, man is one. Through his bodily composition he gathers to himself the elements of the material world. Thus they reach their crown through him and through him raise their voice in free praise of the Creator.

"For this reason man is not allowed to despise his bodily life. Rather, he is obliged to regard his body as good and honorable since God has created it and will raise it up on the last day. Nevertheless, wounded by sin, man experiences rebellious stirrings in his body. But the very dignity of man postulates that man glorify God in his body and forbid it to serve the evil inclinations of his heart." (*Modern World,* 14).

555. Volumes could be written on the asceticism urged upon priests and religious in the decrees published for their direction by Vatican II. Many of these texts which were necessarily brief have been quoted in previous chapters of this book (Chapters 7 and 8). Suffice it here to add only three more texts which indicate a few of the basic ground rules for every form of the spiritual life. They remind us that of ourselves we can do nothing but that Christ is ever willing to provide the necessary help.

556. "By himself and by his own power, no one is freed from sin or raised above himself or completely rid of his sickness or his solitude or his servitude. On the contrary, all stand in need of Christ, their Model, . . . their Liberator, their Savior and their Source of life." (*Missions,* 8).

557. "All the sons of the Church should remember that their exalted status is to be attributed not to their own merits, but to the special grace of Christ. If they fail, moreover, to respond to that grace in thought, word and deed, not only will they not be saved, but they will be more severely judged." (*Church,* 14).

558. "Undergoing death itself for all of us sinners, He taught us by example that we too must shoulder that cross which the world and the flesh inflict upon those who search after peace and justice. Appointed Lord by His resurrection and given plenary power in heaven and on earth, Christ is now at work in the hearts of men through the energy of His Spirit. He arouses not only a desire for the age to come, but, by that very fact, He animates, purifies and strengthens those noble longings too by which the human family strives to make its life more human and render the whole earth submissive to this goal." (*Modern World,* 38).

PRAYER

559. It was not the purpose of Vatican II to give us a systematic treatise on prayer of which so many definitions have been provided and about which so many hundreds of books have been written. With telegraphic brevity, however, the Council did point out the essential qualities of prayer, its purpose and functions and the fruits it can produce. Thus, the Council declares that seminarians should "learn to live in familiar and constant companionship with the Father, through Jesus Christ, His Son, in the Holy Spirit." As friends of Christ "they should be used to loyal association with Him through a profound identification of their whole lives with Him." (*Priestly Formation,* 8). Priests should "penetrate ever more deeply through prayer into the Mystery of Christ" (*Priests,* 14), and should "prize daily conversation with Christ the Lord by visits of personal devotion to the Most Holy Eucharist." (*Priests,* 18). Priests should likewise beg of God that spirit of genuine adoration by which they themselves and the people entrusted to them can unite themselves intimately with Christ, the Mediator of the New Testament." (*Priests,* 18).

560. Since prayer is presented to us as companionship and conversation with God, it is not merely a one-sided affair. It must be a response to one or more of the many relationships that bind us to God. He is the Creator of the universe and of each individual soul. We are His creatures. In His loving kindness He looks upon Himself as our Father. We are His children. He loves us and wants us to love Him. He is our benefactor and we are the recipients of His favors. He is our Helper and we are the ones who are helped. We often find ourselves in doubt or perplexity and He wants to guide us.

561. This list of relationships could be lengthened indefinitely but all of our relationships challenge us to respond in some way, be it by adoration, praise, thanks, love, confidence, petition or any of the other things we can say to or do for God.

562. Vatican II reminds us that "only the Lord can give fruitfulness and increase to the works" in which we are engaged. 'Without me,' He said, 'you can do nothing' (John 15:5). That is why the apostles appointing deacons, said: 'We will devote ourselves to prayer and to the ministry of the Word' (Acts 6:4)." (*Liturgy*, 86).

THE BREVIARY

563. In accordance with the millennial practice of the Church, Vatican II again stressed the importance of the divine Office. Especially noteworthy is the fact that the Council placed strong emphasis on the recitation of at least a part of the Breviary by the laity also. The reasons for stressing the recitation of the Breviary and the seriousness of the obligation for men in major orders are explained in the following texts.

564. "Christ Jesus, high priest of the new and eternal covenant, taking human nature, introduced into this earthly exile that hymn which is sung throughout all ages in the halls of heaven. He joins the entire community of mankind to Himself, associating it with His own singing of this canticle of divine praise.

"For He continues His priestly work through the agency of His Church, which is ceaselessly engaged in praising the Lord and interceding for the salvation of the whole world. This she does not only by celebrating the Eucharist, but also in other ways, especially by praying the divine Office." (*Liturgy*, 83).

565. "By tradition going back to early Christian times, the divine Office is arranged so that the whole course of the day and night is made holy by the praises of God. Therefore, when this wonderful song of praise is worthily rendered by priests and others who are deputed for this purpose by Church ordinance, or by the faithful praying together with the priest in an approved form then it is truly the voice of the bride addressing her bridegroom; it is the very prayer which Christ Himself, together with His Body, addresses to the Father." (*Liturgy*, 84).

566. "All who perform this service (Breviary) are not only fulfilling a duty of the Church, but also are sharing in the greatest honor accorded to Christ's spouse, for by offering these praises to God they are standing before God's throne in the name of the Church their Mother." (*Liturgy*, 85).

567. "By reciting the divine Office, they (priests) lend their voice to

the Church as in the name of humanity she perseveres in prayer along with Christ, Who 'lives always to make intercession for us' (Heb. 7:25)." (*Priests*, 13).

568. "Priests themselves extend to the different hours of the day the praise and thanksgiving of the Eucharistic celebration by reciting the divine Office. Through it they pray to God in the name of the Church on behalf of the whole people entrusted to them and indeed for the whole world." (*Priests*, 5).

569. "Priests engaged in the sacred pastoral ministry will offer the praises of the hours with fervor to the extent that they vividly realize that they must heed St. Paul's exhortation: 'Pray without ceasing' (1 Th. 5:17). For only the Lord can give fruitfulness and increase to the works in which they are engaged. 'Without me,' He said, 'you can do nothing' (John 15:5). That is why the apostles, appointing deacons, said: 'We will devote ourselves to prayer and to the ministry of the Word' (Acts 6:4)." (*Liturgy*, 86).

570. "All members of the aforementioned communities who are in major orders or who are solemnly professed, except for lay Brothers, are bound to recite individually those canonical hours which they do not pray in choir." (*Liturgy*, 95 c).

"Clerics not bound to Office in choir, if they are in major Orders, are bound to pray the entire Office every day, either in common or individually, as laid down in article 89." (*Liturgy*, 96).

"Appropriate instances are to be defined by the rubrics in which a liturgical service may be substituted for the divine Office. In particular cases, and for a just reason, ordinaries can dispense their subjects wholly or in part from the obligation of reciting the divine Office, or may commute the obligation." (*Liturgy*, 97).

571. "Since the divine Office is the voice of the Church, that is, of the whole Mystical Body publicly praising God, those clerics who are not obliged to Office in choir, especially priests who live together or who assemble for any purpose, are urged to pray at least some part of the divine Office in common . . ." (*Liturgy*, 99). "Pastors of souls should see to it that the chief hours, especially Vespers, are celebrated in common in Church on Sundays and the more solemn feasts. And the laity, too, are encouraged to recite the divine Office, either with the priests, or among themselves, or even individually." (*Liturgy*, 100).

DEVOTIONS TO THE SAINTS AND ANGELS

572. Since the Second Council of the Vatican devoted the whole of Chapter Seven of the Dogmatic Constitution on the Church to the

Church's eschatological nature, it was logical for the Council to draw practical conclusions concerning the intimate relationship existing between the faithful on earth and the saints in heaven. Angels, strictly speaking, do not belong to the Church but they do belong to God's family and have always rendered inestimable services to God's other children who make up the human race. It was not the purpose of the Council to expatiate on the Scriptural or dogmatic texts concerning angels, but the casual mention of angels found here and there gives valuable testimony to the traditional doctrine concerning them — a testimony which is especially valuable at a time when so many writers question the very existence of angels — and therefore also of devils.

573. "The Church has always believed that the apostles, and Christ's martyrs who had given the supreme witness of faith and charity by the shedding of their blood, are quite closely joined with us in Christ. She has always venerated them with special devotion, together with the Blessed Virgin Mary and the holy angels. The Church has devoutly implored the aid of their intercession. To these were soon added those who had imitated Christ's virginity and poverty more exactly, and finally others whom the outstanding practice of the Christian virtues and the divine charisms recommended to the pious devotion and imitation of the faithful." (*Church*, 50).

574. "It is not only by the title of example that we cherish the memory of those in heaven. We do so still more in order that the union of the whole Church may be strengthened in the Spirit by the practice of fraternal charity (Eph. 4:1-6). For just as the communion among wayfarers brings us closer to Christ, so companionship with the saints joins us to Christ, from Whom as from their fountain and head issue every grace and the life of God's people itself." (*Church*, 50).

575. "By reason of the fact that those in heaven are more closely united with Christ, they establish the whole Church more firmly in holiness, lend nobility to the worship which the Church offers on earth to God and in many ways contribute to its greater upbuilding (1 Cor. 12:12-27). For after they have been received into their heavenly home and are present to the Lord (2 Cor. 5:8), through Him and with Him and in Him, they do not cease to intercede with the Father for us. Rather, they show forth the merits which they won on earth through the one Mediator between God and men, Christ Jesus (1 Tim. 2:5). There they served God in all things and filled up in their flesh whatever was lacking of the sufferings of Christ on behalf of His body which is the Church (Col. 1:24). Thus by their brotherly interest, our weakness is very greatly strengthened." (*Church*, 49).

576. "The Church has also included in the annual cycle, days devoted to the memory of the martyrs and other saints. Raised up to perfection

by the manifold grace of God, and already in possession of eternal salvation, they sing God's perfect praise in heaven and offer prayers for us. By celebrating the passage of these saints from earth to heaven, the Church proclaims the paschal mystery as achieved in the saints who have suffered and been glorified with Christ; she proposes them to the faithful as examples who draw all to the Father through Christ, and through their merits she pleads for God's favors." (*Liturgy,* 104).

577. "When we look at the lives of those who have faithfully followed Christ, we are inspired with a new reason for seeking the city which is to come (Heb. 13:14; 11:10). At the same time we are shown a most safe path by which, among the vicissitudes of this world and in keeping with the state in life and condition proper to each of us, we will be able to arrive at perfect union with Christ, that is, holiness. In the lives of those who shared in our humanity and yet were transformed into especially successful images of Christ (2 Cor. 2:18), God vividly manifests to man His presence and His face. He speaks to us in them, and gives us a sign of His kingdom, to which we are powerfully drawn, surrounded as we are by so many witnesses (Heb. 12:1) and having such an argument for the truth of the gospel." (*Church,* 50).

578. "Let the faithful be taught that the authentic cult of the saints consists not so much in the multiplying of external acts, but rather in the intensity of our active love. By such love, for our own greater good and that of the Church, we seek from the saints 'example in their way of life, fellowship in their communion, and aid by their intercession.' At the same time, let the people be instructed that our communion with those in heaven, provided that it is understood in the more adequate light of faith, in no way weakens, but conversely, more thoroughly enriches the supreme worship we give to God, the Father, through Christ in the Spirit." (*Church,* 51).

579. "It is supremely fitting, therefore, that we love those friends and fellow-heirs of Jesus Christ, who are also our brothers and extraordinary benefactors, that we render due thanks to God for them and 'suppliantly invoke them and have recourse to their prayers, their power and help in obtaining benefits from God through His Son, Jesus Christ, our Lord, Who is our sole Redeemer and Savior' *(Trent).* For by its very nature every genuine testimony of love which we show to those in heaven tends towards, and terminates, in Christ, Who is the 'crown of all saints.' Through Him, it tends towards and terminates in God, Who is wonderful in His saints and is magnified in them." (*Church,* 50).

580. "The saints have been traditionally honored in the Church and their authentic relics and images held in veneration. For the feasts of the saints proclaim the wonderful works of Christ in His servants, and display to the faithful fitting examples for their imitation."

"Lest the feasts of the saints, however, take precedence over the feasts which commemorate the very mysteries of salvation, many of them should be left to be celebrated by a particular Church or nation or religious community; only those should be extended to the universal Church which commemorate saints who are truly of universal significance." (*Liturgy*, 111).

MARY, MOTHER OF GOD AND OUR MOTHER

581. The importance which the Second Council of the Vatican attached to the Blessed Virgin in the economy of salvation and to her place in the Church is evident from the fact that it devoted the whole of Chapter Eight of the Dogmatic Constitution on the Church to the discussion of these topics. The following texts are basic for an understanding of Mary's position in the faith and the spiritual life of the people.

582. "Mary was involved in the mysteries of Christ. As the most holy Mother of God, she was, after her Son, exalted by divine grace above all angels and men. Hence the Church appropriately honors her with special reverence. Indeed, from most ancient times, the Blessed Virgin has been venerated under the title of 'God-bearer.' In all perils and needs, the faithful have fled prayerfully to her protection. Especially after the Council of Ephesus, the cult of the People of God towards Mary wonderfully increased in veneration and love, in invocation and imitation, according to her own prophetic words: 'All generations shall call me blessed; because He Who is mighty has done great things for me' (Lk. 1:48)." (*Church*, 66).

583. "Rightly the holy Fathers see her (Mary) as used by God not merely in a passive way, but as cooperating in the work of human salvation through free faith and obedience. For, as St. Irenaeus says, she, 'being obedient, became the cause of salvation for herself and the whole human race.' Hence in their preaching not a few of the early Fathers gladly assert with him: 'The knot of Eve's disobedience was untied by Mary's obedience. What the virgin Eve bound through her unbelief, Mary loosed by her faith.' Comparing Mary with Eve, they call her 'the mother of the living' and still more often they say: 'Death through Eve, life through Mary.' " (*Church*, 56).

584. "The Blessed Virgin was eternally predestined . . . to be the Mother of God. . . . She cooperated by her obedience, faith, hope and burning charity in the Savior's work of restoring supernatural life to souls. For this reason she is a mother to us in the order of grace." (*Church*, 61).

"This maternity of Mary in the order of grace began with the consent which she gave in faith at the Annunciation and which she sustained without wavering beneath the cross. This maternity will last without interruption until the eternal fulfillment of all the elect. For, taken up to heaven, she did not lay aside this saving role, but by her manifold acts of intercession continues to win for us gifts of eternal salvation." (*Church,*, 62).

585. "She is 'clearly the mother of the members of Christ . . . since she cooperated out of love so that there might be born in the Church the faithful who are members of their Head' (Augustine). Therefore she is also hailed as a pre-eminent and altogether singular member of the Church, and as the Church's model and exemplar in faith and charity. Taught by the Holy Spirit, the Catholic Church honors her with filial affection and piety as a most beloved mother." (A footnote added at the bottom of the page here tells us: "The Council here comes close to calling her 'Mother of the Church,' the title given her by Pope Paul VI in his closing allocution at the end of the Third Session on November 21, 1964.") (*Church,* 53).

586. "By her maternal charity, Mary cares for the brethren of her Son who still journey on earth surrounded by dangers and difficulties, until they are led to their happy fatherland. Therefore the Blessed Virgin is invoked by the Church under the titles of Advocate, Auxiliatrix, Adjutrix, and Mediatrix. These, however, are to be so understood that they neither take away from nor add anything to the dignity and efficacy of Christ the one Mediator.

"For no creature could ever be classed with the Incarnate Word and Redeemer. But just as the priesthood of Christ is shared in various ways both by sacred ministers and by the faithful, and as the one goodness of God is in reality communicated diversely to His creatures, so also the unique mediation of the Redeemer does not exclude but rather gives rise among creatures to a manifold cooperation which is but a sharing in this unique source.

"The Church does not hesitate to profess this subordinate role of Mary. She experiences it continuously and commends it to the hearts of the faithful, so that, encouraged by this maternal help, they may more closely adhere to the Mediator and Redeemer." (*Church,* 62).

MARY AND JESUS

587. "The Church in her apostolic work . . . rightly looks to her who brought forth Christ, conceived by the Holy Spirit and born of the Virgin, so that through the Church Christ may be born and grow in the hearts of the faithful also." (*Church,* 65).

588. "This most holy Synod ... admonishes all the sons of the Church that the cult, especially the liturgical cult, of the Blessed Virgin, be generously fostered. It charges that practices and exercises of devotion towards her be treasured as recommended in the course of centuries, and that those decrees issued in earlier times regarding the veneration of images of Christ, the Blessed Virgin and the saints be religiously observed." (*Church*, 67).

589. "The Blessed Mary, Mother of God, is joined by an inseparable bond to the saving work of her Son. In her the Church holds up and admires the most excellent fruit of the redemption, and joyfully contemplates as a faultless model, that which she herself wholly desires and hopes to be." (*Liturgy*, 103).

590. "Embracing God's saving will with a full heart and impeded by no sin, she (Mary) devoted herself totally as a handmaid of the Lord to the Person and work of her Son. In subordination to Him and alone with Him, by the grace of almighty God, she served the mystery of the redemption." (*Church*, 56).

591. "Thus the Blessed Virgin advanced in her pilgrimage of faith, and loyally persevered in her union with her Son unto the cross. There she stood, in keeping with the divine plan (John 19:25) suffering grievously with her only-begotten Son. There she united herself with a maternal heart to His sacrifice and lovingly consented to the immolation of this Victim Which she herself had brought forth. Finally, the same Christ Jesus, dying on the cross, gave her as a mother to His disciple. This He did when He said: 'Woman, behold thy son' (John 19:26-27)." (*Church*, 58).

MARY PRAISED BY THE ANGEL AND BY HER SON

592. "Adorned from the first instant of her conception with the splendors of an entirely unique holiness, the Virgin of Nazareth is, on God's command, greeted by an angel messenger as 'full of grace' (Lk. 1:28). To the ... messenger she replies: 'Behold the handmaid of the Lord; be it done to me according to thy word' (Lk. 1:38)." (*Church*, 56).

593. "In the course of her Son's preaching, she received His praise when in extolling a kingdom beyond the calculations and bonds of flesh and blood, He declared blessed (Mk. 3:35 par.; Lk. 11:27-28) those who heard and kept the word of God, as she was faithfully doing (Lk. 2:19, 51)." (*Church*, 58).

DEVOTION TO MARY

594. "As it has always existed in the Church, this cult (of Mary) is al-

together special. Still, it differs essentially from the cult of adoration which is offered to the Incarnate Word, as well as to the Father and the Holy Spirit. Yet devotion to Mary is most favorable to this supreme cult. The Church has endorsed many forms of piety toward the Mother of God, provided that they are within the limits of sound and orthodox doctrine. These forms have varied according to the circumstances of time and place and have reflected the diversity of native characteristics and temperament among the faithful. While honoring Christ's Mother, these devotions cause her Son to be rightly known, loved and glorified and all His commands observed. Through Him all things have their being (Col. 1:15-16) and in Him 'it has pleased (the eternal Father) that . . . all His fullness should dwell' (Col. 1:19)." (*Church,* 66).

595. "This most holy Synod deliberately teaches this doctrine (concerning Mary). At the same time, it admonishes all the sons of the Church that the cult, especially the liturgical cult, of the Blessed Virgin be generously fostered. It charges that practices and exercises of devotion towards her be treasured as recommended by the teaching authority of the Church in the course of centuries, and that those decrees issued in earlier times regarding the veneration of images of Christ, the Blessed Virgin and the saints be religiously observed." (*Church,* 67).

596. "Let the faithful remember that true devotion consists neither in fruitless and passing emotion, nor in a certain vain credulity. Rather, it proceeds from true faith by which we are led to know the excellence of the Mother of God, and are moved to a filial love towards our Mother and to the imitation of her virtues." (*Church,* 67).

597. "Mary shines forth on earth until the day of the Lord shall come (2 Pet. 3:10), as a sign of sure hope and solace for the pilgrim People of God." (*Church,* 68).

"Let the entire body of the faithful pour persevering prayer to the Mother of God and the Mother of men. Let them implore that she who aided the beginning of the Church by her prayers, may now, exalted as she is in heaven above all the saints and angels, intercede with her Son in the fellowship of all the saints." (*Church,* 69).

SACRED IMAGES IN CHURCHES

598. "The practice of placing sacred images in churches so that they may be venerated by the faithful is to be firmly maintained. Nevertheless, their number should be moderate and their relative location should reflect right order. Otherwise they may create confusion among the Christian people and promote a faulty sense of devotion." (*Liturgy,* 125).

PIOUS PRACTICES

599. It was not the purpose of Vatican II to give us a systematic treatise concerning the pious practices which are necessary for the normal development of our spiritual life. In the pursuit of its pastoral aim, the Council did, however, strongly recommend such practices as frequent attendance at Mass, reception of Holy Communion, visits to the Blessed Sacrament, frequent confession along with daily examination of one's conscience, prayer, meditation, contemplation, spiritual reading, Scripture reading, and so on. So inspiring in fact are the decrees of the Council itself that the Holy Father, Pope Paul VI, himself in his general audience in St. Peter's Basilica on September 30, 1970, spoke of the conciliar documents in the following terms:

600. "The volume containing the Council's Constitutions and Decrees can serve as a book of spiritual reading and meditation. It has beautiful passages, full of wisdom and historical and human experience. They deserve meditation and can become food for the soul. God's Word is so widespread now and so responsive to the human requirements of our age, that we can go to school to it. Its lesson ought not to be missed, for it can well lead Christians of today towards the call of a listening silence, the vocation of the heart which allows the Lord's truth to become the spirit and life of its existence. The simple, plain, authoritative form of the Council's teachings is itself a lesson in evangelical temperament, pastoral style and imitation of the Lord. He made Himself our Model: 'Learn of me, for I am meek and humble of heart' (Mt. 11:29)." (*L'Osservatore Romano,* October 8, 1970).

601. With regard to popular devotions current among the Christian people, the Council declared that they "are warmly commended provided they accord with the laws and norms of the Church. Such is especially the case with devotions called for by the Apostolic See. . . . Nevertheless, these devotions should be so drawn up that they harmonize with the liturgical seasons, accord with the sacred liturgy, are in some fashion derived from it and lead people to it, since the liturgy by its very nature far surpasses any of them." (*Liturgy,* 13).

ROSARY — STATIONS OF THE CROSS

602. It is true that the Council does not make explicit mention of the Rosary or the Stations of the Cross but hardly any other devotion has been recommended more frequently or with greater insistence than these two pious practices. It is also true that in practice the Rosary seems to have lost much of its popularity in recent years, but one may

well wonder whether this is not due to the fact that people have not been properly trained to meditate on the mysteries of the Rosary and therefore found little inspiration in merely reciting the words of the Hail Mary by rote.

603. The same may well be true concerning the Stations of the Cross due to the fact that too many people merely read what is written in their prayer books without really meditating on what they read or making any practical application of the Mysteries of the Passion to their own lives. Those who do meditate on the Mysteries of the first and second Stations, for example, will naturally ask themselves *why* Christ accepted the sentence, the scourging, the crowning with thorns, the cross and death itself and will quickly realize that He accepted all of this to satisfy the demands of His Father's Justice by making atonement for all the sins of all of us. They will also realize, however, that the things that really sent Christ to Calvary were the necessity for Christ to atone for us, His Father's love for His children, and the Father's mercy towards sinners.

604. People who do meditate on these points will also realize that since Christ did finish His work in this way, He certainly wishes that we, who have benefited by it and are members of His Mystical Body, should now join Him in making atonement not only for our sins but for the sins of all men and should join Christ in showing love for all men simply because they are God's children and brothers of Christ. We should also be merciful towards sinners not only in thought, word and deed, but especially in our way of judging them. Equally fruitful meditations are possible with regard to all of the Stations of the Cross provided people are taught how to meditate on the lessons conveyed by them.

605. Certainly the mind of the Church with regard to the Rosary, the Stations of the Cross, visits to the Blessed Sacrament, and other devotions is clearly revealed in the fact that though many other plenary indulgences have been abrogated, it is still possible to obtain a plenary indulgence once a day, under the usual conditions, either by reciting the Rosary in a church or chapel, making the Stations of the Cross or by making a visit of adoration to the Blessed Sacrament for half an hour. (*Enchiridion Indulgentiarum*).

606. With regard to other pious practices, Vatican II stresses meditation as a way to "look for Christ" (*Priestly Formation*, 8), while priests' activities "should be fed and fostered by a wealth of meditation to the delight of the whole Church of God." (*Church*, 41). Spiritual reading is recommended to priests as a means to "detect the signs of God's will and the impulses of His grace in the various happenings of life" (*Priests*, 18) and priests should also gladly undertake spiritual retreats and highly esteem spiritual direction even for themselves. (*Priests*, 18). In major

seminaries it is especially with the help of the spiritual director that students should "learn to live in familiar companionship with the Father through Jesus Christ, His Son, in the Holy Spirit." (*Priestly Formation*, 8). The formation given in minor seminaries should give "first place to spiritual direction." (*Priestly Formation*, 3). The Council's recommendation concerning daily conversation with Christ in visits of devotion to the Blessed Sacrament has already been noted.

SCRIPTURE READING

607. In explaining why the Church promotes the study and reading of sacred Scripture, Vatican II tells us that the Church wishes thereby to provide "nourishment of the Scriptures for the People of God, thereby enlightening their minds, strengthening their wills and setting their hearts on fire with the love for God." (*Revelation*, 23).

608. "In the sacred books, the Father Who is in heaven meets His children with great love and speaks with them; and the force and power in the word of God is so great that it remains the support and energy of the Church, the strength of faith for her sons, the food of the soul, the pure and perennial source of spiritual life." (*Revelation*, 21).

609. "This sacred tradition, therefore, and sacred Scripture of both the Old and the New Testament are like a mirror in which the pilgrim Church on earth looks at God from Whom she has received everything, until she is brought finally to see Him as He is face-to-face (1 John 3:2)." (*Revelation*, 7).

610. "This sacred Synod earnestly and specifically urges all the Christian faithful, too, especially religious, to learn by frequent reading of the divine Scriptures the 'excelling knowledge of Jesus Christ' (Phil. 3:8). 'For ignorance of the Scriptures is ignorance of Christ' (St. Jerome). Therefore, they should gladly put themselves in touch with the sacred text itself. . . . Let them remember that prayer should accompany the reading of the sacred Scripture, so that God and man may talk together; for 'we speak to Him when we pray; we hear Him when we read the divine sayings' (St. Jerome)." (*Revelation*, 25).

12. Sanctification Through Liturgy and Sacraments

LITURGY

611. "Christ is always present in His Church, especially in her liturgical celebrations. He is present in the sacrifice of the Mass, not only in the person of His minister, 'the same one now offering through the ministry of priests, Who formerly offered Himself on the cross' *(Trent)*, but especially under the Eucharistic species. By His power He is present in the sacraments, so that when a man baptizes, it is really Christ Who baptizes.

"Rightly then, the liturgy is considered as an exercise of the priestly office of Jesus Christ. In the liturgy the sanctification of man is manifested by signs perceptible to the senses and is effected in a way which is proper to each of these signs; in the liturgy full public worship is performed by the Mystical Body of Jesus Christ, that is by the Head and His members." (*Liturgy,* 7).

612. "From the liturgy, therefore, and especially from the Eucharist as from a fountain, grace is channeled into us; and the sanctification of men in Christ and the glorification of God, to which all other activities of the Church are directed as to their goal, are most powerfully achieved." (*Liturgy,* 10).

613. "The minds of the faithful must be directed primarily towards the feasts of the Lord in which the mysteries of salvation are celebrated in the course of the year. Therefore, the Proper of the Time shall be given the preference which is due over the feasts of the saints, so that the entire cycle of the mysteries of salvation can be suitably recalled." (*Liturgy,* 108).

614. The "life of intimate union with Christ in the Church is nourished by spiritual aids which are common to all the faithful, especially active participation in the sacred liturgy. These are to be used by the laity in such a way that while properly fulfilling their secular duties

in the ordinary conditions of life, they do not dissociate union with Christ from life." (*Laity*, 4).

615. "Day by day the liturgy builds up those within the Church into the Lord's holy temple, into a spiritual dwelling for God (Eph. 2:21-22), an enterprise which will continue until Christ's full stature is achieved (Eph. 4:13)." (*Liturgy*, 2).

SACRAMENTS IN GENERAL

616. "For well-disposed members of the faithful, the liturgy of the sacraments and sacramentals sanctifies almost every event in their lives; they are given access to the stream of divine grace which flows from the paschal mystery of the passion, death and resurrection of Christ, the fountain from which all sacraments and sacramentals draw their power. There is hardly any proper use of material things which cannot be directed toward the sanctification of men and the praise of God." (*Liturgy*, 61).

617. "The purpose of the sacraments is to sanctify men, to build up the body of Christ, and finally, to give worship to God. Because they are signs they also instruct. They not only presuppose faith, but by words and objects they also nourish, strengthen and express it; this is why they are called 'sacraments of faith.' They do indeed impart grace, but in addition, the very act of celebrating them disposes the faithful most effectively to receive this grace in a fruitful manner, to worship God duly and to practice charity.

"It is therefore of capital importance that the faithful easily understand the sacramental signs, and with great eagerness have frequent recourse to those sacraments which were instituted to nourish the Christian life." (*Liturgy*, 59).

THE SACRAMENT OF BAPTISM

618. "When in the womb of the baptismal font," the Holy Spirit "begets to a new life those who believe in Christ, He gathers them into the one People of God which is 'a chosen race, a royal priesthood, a holy nation, a purchased people' (1 Pet. 2:9)." (*Missions*, 15). It is through baptism also that men are incorporated into the Mystical Body of Christ. (*Laity*, 3).

619. In that Mystical Body, "the life of Christ is poured into the believers who, through the sacraments are united in a hidden and real way to Christ Who suffered and was glorified. Through baptism we are

143

formed in the likeness of Christ: 'For, in one Spirit we were all baptized into one body' (1 Cor. 12:13). In this sacred rite, a union with Christ's death and resurrection is both symbolized and brought about: 'For we were buried with Him by means of baptism unto death.' And if 'we have been united with Him in the likeness of His death, we shall be so in the likeness of His resurrection also' (Rom. 6:4-5)." (*Church*, 7).

620. "The followers of Christ are called by God, not according to their accomplishments, but according to His own purpose and grace. They are justified in the Lord Jesus, and through baptism sought in faith they truly become sons of God and sharers in the divine nature. In this way they are really made holy. Then, too, by God's gifts they must hold on to and complete in their lives this holiness which they have received. They are warned by the apostle to live 'as becomes saints' (Eph. 5:3), and to put on 'as God's chosen ones, holy and beloved, a heart of mercy, kindness, humility, meekness, patience' (Col. 3:12), and to possess the fruits of the Spirit unto holiness (Gal. 5:22; Rom. 6:22). Since we all truly offend in many things (Jas. 3:2), we all need God's mercy continuously and must daily pray: 'Forgive us our debts.' " (*Church*, 40).

CONFIRMATION

621. "Incorporated into Christ's Mystical Body through baptism and strengthened by the power of the Holy Spirit through confirmation, the laity are assigned to the apostolate by the Lord Himself." (*Laity*, 3).

622. By the sacrament of confirmation, the laity are "bound more intimately to the Church" and are "endowed by the Holy Spirit with special strength. Hence they are more strictly obliged to spread and defend the faith both by word and by deed as true witnesses of Christ." (*Church*, 11).

THE EUCHARIST

623. "The Lord left behind a pledge of this hope and strength for life's journey in that sacrament of faith where natural elements refined by man are changed into His glorified Body and Blood, providing a meal of brotherly solidarity and a foretaste of the heavenly banquet." (*Modern World*, 38).

624. "The other sacraments, as well as every ministry of the Church and every work of the apostolate, are linked with the Holy Eucharist and are directed towards it, for the most Holy Eucharist contains the

Church's entire spiritual wealth, that is, Christ Himself, our Passover and living bread. Through His very flesh, made vital and vitalizing by the Holy Spirit, He offers life to men. They are thereby invited and led to offer themselves, their labors and all created things together with Him." (*Priests,* 5).

625. "In any community existing around an altar, under the sacred ministry of the bishop, there is manifested a symbol of that charity and 'unity of the Mystical Body, without which there can be no salvation' (St. Thomas Aquinas). In these communities, though frequently small and poor, or living far from any other, Christ is present. By virtue of Him, the one, holy, catholic and apostolic Church gathers together (St. Augustine). For 'the partaking of the Body and Blood of Christ does nothing other than transform us into that which we consume' (St. Leo the Great)." (*Church,* 26).

THE HOLY SACRIFICE

626. "At the Last Supper, on the night when He was betrayed, our Savior instituted the Eucharistic Sacrifice of His Body and Blood. He did this in order to perpetuate the sacrifice of the cross throughout the centuries until He should come again, and to entrust to His beloved spouse, the Church, a memorial of His death and resurrection: a sacrament of love, a sign of unity, a bond of charity, a paschal banquet in which Christ is consumed, the mind is filled with grace, and a pledge of future glory is given to us." (*Liturgy,* 47).

627. "Taking part in the Eucharistic Sacrifice which is the fount and apex of the whole Christian life," the faithful "offer the divine Victim to God and offer themselves along with it. Thus, both by the act of oblation and through holy Communion, all perform their proper part in this liturgical service, not indeed, all in the same way but each in that way which is appropriate to himself. Strengthened anew at the holy table by the Body of Christ, they manifest in a practical way that unity of God's People which is suitably signified and wondrously brought about by this most awesome sacrament." (*Church,* 11).

628. "Through the hands of priests and in the name of the whole Church, the Lord's sacrifice is offered in the Eucharist in an unbloody and sacramental manner until He returns." (*Priests,* 2).

629. "Through the ministry of priests, the spiritual sacrifice of the faithful is made perfect in union with the sacrifice of Christ, the sole Mediator." (*Priests,* 2).

630. "In the Eucharistic Sacrifice . . . are fulfilled the words of God, spoken through His prophet: 'From the rising of the sun even to the

going down, my name is great among the gentiles, and in every place there is sacrifice and there is offered to my name a clean oblation' (Mal. 1:11). In this way the Church simultaneously prays and labors in order that the entire world may become the People of God, the Body of the Lord and the Temple of the Holy Spirit, and that in Christ, the Head of all, there may be rendered to the Creator and Father of the universe all honor and glory." (*Church,* 17).

631. "The ministry of priests . . . derives its power and force from the sacrifice of Christ. Its aim is that 'the entire commonwealth of the redeemed, that is the community and society of the saints, be offered as a universal sacrifice to God through the High Priest Who in His Passion offered His very self for us that we might be the body of so exalted a Head' (St. Augustine)." (*Priests,* 2).

THE EUCHARIST AND THE CHURCH

632. "As often as the sacrifice of the cross in which 'Christ, our passover, has been sacrificed' (1 Cor. 5:7) is celebrated on an altar, the work of our redemption is carried on. At the same time, in the sacrament of the Eucharistic bread the unity of all believers who form one body in Christ (1 Cor. 10:17) is both expressed and brought about. All men are called to this union with Christ, Who is the light of the world, from Whom we go forth, through Whom we live and towards Whom our journey leads us." (*Church,* 3).

633. "In discharging their duty to sanctify their people, pastors should arrange for the celebration of the Eucharistic Sacrifice to be the center and culmination of the whole life of the Christian community. They should labor to see that the faithful are nourished with spiritual food through the devout and frequent reception of the sacraments and through intelligent and active participation in the liturgy." (*Bishops,* 30).

634. "Thus the Eucharistic Action is the very heartbeat of the congregation of the faithful over which the priest presides. So priests must instruct them to offer to God the Father the divine Victim in the sacrifice of the Mass, and to join to it the offering of their own lives." (*Priests,* 5).

635. "No Christian community can be built up unless it has its basis and center in the celebration of the most Holy Eucharist. Here, therefore, all education in the spirit of community must originate. If this celebration is to be sincere and thorough, it must lead to various works of charity and mutual help, as well as to missionary activity and to different forms of Christian witness." (*Priests,* 6).

636. "The Eucharist shows itself to be the source and the apex of the whole work of preaching the gospel. Those under instruction are introduced by stages to a sharing in the Eucharist. The faithful, already marked with the sacred seal of baptism and confirmation, are through the reception of the Eucharist, fully joined to the Body of Christ." (*Priests*, 5).

THE EUCHARIST, BOND OF UNION

637. "Celebrating the Eucharistic Sacrifice, we are most closely united to the worshipping Church in heaven as we join with and venerate the memory first of all of the glorious ever-Virgin Mary, of Blessed Joseph and the blessed apostles and martyrs and of all the saints." (*Church*, 50).

638. "Truly partaking of the Body of the Lord in the breaking of the Eucharistic bread, we are taken up into communion with Him and with one another. 'Because the bread is one, we, though many, are one body, all of us who partake of the one bread' (1 Cor. 10:17). In this way all of us are made members of His Body (1 Cor. 12:27), 'but severally members one of another' (Rom. 12:5)." (*Church*, 7).

639. "In the house of prayer the most Holy Eucharist is celebrated and preserved. There the faithful gather, and find help and comfort through venerating the presence of the Son of God, our Savior, offered for us on the sacrificial altar. This house must be well kept and suitable for prayer and sacred functions. There, pastors and faithful are called to respond with grateful hearts to the gift of Him Who through His humanity constantly pours divine life into the members of His Body." (*Priests*, 5).

640. "The Church earnestly desires that Christ's faithful, when present at this mystery of faith (the Mass), should not be there as strangers or silent spectators. On the contrary, through a proper appreciation of the rites and prayers they should participate knowingly, devoutly, and actively. They should be instructed by God's word and be refreshed at the table of the Lord's Body; they should give thanks to God; by offering the Immaculate Victim, not only through the hands of the priest but also with him, they should learn to offer themselves too. Through Christ the Mediator, they should be drawn day by day into ever closer union with God and with each other, so that finally God may be all in all." (*Liturgy*, 48).

641. "The liturgy in its turn inspires the faithful to become 'of one heart in love,' when they have tasted to their full of the paschal mysteries; it prays that 'they may grasp by deed what they hold by creed.'

The renewal in the Eucharist of the covenant between the Lord and man draws the faithful into the compelling love of Christ and sets them afire. From the liturgy, therefore, and especially from the Eucharist, as from a fountain, grace is channelled into us; and the sanctification of men in Christ and the glorification of God, to which all other activities of the Church are directed as towards their goal, are most powerfully achieved." (*Liturgy,* 10).

THE SACRAMENT OF PENANCE

642. "In the spirit of Christ the Shepherd, priests should train 'the faithful' to submit their sins with a contrite heart to the Church in the sacrament of penance. Thus, mindful of the Lord's words: 'Repent, for the kingdom of God is at hand' (Mt. 4:17), the people will be drawn closer to Him each day." (*Priests,* 5).

643. "Those who approach the sacrament of penance, obtain pardon from the mercy of God for offenses committed against Him. They are at the same time reconciled with the Church, which they wounded by their sins, and which by charity, example and prayer seeks their conversion." (*Church,* 11).

644. With regard to the sacrament of penance, the Council reminds priests that "this sacrament, prepared for by a daily examination of conscience greatly fosters the necessary turning of the heart towards the love of the Father of mercies." (*Priests,* 18). The Council also urges pastors to "be mindful of how much the sacrament of penance contributes to developing the Christian life" and says that pastors "should make themselves available to hear the confessions of the faithful." (*Bishops,* 30).

645. It will not be out of place here to cite the opinion of those who hold that never in the history of humanity has a more effective method been found for the correction of personal faults than has been provided for us by the sacrament of penance with its sixfold program of examination, contrition, purpose of amendment, confession, absolution and satisfaction. For those of us who are priests, a fruitful lesson is provided by a remark made half a century ago by Fr. Walter Elliott, who was then one of the best known and deeply admired priests in the United States. He had been a captain in the American Civil War before becoming a priest and owed his fame to his marvelous work in preaching retreats and parish missions throughout the United States for nearly fifty years. Reminiscing at the dinner table one evening he told those present, "I have but one regret and that is that I was not more kind in the confessional."

148

SACRAMENT OF THE SICK

646. "By the sacred anointing of the sick and the prayer of her priests, the whole Church commends those who are ill to the suffering and glorified Lord, asking that He may lighten their sufferings and save them (Jas. 5:14-16). She exhorts them moreover to contribute to the welfare of the whole People of God by associating themselves freely with the passion and death of Christ (Rom. 8:17; Col. 1:24; 2 Tim. 2:11-12; 1 Pet. 4:13)." (*Church*, 11).

THE SACRAMENT OF MATRIMONY ESTABLISHED BY GOD HIMSELF

647. "The intimate partnership of married life and love has been established by the Creator and qualified by His laws. It is rooted in the conjugal covenant of irrevocable personal consent. Hence, by that human act whereby spouses mutually bestow and accept each other, a relationship arises which by divine will and in the eyes of society too is a lasting one. For the good of the spouses and their offspring as well as of society, the existence of this sacred bond no longer depends on human decisions alone." (*Modern World*, 48).

648. "Let the spouses themselves, made to the image of the living God and enjoying the authentic dignity of persons, be joined together in equal affection, harmony of mind, and the work of mutual sanctification. Thus they will follow Christ Who is the principle of life. Thus, too, by the joys and sacrifices of their vocation and through their faithful love, married people will become witnesses of the mystery of that love which the Lord revealed to the world by His dying and His rising to life again." (*Modern World*, 52).

649. "The Christian family, which springs from marriage as a reflection of the loving covenant uniting Christ with the Church, and as a participation in that covenant, will manifest to all men the Savior's living presence in the world, and the genuine nature of the Church. This the family will do by the mutual love of the spouses, by their generous fruitfulness, their solidarity and faithfulness, and by the loving way in which all members of the family work together." (*Modern World*, 48).

650. "Authentic married love is caught up into divine love and is governed and enriched by Christ's redeeming power and the saving activity of the Church. Thus this love can lead the spouses to God with powerful effect and can aid and strengthen them in the sublime office of being a father or a mother." (*Modern World*, 48).

651. "Christ the Lord abundantly blessed this many-faceted love,

welling up as it does from the fountain of divine love and structured as it is on the model of His union with the Church. For as God of old made Himself present to His people through a covenant of love and fidelity, so now the Savior of men and the Spouse of the Church, comes into the lives of married Christians through the sacrament of matrimony. He abides with them thereafter so that, just as He loved the Church and handed Himself over on her behalf, the spouses may love each other with perpetual fidelity through mutual love and self-bestowal." (*Modern World,* 48).

HUSBAND AND WIFE

652. "A man and a woman, who by the marriage covenant of conjugal love 'are no longer two, but one flesh' (Mt. 19:6) render mutual help and service to each other through an intimate union of their persons and of their actions. Through this union they experience the meaning of their oneness and attain to it with growing perfection day by day. As a mutual gift of two persons, this intimate union, as well as the good of the children, imposes total fidelity on the spouses and argues for an unbreakable oneness between them." (*Modern World,* 48).

653. "Husband and wife find their proper vocation in being witnesses to one another and to their children of faith in Christ and love for Him. The Christian family loudly proclaims both the present virtues of the kingdom of God and the hope of a blessed life to come. Thus by its example and its witness it accuses the world of sin and enlightens those who seek the truth." (*Church,* 35).

654. "Christian spouses have a special sacrament by which they are fortified and receive a kind of consecration in the duties and dignity of that state. By virtue of this sacrament, as spouses fulfill their conjugal and family obligations, they are penetrated with the spirit of Christ. This spirit suffuses their whole lives with faith, hope and charity. Thus they increasingly advance their own perfection as well as their mutual sanctification and hence contribute jointly to the glory of God." (*Modern World,* 48).

655. "Trusting in divine Providence and refining the spirit of sacrifice, married Christians glorify the Creator and strive toward fulfillment in Christ when, with a generous human and Christian sense of responsibility, they acquit themselves of the duty to procreate. Among the couples who fulfill their God-given task in this way, those merit special mention who, with wise and common deliberation, and with a gallant heart, undertake to bring up suitably even a relatively large family.

"Marriage to be sure is not instituted solely for procreation. Rather, its very nature as an unbreakable compact between persons, and the welfare of the children, both demand that the mutual love of the spouses, too, be embodied in a rightly ordered manner, that it grow and ripen. Therefore, marriage persists as a whole manner and communion of life, and maintains its value and indissolubility, even when offspring are lacking — despite, rather often, the very intense desire of the couple." (*Modern World,* 50).

656. "Married couples and Christian parents should follow their own proper path to holiness by faithful love, sustaining one another in grace through the entire length of their lives. They should imbue their offspring, lovingly welcomed from God, with Christian truths and evangelical virtues. For thus they can offer all men an example of unwearying and generous love, build up the brotherhood of charity, and stand as witnesses to and cooperators in the fruitfulness of Holy Mother Church. By such lives, they signify and share in that very love with which Christ loved His Bride and because of which He delivered Himself up on her behalf. A like example, but one given in a different way, is that offered by widows and single people, who are able to make great contributions toward holiness and apostolic endeavor in the Church." (*Church,* 41).

PARENTS AND THEIR CHILDREN

657. "It is particularly in the Christian family, enriched by the grace and the office of the sacrament of matrimony, that from their earliest years children should be taught, according to the faith received in baptism, to have a knowledge of God, to worship Him, and to love their neighbor." (*Education,* 3).

658. "With their parents leading the way by example, and family prayer, children and indeed everyone gathered around the family hearth will find a readier path to human maturity, salvation and holiness. Graced with the dignity and office of fatherhood and motherhood, parents will energetically acquit themselves of a duty which devolves primarily on them, namely education, and especially religious education." (*Modern World,* 48).

659. "Since parents have conferred life on their children, they have a most solemn obligation to educate their offspring. Hence, parents must be acknowledged as the first and foremost educators of their children. Their role as educators is so decisive that scarcely anything can compensate for their failure in it. For it devolves on parents to create a family atmosphere so animated with love and reverence for God and men that a well-rounded personal and social development will be fostered

among the children. Hence, the family is the first school of those social virtues which society needs." (*Education*, 3).

660. "As living members of the family, children contribute in their own way to making their parents holy. For they will respond to the kindness of their parents with sentiments of gratitude, with love and trust. They will stand by them as children should when hardships overtake their parents and old age brings its loneliness." (*Modern World*, 48).

661. "By a truly Christian life, families must become nurseries of the lay apostolate and of vocations to the priesthood and the religious life." (*Missions*, 19).

13. Virtues

662. In the Fifth Chapter of its Dogmatic Constitution on the Church, Vatican II reminds us of St. Paul's admonition to the Ephesians that they should live "as becomes saints." This whole chapter which is entitled "The Call of the Whole Church to Holiness" might be described as a litany of all the virtues needed for that perfection which Christ Himself urged upon all of His followers when He said: "You therefore are to be perfect, even as your heavenly Father is perfect (Mt. 5:48)."

FAITH

663. As was to be expected, few spiritual concepts were stressed as strongly by Vatican II as was the concept of faith. As Pope John XXIII in his opening address on October 11, 1962, said to the Council Fathers: "The greatest concern of the Ecumenical Council is that the sacred deposit of Christian doctrine should be guarded and taught more efficaciously." He went on to say that "the Twenty-first Ecumenical Council . . . wishes to transmit the doctrine pure and integral, without any attenuation or distortion, which throughout twenty centuries, notwithstanding difficulties and contrasts, has become the common patrimony of men. It is a patrimony not well received by all, but always a rich treasure available to men of good will." (*Documents of Vatican II*).

664. "From the renewed, serene and tranquil adherence to all the teaching of the Church in its entirety and preciseness, as it still shines forth in the Acts of the Council of Trent and First Vatican Council, the Christian, Catholic and apostolic spirit of the whole world expects a step forward toward a doctrinal penetration and a formation of consciousness in faithful and perfect conformity to the authentic doctrine, which, however, should be studied and expounded through the methods of research and through the literary forms of modern thought. The sub-

stance of the ancient doctrine of the deposit of faith is one thing, and the way in which it is presented is another. And it is the latter that must be taken into great consideration with patience if necessary, everything being measured in the forms and proportions of a magisterium which is predominantly pastoral in character." *(Documents of Vatican II)*.

665. Many texts concerning the faith have already been quoted in previous chapters of this book. The following are added merely as a kind of supplement.

666. "It is through the gift of the Holy Spirit that man comes by faith to the contemplation and appreciation of the divine plan." *(Modern World, 15)*.

667. "The Holy Spirit, Who calls all men to Christ by the seeds of the Word and by the preaching of the gospel, stirs up in their hearts the obedience of faith. When in the womb of the baptismal font, He begets to a new life those who believe in Christ, He gathers them into the one People of God which is 'a chosen race, a royal priesthood, a holy nation, a purchased people.' " *(Missions, 15)*.

668. " 'The obedience of faith' (Rom. 16:26; 1:5; 2 Cor. 10:5-6) must be given to God Who reveals, an obedience by which man entrusts his whole self freely to God, offering 'the full submission of intellect and will to God Who reveals' *(Vatican I),* and freely assenting to the truth revealed by Him. If this faith is to be shown, the grace of God and the interior help of the Holy Spirit must precede and assist, moving the heart and turning it to God, opening the eyes of the mind, and giving 'joy and ease to everyone in assenting to the truth and believing it.' To bring about an ever deeper understanding of revelation, the same Holy Spirit constantly brings faith to completion by His gifts." *(Revelation, 5)*.

669. "It is one of the major tenets of Catholic doctrine that man's response to God in faith must be free. Therefore, no one is to be forced to embrace the Christian faith against his own will. This doctrine is contained in the Word of God and it was constantly proclaimed by the Fathers of the Church. The act of faith is of its very nature a free act. Man, redeemed by Christ the Savior, and through Christ Jesus called to be God's adopted son, cannot give his adherence to God revealing Himself unless the Father draw him to offer to God the reasonable and free submission of faith." *(Religious Liberty, 10)*.

670. "It is the function of the Church, led by the Holy Spirit Who renews and purifies her ceaselessly, to make God the Father and His Incarnate Son present and in a sense visible.

"This result is achieved chiefly by the witness of a living and mature faith, namely, one trained to see difficulties clearly and to master them. Very many martyrs have given luminous witness to this faith and continue to do so. This faith needs to prove its fruitfulness by penetrating the believer's entire life, including its worldly dimensions, and by activating him towards justice and love, especially regarding the needy. What does the most to reveal God's presence, however, is the brotherly charity of the faithful who are united in spirit as they work together for the faith of the gospel and who prove themselves a sign of unity." (*Modern World, 21*).

671. "To every thoughtful man, a solidly established faith provides the answer to his anxiety about what the future holds for him. At the same time, faith gives him the power to be united in Christ with his beloved ones who have already been snatched away by death. Faith arouses the hope that they have found true life with God." (*Modern World, 18*).

672. "Not only when things are read 'which have been written for our instruction' (Rom. 15:4), but also when the Church sings or prays or acts, the faith of those taking part is nourished and their minds are raised to God, so that they may offer Him the worship which reason requires and more copiously receive His grace." (*Liturgy, 33*).

HOPE

673. Vatican II rarely made explicit mention of the theological virtue of hope but the thought of this virtue was implicit in the Council's frequent reference to the eternal destiny of man even in the Pastoral Constitution on the Church in the Modern World. One might well go so far as to say that hope, both for betterment of man's condition here on earth and especially for his eternal welfare, was characteristic of Vatican II in most of its declarations. Examples of its reference to the theological virtue of hope are the following:

674. "Pressing upon the Christian, to be sure, are the need and the duty to battle against evil through manifold tribulations and even to suffer death. But linked with the paschal mystery and patterned on the dying Christ, he will hasten forward to resurrection in the strength which comes from hope." (*Modern World, 22*).

675. "They who have this faith live in the hope of what will be revealed to the sons of God and bear in mind the cross and resurrection of the Lord.

"In the pilgrimage of this life, hidden with Christ in God and free from enslavement to wealth, they aspire to those riches which remain forever, and generously dedicate their entire selves to spreading God's kingdom and to fashioning and perfecting the sphere of earthly things according to the spirit of Christ. Among the struggles of this life, they find strength in hope, convinced that 'the sufferings of the present time are not worthy to be compared with the glory to come that will be revealed to us' (Rom. 8:18)." (*Laity*, 4).

CHARITY — LOVE FOR GOD AND NEIGHBOR

676. The virtue mentioned most frequently by Vatican II is charity. Here the most basic element, of course, is God's love for us and the Council reminds us that man simply would not exist if he had not been "created by God's love and constantly preserved by it." (*Modern World*, 19). Furthermore, the Council not only reminds us in various texts that the first and greatest commandment is love for God but tells us that only God can satisfy the deepest aspirations of the human heart. (*Modern World*, 41).

677. Since the basic aim of the Council was pastoral, it is not surprising that the Council placed very heavy emphasis on love of neighbor but to forestall possible misinterpretations it also declares that the basis of real love for neighbor is love for God: we must love our neighbor "because of God." (Cf. 679 below).

678. "The Christian man, conformed to the likeness of that Son Who is the firstborn of many brothers, receives 'the first fruits of the Spirit' (Rom. 8:23) by which he becomes capable of discharging the new law of love. Through this Spirit Who is the 'pledge of our inheritance' (Eph. 1:14), the whole man is renewed from within, even to the achievement of the 'redemption of the body' (Rom. 8:23): 'If the Spirit of Him Who raised Jesus from the death dwells in you, then He Who raised Jesus Christ from the dead will also bring to life your mortal bodies because of His Spirit Who dwells in you (Rom. 8:11)." (*Modern World,* 22).

679. " 'God is love, and he who abides in love abides in God and God in him' (1 John 4:16). God pours out His love into our hearts through the Holy Spirit, Who has been given to us (Rom. 5:5). Thus the first and most necessary gift is that charity by which we love God above all things and our neighbor because of God. If that love, as good seed, is to grow and bring forth fruit in the soul, each one of the faithful must willingly hear the Word of God and with the help of His grace act to fulfill His will." (*Church*, 42).

680. "The Lord Jesus . . . Himself stands as the author and finisher of this holiness of life. For He sent the Holy Spirit upon all men so that He might inspire them from within to love God with their whole heart and their whole soul, with all their mind and all their strength (Mk. 12:30) and that they might love one another as Christ loved them (John 13:34; 15:12)." (*Church*, 40).

681. "The Spirit, too, has been bestowed on us by the Father, that living the life of God, we might love God and the brethren who are all of us one in Christ." *(Message to Humanity.)*

682. "Love for God and neighbor is the first and greatest commandment. Holy Scripture, however, teaches us that the love for God cannot be separated from love of neighbor: 'If there is any other commandment, it is summed up in this saying. Thou shalt love thy neighbor as thyself.... Love therefore is the fulfillment of the law' (Rom. 13:9-10; 1 John 4:20). To men growing daily more dependent on one another, and to a world becoming more unified every day, this truth proves to be of paramount importance." *(Modern World,* 24).

683. "The Lord Jesus, when He prayed to the Father 'that all may be one ... as we are one' (John 17:21-22) opened up vistas closed to human reason. For He implied a certain likeness between the union of the Divine Persons and in the union of God's sons in truth and charity. This likeness reveals that man, who is the only creature on earth which God willed for itself, cannot fully find himself except through a sincere gift of himself." *(Modern World,* 24).

684. Each one of the faithful "must share frequently in the sacraments, the Eucharist especially, and in liturgical rites. Each must apply himself constantly to prayer, self-denial, active brotherly service, and the exercise of all the virtues. For charity, as the bond of perfection and the fulfillment of the law (Col. 3:14; Rom. 13:10) rules over all the means of attaining holiness, gives life to them, and makes them work. Hence it is the love of God and of neighbor which points out the true disciple of Christ." *(Church,* 42).

685. "Thus it is evident to everyone that all the faithful of Christ of whatever rank or status are called to the fullness of the Christian life and to the perfection of charity. By this holiness a more human way of life is promoted even in this earthly society. In order that the faithful may reach this perfection they must use their strength according as they have received it, as a gift from Christ. In this way they can follow in His footsteps and mold themselves in His image, seeking the will of the Father in all things, devoting themselves with all their being to the glory of God and the service of their neighbor. In this way, too, the holiness of the People of God will grow into an abundant harvest of good, as is brilliantly proved by the lives of so many saints in Church history." *(Church,* 40).

686. To further Christian maturity, "priests should help men see what is required and what is God's will in the great and small events of life. Christians should also be taught that they do not live for themselves alone, but, according to the demands of the new law of charity, every man must administer to others the grace he has received. In this

way, all will discharge in a Christian manner their duties within the community of men." (*Priests,* 6).

LOVE OF NEIGHBOR

687. Christ "gave His followers a new commandment of mutual love (John 13:34), and promised the Spirit, their advocate (John 16:7), Who, as Lord and life-giver, would abide with them forever." (*Ecumenism,* 2).

688. "The greatest commandment in the law is to love God with one's whole heart and one's neighbor as oneself (Mt. 22:37-40). Christ made this commandment of love of neighbor His own and enriched it with a new meaning. For He wanted to identify Himself with His brethren as the object of this love when He said: 'As long as you did it for one of these, the least of my brethren, you did it for me' (Mt. 25:40). Taking on human nature, He bound the whole human race to Himself as a family through a certain supernatural solidarity and established charity as the mark of His disciples, saying: 'By this will all men know that you are my disciples, if you have love for one another' (John 13:35)." (*Laity,* 8).

689. "Not everyone who cries, 'Lord, Lord,' will enter into the kingdom of heaven, but those who do the Father's will and take a strong grip on the work at hand. Now, the Father wills that in all men we recognize Christ our Brother and love Him effectively in word and deed. By thus giving witness to the truth, we will share with others the mystery of the heavenly Father's love. As a consequence, men throughout the world will be aroused to a lively hope — the gift of the Holy Spirit — that they will finally be caught up in peace and utter happiness in that fatherland radiant with the splendor of the Lord." (*Modern World,* 93).

690. "We cannot in truthfulness call upon that God Who is the Father of all if we refuse to act in a brotherly way toward certain men, created though they be to God's image. A man's relationship with God the Father and his relationship with his brother men are so linked together that Scripture says: 'He who does not love does not know God' (1 John 4:8)." (*Non-Christian Religions,* 5).

691. "This Council lays stress on reverence for man; everyone must consider his every neighbor without exception as another self, taking into account first of all his life and the means necessary to living it with dignity, so as not to imitate the rich man who had no concern for the poor man Lazarus.

"In our times a special obligation binds us to make ourselves the neighbor of absolutely every person, and of actively helping him when he comes across our path, whether he be an old person abandoned by all, a foreign laborer unjustly looked down upon, a refugee, a child born out of an unlawful union and wrongly suffering for a sin he did not commit, or a hungry person who disturbs our conscience by recalling the voice of the Lord: 'As long as you did it for one of these, the least of my brethren, you did it for me' (Mt. 25:40)." (*Modern World, 27*).

692. "The presence of the Christian faithful in these human groups should be animated by that charity with which God has loved us, and with which He wills that we should love one another (1 John 4:11). Christian charity truly extends to all, without distinction of race, social condition or religion. It looks for neither gain nor gratitude. For as God has loved us with a spontaneous love, so also the faithful should in their charity care for the human person himself by loving him with the same affection with which God sought out man." (*Missions, 12*).

693. "Respect and love ought to be extended also to those who think or act differently than we do in social, political and religious matters, too. In fact, the more deeply we come to understand their ways of thinking through such courtesy and love, the more easily will we be able to enter into dialogue with them.

"This love and good will, to be sure, must in no way render us indifferent to truth and goodness. Indeed, love itself impels the disciples of Christ to speak the saving truth to all men. But it is necessary to distinguish between error, which always merits repudiation, and the person in error, who never loses the dignity of being a person, even when he is flawed by false or inadequate religious notions. God alone is the Judge and Searcher of hearts; for that reason He forbids us to make judgments about the internal guilt of anyone.

"The teaching of Christ even requires that we forgive injuries and extends the law of love to include every enemy, according to the New Law: 'You have heard that it was said, "Thou shalt love thy neighbor, and shalt hate thy enemy." But I say to you, love your enemies, do good to those who hate you, and pray for those who persecute and calumniate you' (Mt. 5:43-44)." (*Modern World, 28*).

CAUTION

694. Though it is next to impossible to exaggerate the importance of love for one's neighbor, caution is necessary with regard to the opinion of those who feel that it is not possible to love God except in our neighbor. It is quite true that even great saints rarely felt any deep emotional love for God and, on the contrary, spoke quite commonly about spiritual aridity. Yet their deep spiritual love was revealed by their conform-

ity to God in mind, heart and will, which is known as the love of conformity, the highest type of love. Some have ventured the opinion that Christ Himself, in His human nature, felt no emotional love for His Father when He was in the garden or on the cross, but they feel that His spiritual love for His Father was never shown more clearly than on those two occasions.

GOOD WORKS

695. "Christ was sent by the Father to 'bring good news to the poor, to heal the contrite of heart' (Lk. 4:18), 'to seek and save what was lost' (Lk. 19:10). Similarly, the Church encompasses with love all those who are afflicted with human weakness. Indeed, she recognizes in the poor and the suffering the likeness of her poor and suffering Founder. She does all she can to relieve their need and in them she strives to serve Christ." (*Church,* 8).

696. The Church must win the believers "to all the works of charity, piety and the apostolate. For all these activities make it clear that Christ's faithful, though not of this world, are the light of the world and give glory to the Father in the sight of men." (*Liturgy,* 9).

697. "By charity, prayer, example and works of penance, the Church community exercises a true motherhood toward souls who are to be led to Christ. For this community constitutes an effective instrument by which the path to Christ and to His Church is pointed out and made smooth for unbelievers, and by which the faithful are aroused, nourished and strengthened for spiritual combat." (*Priests,* 6).

698. "In her very early days, the holy Church added the 'agape' to the Eucharistic Supper and thus showed herself to be wholly united around Christ by the bond of charity. So, too, in every era she is recognized by the sign of love, and while she rejoices in the undertakings of others, she claims works of charity as her own inalienable duty and right. For this reason, pity for the needy and the sick, and works of charity and mutual aid intended to relieve human needs of every kind are held in special honor by the Church." (*Laity,* 8).

699. "At the present time, when the means of communication have grown more rapid, the distances between men have been overcome in a sense, and the inhabitants of the whole world have become like members of a single family, these actions and works have grown much more urgent and extensive." (*Laity,* 8).

700. "These charitable enterprises can and should reach out to absolutely every person and every need. Wherever there are people in need of food and drink, clothing, housing, medicine, employment, educa-

tion; wherever men lack the facilities necessary for living a truly human life or are tormented by hardships or poor health, or suffer exile or imprisonment, there Christian charity should seek them out and find them, console them with eager care and relieve them with the gift of help. This obligation is imposed above all upon every prosperous person and nation." (*Laity*, 8).

701. "That the exercise of such charity may rise above any deficiencies in fact and even in appearance, certain fundamentals must be observed. Thus, attention is to be paid to the image of God in which our neighbor has been created, and also to Christ the Lord to Whom is really offered whatever is given to a needy person. The freedom and dignity of the person being helped should be respected with the utmost delicacy, and the purity of one's charitable intentions should not be stained by a quest for personal advantage or by any thirst for domination. The demands of justice should first be satisfied, lest the giving of what is due in justice be represented as the offering of a charitable gift. Not only the effects but also the causes of various ills must be removed. Help should be given in such a way that the recipients may gradually be freed from dependence on others and become self-sufficient." (*Laity*, 8).

702. "Therefore the laity should hold in high esteem and, according to their ability, aid the works of charity and projects for social assistance, whether public or private, including international programs whereby effective help is given to needy individuals and peoples. In so doing, they should cooperate with all men of good will." (*Laity*, 8).

SUFFERING

703. "Those who are oppressed by poverty, infirmity, sickness or various other hardships, as well as those who suffer persecution for justice' sake — may they all know that in a special way they are united with the suffering Christ for the salvation of the world. The Lord called them blessed in His gospel. They are those whom 'the God of all grace, Who has called us unto His Glory in Christ Jesus, will Himself, after we have suffered a little while, perfect, strengthen and establish' (1 Pet. 5:10)." (*Church*, 41).

704. We learn from St. Paul "that we must always carry about in our body the dying of Jesus, so that the life of Jesus too may be made manifest in our bodily frame (2 Cor. 4:10-11). This is why we ask the Lord in the sacrifice of the Mass that 'receiving the offering of the spiritual Victim,' He may fashion us for Himself 'as an eternal gift.' " (*Liturgy*, 12).

705. "Prompted by the Holy Spirit, the Church must walk the same

161

road which Christ walked, a road of poverty and obedience, of service and self-sacrifice to the death, from which death He came forth a victor by His resurrection. For thus did all the apostles walk in hope. On behalf of Christ's Body, which is the Church, they supplied what was wanting of the sufferings of Christ by their own many trials and sufferings (Col. 1:24). Often, too the blood of Christians was like a seed." (*Missions*, 5).

706. "Let each one remember that he can have an impact on all men and contribute to the salvation of the whole world by public worship and prayer as well as by penance and voluntary acceptance of the labors and hardships of life. By such means does the Christian grow in likeness to the suffering Christ (2 Cor. 4:10; Col. 1:24)." (*Laity*, 16).

TEMPTATION, SIN AND THE DEVIL

707. The dangers involved in temptations and the steps needed to overcome them are referred to by Vatican II in several of its documents concerning the Church and the groups that make up the People of God. As examples of a more general character, suffice it to quote the following:

708. "A monumental struggle against the powers of darkness pervades the whole history of man. The battle was joined from the very origins of the world and will continue until the last day, as the Lord has attested. Caught in this conflict, man is obliged to wrestle constantly if he is to cling to what is good. Nor can he achieve his own integrity without valiant efforts and the help of God's grace." (*Modern World*, 37).

709. "The weakness of human flesh can be healed by the holiness of Him Who has become for our sake a High Priest, 'holy, innocent, undefiled, set apart from sinners' (Heb. 7:26)." (*Priests*, 12).

710. " 'While we are in the body, we are exiled from the Lord' (2 Cor. 5:6) and having the first fruits of the Spirit we groan within ourselves (Rom. 8:23) and desire to be with Christ (Phil. 1:23). A common love urges us to live more for Him Who died for us and rose again (2 Cor. 5:15). We strive therefore to please the Lord in all things (2 Cor. 5:9). We put on the armor of God that we may be able to stand against the wiles of the devil and resist on the evil day (Eph. 6:11-13)." (*Church*, 48).

711. "Christ the Lord, Son of the living God, came that He might save His people from their sins and that all men might be made holy. Just as He Himself was sent by the Father, so He also sent His apostles. Therefore, He sanctified them, conferring on them the Holy Spirit, so that they too might glorify the Father upon earth and save men, 'for the

162

building up of the Body of Christ' (Eph. 4:12) which is the Church." (*Bishops*, 1).

712. "While Christ, 'holy, innocent, undefiled' (Heb. 7:26) knew nothing of sin (2 Cor. 5:21) but came to expiate only the sins of the people (Heb. 2:17), the Church, embracing sinners in her bosom is at the same time holy and always in need of being purified and incessantly pursues the path of penance and renewal." (*Church*, 8).

713. "St. John has testified: 'If we say that we have not sinned, we make Him a liar, and His word is not in us' (1 John 1:10)." (*Ecumenism*, 7).

714. "The Council focuses its attention on the world of man, the whole human family along with the sum of those realities in the midst of which the family lives. It gazes upon that world which is the theater of man's history, and carries the marks of his energies, his tragedies and his triumphs; that world which the Christian sees as created by its Maker's love, fallen, indeed, into the bondage of sin, yet emancipated now by Christ. He was crucified and rose again to break the stranglehold of personified Evil, so that this world might be fashioned anew according to God's design and reach its fulfillment." (*Modern World*, 2).

715. "As regards instruction, it is important to impress on the minds of the faithful not only the social consequences of sin but also the fact that the real essence of the virtue of penance is hatred for sin as an offense against God; the role of the Church in penitential practices is not to be passed over, and the people must be exhorted to pray for sinners." (*Liturgy*, 109).

CONSCIENCE

716. "In the depths of his conscience, man detects a law which he does not impose upon himself, but which holds him to obedience. Always summoning him to love good and avoid evil, the voice of conscience can when necessary speak to his heart more specifically: do this, shun that. For man has in his heart a law written by God. To obey it is the very dignity of man; according to it he will be judged.

"Conscience is the most secret core and sanctuary of a man. There he is alone with God, whose voice echoes in his depths. In a wonderful manner conscience reveals that law which is fulfilled by love of God and neighbor." (*Modern World*, 16).

717. "In all his activity a man is bound to follow his conscience faithfully in order that he may come to God for Whom he was created." (*Religious Freedom*, 3).

718. "God calls men to serve Him in spirit and in truth. Hence they

are bound in conscience but they stand under no compulsion. God has regard for the dignity of the human person whom He Himself created; man is to be guided by his own judgment and he is to enjoy freedom." (*Religious Freedom*, 11).

719. "Conscience frequently errs from invincible ignorance without losing its dignity. The same cannot be said of a man who cares but little for truth and goodness, or of a conscience which by degrees grows practically sightless as a result of habitual sin." (*Modern World*, 16).

720. "In the formation of their consciences, the Christian faithful ought carefully to attend to the sacred and certain doctrine of the Church. The Church is, by the will of Christ, the teacher of the truth. It is her duty to give utterance to, and authoritatively to teach, that truth which is Christ Himself, and also to declare and confirm by her authority those principles of the moral order which have their origin in human nature itself." (*Religious Freedom*, 14).

721. "It is worth noting that the Declaration (on Religious Freedom) does not base the right to the free exercise of religion on the 'freedom of conscience.' Nowhere does this phrase occur. The Declaration nowhere lends its authority to the theory for which the phrase frequently stands, namely, that I have the right to do what my conscience tells me to do, simply because my conscience tells me to do it. This is a perilous theory. Its particular peril is subjectivism — the notion that, in the end, it is my conscience, and not the objective truth which determines what is right or wrong, true or false." (*Religious Freedom*, 2, footnote).

14. Spiritual Duties Toward the Temporal Order

722. While the spiritual teaching of Vatican II is essentially directed toward God and the eternal salvation of men, it is by no means indifferent to the things of this world or the temporal concerns of mankind. The Council does indeed remind us that we must "not be conformed to this world" (Rom. 12:2) but tells us that in this context the word "world" refers to that "spirit of vanity and malice which transforms into an instrument of sin those human energies which are intended for the service of God and man." (*Modern World,* 37). Even the material universe is something sacred and is destined to have a share in man's own eternal destiny. For "through his bodily composition he (man) gathers to himself the elements of the material world. Thus they reach their crown through him, and through him raise their voice in free praise of the Creator." (*Modern World,* 14). It was through the Word that God not only created all things and keeps them in existence, but also "gives men an enduring witness to Himself in created realities." (*Revelation,* 3).

723. The world of men which is entrusted "to the loving ministry of the pastors of the Church is that world which God so loved that He gave His only Son for it. The truth is that though entangled in many sins, this world is also endowed with great talents and provides the Church with the living stones to be built up into the dwelling place of God in the Spirit." (*Priests,* 22).

724. "God, Who has fatherly concern for everyone, has willed that all men should constitute one family and treat one another in a spirit of brotherhood. For, having been created in the image of God, Who 'from one man has created the whole human race and made them live all over the face of the earth' (Acts 17:26), all men are called to one and the same goal, namely, God Himself." (*Modern World,* 24).

725. "Christ is now at work in the hearts of men through the energy of His Spirit. He arouses not only a desire for the age to come, but by

that very fact, He animates, purifies and strengthens those noble longings too by which the human family strives to make its life more human
and to render the whole earth submissive to this goal." (*Modern World,*
38).

726. "In fulfilling the mandate she has received from her divine
Founder to proclaim the mystery of salvation to all men, and to restore
all things in Christ, Holy Mother the Church must be concerned with
the whole of man's life, even the earthly part of it insofar as that has a
bearing on his heavenly calling." (*Education,* Intro).

COOPERATION WITH GOD IN THE TEMPORAL ORDER

727. The documents of Vatican II contain innumerable texts concerning the Christian's duty to work for a human world order. Suffice it to
quote only the following:

"Christians, on pilgrimage towards the heavenly city, should seek
and savor the things which are above. This duty in no way decreases,
but rather increases, the weight of their obligation to work with all men
in constructing a more human world. In fact, the mystery of the Christian faith furnishes them with excellent incentives and helps toward
discharging this duty more energetically and especially toward uncover-
ing the full meaning of this activity, a meaning which gives human culture its eminent place in the integral vocation of man." (*Modern World,*
57).

728. The elements of the temporal order "not only aid in the attainment of man's ultimate goal but also possess their own intrinsic value.
This value has been implanted in them by God, whether they are considered in themselves or as parts of the temporal order. 'God saw all
that He had made, and it was very good.' " (*Laity,* 7).

729. "Far from thinking that works produced by man's own talent
and energy are in opposition to God's power, and that the rational creature exists as a kind of rival to the Creator, Christians are convinced
that the triumphs of the human race are a sign of God's greatness and
the flowering of His own mysterious design. For the greater man's
power becomes, the farther his individual and community responsibility
extends. Hence it is clear that men are not deterred by the Christian
message from building up the world, or impelled to neglect the welfare
of their fellows. They are, rather, more stringently bound to do these
very things." (*Modern World,* 34).

730. "When by the work of his hands or with the aid of technology,
man develops the earth so that it can bear fruit and become a dwelling

worthy of the whole human family, and when he consciously takes part in the life of social groups, he carries out the design of God. Manifested at the beginning of time, the divine plan is that man should subdue the earth, bring creation to perfection, and develope himself. When a man so acts, he simultaneously obeys the Christian commandment that he place himself at the service of his brother men." (*Modern World,* 57).

A TEMPORAL ORDER ACCORDING TO GOD'S PLAN

731. Vatican II admits that earthly affairs have an autonomy of their own in the sense that "created things and societies enjoy their own laws and values which must be gradually deciphered, put to use and regulated by men. . . . Such is not merely required by modern men, but harmonizes with the will of the Creator. For, by the very circumstance of their having been created, all things are endowed with their own stability, truth, goodness, proper laws and order." (*Modern World,* 36).

732. The Council declares, however, that in all things "the primacy of the objective moral order demands absolute allegiance, for this order alone excels and rightly integrates all other fields of human concern." (*Communications,* 6). Similarly we are told that "even in secular affairs there is no human activity which can be withdrawn from God's dominion." (*Church,* 36).

733. The Church has not only "an eschatological purpose that can be attained only in the future world," but, being composed of men living in this world she must serve "as a leaven and as a kind of soul for human society as it is to be renewed in Christ and transformed into God's family." (*Modern World,* 40). This thought is also stressed by Vatican II in its Dogmatic Constitution on the Church where we are told that "what the soul is to the body, let Christians be to the world." (*Church,* 38).

734. Even charismatic gifts received from the Holy Spirit are to be used not only for the upbuilding of the Church but also "for the good of mankind." (*Laity,* 3).

735. One reason why Pope John XXIII convoked the Second Council of the Vatican was to "give the Church the possibility to contribute more efficaciously to the solution of the problems of the modern age." (*Documents of Vatican II*). The Pope here speaks of the supernatural order but adds that this order must "reflect its efficiency in the other order, the temporal one, which, on so many occasions is unfortunately the only one that occupies and worries man." (*Documents of Vatican II*).

736. Vatican II tells us that "it is the task of the whole Church to labor vigorously so that men may become capable of constructing the

temporal order rightly and directing it to God through Christ." (*Laity,* 7).

737. "As regards activities and institutions in the temporal order, the role of the ecclesiastical hierarchy is to teach and authentically interpret the moral principles to be followed in temporal affairs. Furthermore, it has the right to judge, after careful consideration of all related matters and consultation with experts, whether or not such activities and institutions conform to moral principles. It also has the right to decide what is required for the protection and promotion of values of the supernatural order." (*Laity,* 24).

738. "Let the clergy highly esteem the arduous apostolate of the laity. Let them train the laity to become conscious of the responsibility which as members of Christ, they bear for all men. Let them instruct them deeply in the mystery of Christ, introduce them to practical methods, and be at their side in difficulties, according to the tenor of the Council's Constitution on the Church *(Lumen Gentium)* and its Decree on the Apostolate of the Laity *(Apostolicam Actuositatem)."* (*Missions,* 21).

739. "The laity, by their very vocation, seek the kingdom of God by engaging in temporal affairs and by ordering them according to the plan of God. They live in the world, that is, in each and all of the secular professions and occupations. They live in the ordinary circumstances of family and social life, from which the very web of their existence is woven.

"They are called there by God so that by exercising their proper function and being led by the spirit of the gospel, they can work for the sanctification of the world from within, in the manner of leaven. In this way they can make Christ known to others, especially by the testimony of a life resplendent in faith, hope and charity. The layman is closely involved in temporal affairs of every sort. It is therefore his special task to illumine and organize those affairs in such a way that they may always start out, develope and persist according to Christ's mind, to the praise of the Creator and the Redeemer." (*Church,* 31).

740. "In collaborating as citizens of this world in whatever pertains to the upbuilding and operation of the temporal order, the laity should, under the light of faith, seek for loftier motives of action in their family, professional, cultural and social life and make them known to others when the occasion arises. Let them be aware that by so doing they are cooperating with God the Creator, Redeemer and Sanctifier and are giving praise to Him." (*Laity,* 16).

LOVE FOR ONE'S NEIGHBOR

741. As so many other documents of Vatican II, the Pastoral Consti-

tution on the Church in the Modern World reminds us that "love for God and neighbor is the first and greatest commandment. Holy Scripture, however, teaches us that the love for God cannot be separated from love of neighbor: 'If there is any other commandment, it is summed up in this saying: "Thou shalt love thy neighbor as thyself. . . . Love, therefore is the fulfillment of the law" ' (Rom. 13:9-10; 1 John 4.20). To men growing daily more dependent on one another and to a world becoming more unified every day, this truth proves to be of paramount importance." (*Modern World,* 24).

742. "This Council lays stress on reverence for man; everyone must consider his every neighbor without exception as another self, taking into account first of all his life and the means necessary to living it with dignity, so as not to imitate the rich man who had no concern for the poor man Lazarus.

"In our times a special obligation binds us to make ourselves the neighbor of absolutely every person, and of actively helping him when he comes across our path, whether he be an old person abandoned by all, a foreign laborer unjustly looked down upon, a refugee, a child born out of an unlawful union and wrongly suffering for a sin he did not commit, or a hungry person who disturbs our conscience by recalling the voice of the Lord: 'As long as you did it for one of these, the least of my brethren, you did it for me' (Mt. 25:40)." (*Modern World,* 27).

743. "God's Word, through Whom all things were made, was Himself made flesh and dwelt on the earth of men. Thus He entered the world's history as a perfect man, taking that history up into Himself and summarizing it. He Himself revealed to us that 'God is love' (1 John 4:8). At the same time He taught us that the new command of love was the basic law of human perfection and hence of the world's transformation.

"To those, therefore, who believe in divine love, He gives assurance that the way of love lies open to all men and that the effort to establish a universal brotherhood is not a hopeless one. He cautions them at the same time that this love is not something reserved for important matters, but must be pursued chiefly in the ordinary circumstances of life." (*Modern World,* 38).

744. "The joys and the hopes, the griefs and the anxieties of the men of this age, especially those who are poor or in any way afflicted, these too are the joys and hopes, the griefs and anxieties of the followers of Christ. Indeed, nothing genuinely human fails to raise an echo in their hearts. For theirs is a community composed of men. United in Christ, they are led by the Holy Spirit in their journey to the kingdom of their Father and they have welcomed the news of salvation which is meant for every man. This is why this community realizes that it is truly and

intimately linked with mankind and its history." (*Modern World,* 1).

745. "There is a decline in the individual man's ability to grasp and unify" all branches of knowledge. "Nevertheless, it remains each man's duty to preserve a view of the whole person, a view in which the values of intellect, will, conscience and fraternity are pre-eminent. These values are all rooted in God the Creator and have been wonderfully restored and elevated in Christ." (*Modern World,* 61).

THE PERSON IN THE NATION AND IN THE WORLD

746. "There is a growing awareness of the exalted dignity proper to the human person, since he stands above all things, and his rights and duties are universal and inviolable. Therefore, there must be made available to all men everything necessary for leading a life truly human, such as food, clothing and shelter; the right to choose a state of life freely and to found a family, the right to education, to employment, to a good reputation, to respect, to appropriate information, to activity in accord with the upright norm of one's conscience, to protection of privacy and to rightful freedom in matters religious too.

"Hence the social order and its development must unceasingly work to the benefit of the human person if the disposition of affairs is to be subordinate to the personal realm and not contrariwise, as the Lord indicated when He said that the Sabbath was made for man, and not man for the Sabbath.

"This social order requires constant improvement. It must be founded on truth, built on justice and animated by love; in freedom it should grow every day toward a more human balance. An improvement in attitudes and widespread changes in society will have to take place if these objectives are to be gained.

"God's Spirit, Who with a marvelous providence directs the unfolding of time and renews the face of the earth, is not absent from this development. The ferment of the gospel, too, has aroused and continues to arouse in man's heart the irresistible requirements of his dignity." (*Modern World,* 26).

747. "A vast field for the apostolate has opened up on the national and international levels where most of all the laity are called upon to be stewards of Christian wisdom. In loyalty to their country and in faithful fulfillment of their civic obligations, Catholics should feel themselves obliged to promote the true common good. Thus, they should make the weight of their opinion felt, so that civil authority may act with justice, and laws may conform to moral precepts and the common good. Catholics skilled in public affairs and adequately enlightened by faith and

Christian doctrine should not refuse to administer public affairs, since by performing this office in a worthy manner they can simultaneously advance the common good and prepare the way for the gospel. . . .

"Among the signs of our times, the irresistibly increasing sense of solidarity among all peoples is especially noteworthy. It is a function of the lay apostolate to promote this awareness zealously and to transform it into a sincere and genuine sense of brotherhood. Furthermore, the laity should be informed about the international field and about the questions and solutions, theoretical and practical, which arise in this field, especially with regard to the developing nations." (*Laity,* 14).

SPIRITUAL ASPECTS OF THE ECONOMIC ORDER

748. "In the socio-economic realm, too, the dignity and total vocation of the human person must be honored and advanced along with the welfare of society as a whole. For man is the source, the center, and the purpose of all socio-economic life." (*Modern World,* 63).

749. "The fundamental purpose of this productivity must not be the mere multiplication of products. It must not be profit or domination. Rather, it must be the service of man, and indeed of the whole man, viewed in terms of his material needs, and the demands of his intellectual, moral, spiritual and religious life. And when we say man, we mean every man whatsoever and every group of men of whatever race and from whatever part of the world. Consequently, economic activity is to be carried out according to its own methods and laws but within the limits of morality so that God's plan for mankind can be realized." (*Modern World,* 64).

750. "God intended the earth and all that it contains for the use of every human being and people. Thus, as all men follow justice and unite in charity, created goods should abound for them on a reasonable basis. Whatever the forms of ownership may be, as adapted to the legitimate institutions of people according to diverse and changeable circumstances, attention must always be paid to the universal purpose for which created goods are meant. In using them, therefore, a man should regard his lawful possessions not merely as his own but also as common property in the sense that they should accrue to the benefit of not only himself but of others.

"For the rest, the right to have a share of earthly goods sufficient for oneself and one's family belongs to everyone. The Fathers and Doctors of the Church hold this view, teaching that men are obliged to come to the relief of the poor, and to do so not merely out of their superfluous goods. If a person is in extreme necessity, he has the right to take from the riches of others what he himself needs. Since there are so many people in this world afflicted with hunger, this sacred Council urges all, both individuals and governments, to remember the saying of the Fathers: 'Feed the man dying of hunger, because if you have not fed him you have killed him' (Gratian). According to their ability, let all individuals and governments undertake a genuine sharing of their goods. Let them use these goods especially to provide individuals and nations with the means for helping and developing themselves." (*Modern World*, 69).

751. "By its very nature, private property has a social quality deriving from the law of the communal purpose of earthly goods. If this social quality is overlooked, property often becomes an occasion of greed and of serious disturbances. Thus, to those who attack the concept of private property, pretext is given for calling the right itself into question." (*Modern World*, 71).

752. "Some nations with a majority of citizens who are counted as Christians, have an abundance of this world's goods, while others are deprived of the necessities of life and are tormented with hunger, disease and every kind of misery. This situation must not be allowed to continue, to the scandal of humanity. For the spirit of poverty and of charity are the glory and authentication of the Church of Christ." (*Modern World*, 88).

753. "Christians who take an active part in modern socio-economic development and defend justice and charity should be convinced that they can make a great contribution to the prosperity of mankind and the peace of the world. Whether they do so as individuals or in association, let their example be a shining one. After acquiring whatever skills and experience are absolutely necessary, they should in faithfulness to Christ and His gospel, observe the right order of values in their earthly activities. Thus their whole lives, both individual and social, will be permeated with the spirit of the beatitudes, notably with the spirit of poverty.

"Whoever in obedience to Christ seeks first the kingdom of God will as a consequence receive a stronger and purer love for helping all his brothers and for perfecting the work of justice under the inspiration of charity." (*Modern World*, 72).

SPIRITUAL ASPECTS OF LABOR

754. "Man, created to God's image, received a mandate to subject to himself the earth and all that it contains, and to govern the world with justice and holiness. . . .

172

"This mandate concerns even the most ordinary everyday activities. For while providing the substance of life for themselves and their families, men and women are performing their activities in a way which appropriately benefits society. They can justly consider that by their labor they are unfolding the Creator's work, consulting the advantages of their brother men, and contributing by their personal industry to the realization in history of the divine plan." (*Modern World*, 34).

755. "Human labor which is expended in the production and exchange of goods or in the performance of economic services is superior to the other elements of economic life. For the latter have only the nature of tools.

"Whether it is engaged in independently or paid for by someone else, this labor comes immediately from the person. In a sense, the person stamps the things of nature with his seal and subdues them to his will. It is ordinarily by his labor that a man supports himself and his family, is joined to his fellow men and serves them, and is enabled to exercise genuine charity and be a partner in the work of bringing God's creation to perfection. Indeed, we hold that by offering his labor to God a man becomes associated with the redemptive work itself of Jesus Christ, Who conferred an eminent dignity on labor when at Nazareth He worked with His own hands.

"From all these considerations, there arise every man's duty to labor faithfully and also his right to work. It is the duty of society, moreover, according to the circumstances prevailing in it, and in keeping with its proper role, to help its citizens to find opportunities for adequate employment. Finally, payment for labor must be such as to furnish a man with the means to cultivate his own material, social, cultural and spiritual life worthily and that of his dependents. What this payment should be will vary according to each man's assignment and productivity, the conditions of his place of employment and the common good." (*Modern World*, 67).

756. "Laborers, whose work is often toilsome, should by their human exertions try to perfect themselves, aid their fellow-citizens, and raise all of society, and even creation itself, to a better mode of existence. By their lively charity, joyous hope, and sharing of one another's burdens, let them also truly imitate Christ, Who roughened His hands with carpenter's tools, and Who in union with His Father is always at work for the salvation of all men. By their daily work itself, laborers can achieve greater apostolic sanctity." (*Church*, 41).

ABOUT LABOR UNIONS

757. "Among the basic rights of the human person, must be counted

173

the right of freely founding labor unions. These unions should be truly able to represent the workers and to contribute to the proper arrangement of economic life. Another such right is that of taking part freely in the activity of these unions without risk of reprisal. Through this sort of orderly participation, joined with an ongoing formation in economic and social matters, all will grow day by day in the awareness of their own function and responsibility. Thus they will be brought to feel that according to their own proper capacities and aptitudes they are associates in the whole task of economic and social development and in the attainment of the universal common good." (*Modern World,* 68).

SPIRITUAL ASPECTS OF THE SOCIAL, POLITICAL AND CULTURAL SPHERES

758. "Every day human interdependence grows more tightly drawn and spreads by degrees over the whole world. As a result, the common good, that is, the sum of those conditions of social life which allow social groups and their individual members relatively thorough and ready access to their own fulfillment, today takes on an increasingly universal complexion and consequently involves rights and duties with respect to the whole human race. Every social group must take account of the needs and legitimate aspirations of other groups, and even of the general welfare of the entire human family." (*Modern World,* 26).

759. "Profound and rapid changes make it particularly urgent that no one, ignoring the trend of events or drugged by laziness, content himself with a merely individualistic morality. It grows increasingly true that the obligations of justice and love are fulfilled only if each person, contributing to the common good, according to his own abilities and the needs of others, also promotes and assists the public and private institutions dedicated to bettering the conditions of human life. . . .

"Let everyone consider it his sacred obligation to count social necessities among the primary duties of modern man, and to pay heed to them. For the more unified the world becomes, the more plainly do the offices of men extend beyond particular groups and spread by degrees to the whole world. But this challenge cannot be met unless individual men and their associations cultivate in themselves the moral and social virtues, and promote them in society. Thus, with the needed help of divine grace, men who are truly new and artisans of a new humanity can be forthcoming." (*Modern World,* 30).

760. "Today public opinion exerts massive force and authority over the private and public life of every class of citizen. Hence the necessity arises for every member of society to do what justice and charity require

174

in this matter. With the aid of these instruments (of communication), then, each man should strive to form and to voice worthy views on public affairs. . . .

"Special duties bind those readers, viewers, or listeners who personally and freely choose to receive what these media have to communicate. For good choosing dictates that ample favor be shown to whatever fosters virtue, knowledge or art. People should reject whatever could become a cause or an occasion of spiritual harm to themselves, whatever could endanger others through bad example, and whatever would impede good selections and promote bad ones. The last effect generally results when financial support is given to men who exploit those media for commercial reasons.

"If those who use these media are to honor the moral law, they must not neglect to inform themselves in good time of the judgments made in these affairs by competent authority. These judgments they should respect according to the requirements of a good conscience. By taking pains to guide and settle their conscience with appropriate help, they will more readily thwart less honorable influences and amply support those which are worthy." (*Communications*, 8).

PEACE

761. In a special section devoted to the problem of peace, Vatican II tells us that "the common good of men is, in its basic sense, determined by the eternal law." The Council also says that "peace results from the harmony built into human society by its divine Founder, and actualized by men as they thirst after ever greater justice. . . . Since the human will is unsteady and wounded by sin, the achievement of peace requires that everyone constantly master his passions and that lawful authority keep vigilant.

"But such is not enough. This peace cannot be obtained on earth unless personal values are safeguarded and men freely and trustingly share with one another the riches of their inner spirits and their talents. A firm determination to respect other men and peoples and their dignity, as well as the studied practice of brotherhood, are absolutely necessary for the establishment of peace. Hence peace is likewise the fruit of love, which goes beyond what justice can provide." (*Modern World*, 78).

762. In its zeal for the creation of a better world, Vatican II calls for cooperation even with those "who oppress the Church and harass her in manifold ways. Since God the Father is the origin and purpose of all men, we are called to be brothers. Therefore, if we have been sum-

moned to the same destiny, which is both human and divine, we can and we should work together without violence and deceit in order to build up the world in genuine peace." (*Modern World,* 92).

LAITY AND THE SOCIAL MILIEU

763. "The apostolate of the social milieu, that is, the effort to infuse a Christian spirit into the mentality, customs, laws and structures of the community in which a person lives, is so much the duty and responsibility of the laity that it can never be properly performed by others. In this area the laity can exercise the apostolate of like toward like. It is here that laymen add to the testimony of life the testimony of their speech; it is here in the arena of their labor, profession, studies, residence, leisure and companionship that laymen have a special opportunity to help their brothers.

"To fulfill the mission of the Church in the world, the laity have certain basic needs. They need a life in harmony with their faith, so that they can become the light of the world. They need that undeviating honesty which can attract all men to the love of truth and goodness, and finally to the Church and to Christ. They need the kind of fraternal charity which will lead them to share in the living conditions, labors, sorrows and hope of their brother men, and which will gradually and imperceptibly dispose the hearts of all around them for the saving work of grace. They need full awareness of their role in building up society. . . .

"This apostolate should reach out to all men wherever they can be found; it should not exclude any spiritual or temporal benefit which can possibly be conferred. True apostles, however, are not content with this activity alone, but look for the opportunity to announce Christ to their neighbors through the spoken word as well. For there are many persons who can hear the gospel and recognize Christ only through the laity who live near them." (*Laity,* 13).

AUTHORITY OF THE STATE — ITS RIGHTFUL CLAIMS AND LIMITATIONS

764. It is "obvious that the political community and public authority are based on human nature and hence belong to an order of things divinely foreordained. At the same time, the choice of government and the method of selecting leaders is left to the free will of the citizens.

"It also follows that political authority, whether in the community as such or in institutions representing the state, must always be exercised within the limits of morality and on behalf of the dynamically conceived common good, according to a juridical order enjoying legal status. When such is the case, citizens are conscience-bound to obey. This fact clearly reveals the responsibility, dignity and importance of those who govern." (*Modern World,* 74).

765. "As the Master, so too the apostles recognized legitimate civil authority. 'For there exists no authority except from God,' the apostle teaches, and therefore commands: 'Let everyone be subject to the higher authorities . . . he who resists the authority resists the ordinance of God' (Rom. 13:1-2)." (*Religious Freedom,* 11).

766. "Of its very nature, the exercise of religion consists before all else in those internal, voluntary and free acts whereby man sets the course of his life directly towards God. No merely human power can either command or prohibit acts of this kind." (*Religious Freedom,* 3).

767. "Let all Christians appreciate their special and personal vocation in the political community. This vocation requires that they give conspicuous example of devotion to the sense of duty and of service to the advancement of the common good. Thus they can also show in practice how authority is to be harmonized with freedom, personal initiative with consideration for the bonds uniting the whole social body, and necessary unity with beneficial diversity." (*Modern World,* 75).

768. "Because the very plan of salvation requires it, the faithful should learn to distinguish carefully between those rights and duties which are theirs as members of the Church, and those which they have as members of human society. Let them strive to harmonize the two, remembering that in every temporal affair they must be guided by a Christian conscience. For even in secular affairs, there is no human activity which can be withdrawn from God's dominion. . . . While it must be recognized that the temporal sphere is governed by its own principles since it is properly concerned with the interests of this world, that ominous doctrine must rightly be rejected which attempts to build a society with no regard whatever for religion and which attacks and destroys the religious liberty of its citizens." (*Church,* 36).

769. "Many pressures are brought to bear upon men of our day to the point where the danger arises lest they lose the possibility of acting on their own judgment. On the other hand, not a few can be found who seem inclined to use the name of freedom as the pretext for refusing to submit to authority and for making light of the duty of obedience.

"Therefore, this Vatican Synod urges everyone, especially those who are charged with the task of educating others, to do their utmost to form men who will respect the moral order and be obedient to lawful authority. Let them form men too who will be lovers of true freedom —

men, in other words, who will come to decisions on their own judgment and in the light of truth, govern their activities with a sense of responsibility and strive after what is true and right, willing always to join with others in cooperative effort." (*Religious Freedom,* 8).

SPIRITUAL VIEW OF CULTURE, LEARNING, ETC.

770. In its "Message to Humanity," published at the very beginning of its first session, the Second Council of the Vatican expressed its interest in human and cultural values as follows: "While we hope that the light of faith will shine more clearly and more vigorously as a result of this Council's efforts, we look forward to a spiritual renewal from which will also flow a happy impulse on behalf of human values such as scientific discoveries, technological advances and a wider diffusion of knowledge." *(Documents of Vatican II).*

771. Dealing more specifically with these topics in their relation to human welfare and the Wisdom of God, the Council also declared: "Furthermore, when a man applies himself to the various disciplines of philosophy, of history, and of mathematical and natural science, and when he cultivates the arts, he can do very much to elevate the human family to a more sublime understanding of truth, goodness and beauty, and to the formation of judgments which embody universal values. Thus mankind can be more clearly enlightened by that marvelous wisdom which was with God from eternity, arranging all things with Him, playing upon the earth, delighting in the sons of men.

"In this way, the human spirit grows increasingly free of the bondage to creatures and can be more easily drawn to the worship and contemplation of the Creator. Moreover, under the impulse of grace, man is disposed to acknowledge the Word of God. Before He became flesh in order to save all things and to sum them up in Himself, 'He was in the world' already as 'the true light that enlightens every man' (John 1:9-10)." (*Modern World,* 57).

772. Vatican II reminds us that when scientists think that their methods of investigation can be looked upon as the "supreme rule for discovering the whole truth" they can be led into agnosticism. "These unfortunate results, however, do not necessarily follow from the culture of today, nor should they lead us into the temptation of not acknowledging its positive values. For among these values are these: scientific study and strict fidelity toward truth in scientific research, the necessity of working together with others in technical groups, a sense of international solidarity, an ever clearer awareness of the responsibility of experts to aid men and even to protect them, the desire to make the condi-

tions of life more favorable for all, especially for those who are deprived of the opportunity to exercise responsibility or who are culturally poor.

"All of these values can provide some preparation for the acceptance of the message of the gospel — a preparation which can be animated with divine love by Him Who came to save the world.

"There are many links between the message of salvation and human culture. For God, revealing Himself to His people to the extent of a full manifestation of Himself in the Incarnate Son, has spoken according to the culture proper to different ages." (*Modern World,* 57 and 58).

773. Important for those who are engaged in the field of communications are the principles laid down by the Council in the following paragraph:

"There exists within human society a right to information about affairs which affect men individually or collectively, and according to the circumstances of each. The proper exercise of this right demands that the matter communicated always be true, and as complete as charity and justice allow. The manner of communication should furthermore be honorable and appropriate; this means that in the gathering and publication of news the norms of morality and the legitimate rights and dignity of a man must be held sacred. For knowledge is sometimes unprofitable but 'charity edifies.' " (*Communications,* 5).

774. The best key, perhaps, to the attitude of Vatican II towards the temporal order in this world is to be found in the following words contained in the Decree on Missionary Activity: Through His Son "God made all orders of existence. God further appointed Him heir of all things, so that in the Son, He might restore them all (Eph. 1:10)." (*Missions,* 3).

15. Towards Eternal Life

775. In his address at the opening of the Second Council of the Vatican on October 11, 1962, Pope John XXIII declared that the greatest concern of the Council was "that the sacred deposit of Christian doctrine should be guarded and taught more efficaciously." He added: "That doctrine embraces the whole of man, composed as he is body and soul. And since he is a pilgrim on this earth, it commands him to tend always towards heaven.

"This demonstrates how our mortal life is to be ordered in such a way as to fulfill our duties as citizens of earth and of heaven, and thus attain the aim of life as established by God. That is, all men, whether taken singly or as united in society, today have the duty of tending ceaselessly during their lifetime toward the attainment of heavenly things and to use for this purpose only, the earthly goods, the employment of which must not prejudice their eternal happiness." *(Documents of Vatican II)*.

776. Addressing itself to the world as a whole the Council itself explained God's purpose and His attitude towards us when it declared that "God has called man and still calls him so that with his entire being he might be joined to Him in an endless sharing of a divine life beyond all corruption." *(Modern World,* 18).

777. Referring to the Church "to which we are all called in Christ Jesus, and in which we acquire sanctity through the grace of God," the Council says that she "will attain her full perfection only in the glory of heaven. Then will come the time of the restoration of all things (Acts 3:21). Then the human race as well as the entire world which is intimately related to man and achieves its purpose through him, will be perfectly re-established in Christ (Eph. 1:10; Col. 1:20; 2 Pet. 3:10-13)." *(Church,* 48).

778. The word "Church" in this context means not only the so-called "militant" Church on earth but also the "suffering" Church in Purgatory and the "triumphant" Church in heaven. For Vatican II tells us that

"this most sacred Synod accepts with great devotion the venerable faith of our ancestors regarding this vital fellowship with our brothers who are in heavenly glory or who are still being purified after death. It proposes again the decrees of the Second Council of Nicaea, the Council of Florence and the Council of Trent." (*Church*, 51).

779. The law of this Church, as the People of God, is "the new commandment to love as Christ loved us (John 13:34). Its goal is the kingdom of God which has been begun by God Himself on earth, and which is to be further extended until it is brought to perfection by Him at the end of time." (*Church*, 9).

780. The Head of this Church is Christ. He is the Image of the invisible God and in Him all things came into being. He has priority over everyone and in Him all things hold together. He is the Head of that body which is the Church. He is the beginning, the firstborn from the dead, so that in all things He might have the first place (Col. 1:15-18). By the greatness of His power He rules the things of heaven and the things of earth, and with His all-surpassing perfection and activity He fills the whole body with the riches of His glory (Eph. 1:18-23)." (*Church*, 7).

MAN'S ETERNAL DESTINY

781. "The People of God has no lasting city here below but looks forward to one which is to come." (*Church*, 44). "Man is not restricted to the temporal sphere. While living in history he fully maintains his eternal vocation." (*Modern World*, 76).

782. The Father sent His Son not only to tell men "the innermost realities about God" but also to confirm "with divine testimony what revelation proclaimed: that God is with us to free us from the darkness of sin and to raise us to eternal life." (*Revelation*, 4).

DEATH

783. Vatican II admits that "the mystery of death utterly beggars the imagination" (*Modern World*, 18) and reminds us that we must "battle against evil through manifold tribulations and even suffer death." (*Modern World*, 22). On the very next page, however, the Council declares that "through Christ and in Christ the riddles of sorrow and death grow meaningful." (*Modern World*, 22). "Each one of us can say: 'The Son of God loved me and gave Himself up for me' (Gal. 2:20). By suffering for us He not only provided us with an example for our imita-

181

tion. He blazed a trail and if we follow it, life and death are made holy and take on a new meaning." (*Modern World,* 22).

784. The Council tells us also that "that bodily death from which man would have been immune, had he not sinned, will be vanquished, according to the Christian faith, when man, who was ruined by his own doing, is restored to wholeness by an almighty and merciful Savior. . . . Hence, to every thoughtful man a solidly established faith provides the answer to his anxiety about what the future holds for him. At the same time, faith gives him the power to be united in Christ with his loved ones who have already been snatched away by death. Faith arouses the hope that they have found true life with God." (*Modern World,* 18).

785. "Christ has risen, destroying death by His death. He has lavished life upon us so that, as sons in the Son, we can cry out in the Spirit: 'Abba, Father.' " (*Modern World,* 22).

RESTORATION PROMISED

786. "The promised restoration which we are awaiting has already begun in Christ, is carried forward in the mission of the Holy Spirit, and through Him continues in the Church. There we learn through faith the meaning, too, of our temporal life, as we perform, with hope of good things to come, the task committed to us in this world by the Father, and work out our salvation" (Phil. 2:12).

"The final age of the world has already come upon us (1 Cor. 10:11). The renovation of the world has been irrevocably decreed and in this age is already anticipated in some real way. For even now on this earth the Church is marked with a genuine though imperfect holiness. However, until there is a new heaven and a new earth where justice dwells (2 Pet. 3:13), the pilgrim Church in her sacraments and institutions, which pertain to this present time, takes on the appearance of this passing world. She herself dwells among creatures who groan and travail in pain until now and await the revelation of the sons of God (Rom. 8:19-22)." (*Church,* 48).

787. It is not only the human race which is to share in this restoration. The Council tells us that "the entire world which is intimately related to man and achieves its purpose through him, will be . . . re-established in Christ (Eph. 1:10; Col. 1:20; 2 Pet. 3:10-13)." (*Church,* 48).

AFTER DEATH THE JUDGMENT — HELL

788. "Since we know not the day nor the hour, on our Lord's advice

we must constantly stand guard. Thus when we have finished the one and only course of our earthly life (Heb. 9:27) we may merit to enter into the marriage feast with Him and to be numbered among the blessed (Mt. 25:31-46). Thus we may not be commanded to go into eternal fire (Mt. 25:41) like the wicked and slothful servant (Mt. 25:26), into the exterior darkness where 'there will be weeping and gnashing of teeth' (Mt. 22:13; 25:30). For before we reign with the glorious Christ, all of us will be made manifest 'before the tribunal of Christ, so that each one may receive what he has won through the body, according to his works, whether good or evil' (2 Cor. 5:10). At the end of the world, 'they who have done good shall come forth unto resurrection of life; but who have done evil, unto resurrection of judgment' (John 5:29; Mt. 25:46)." (*Church*, 48).

789. "All the sons of the Church should remember that their exalted status is to be attributed not to their own merits, but to the special grace of Christ. If they fail moreover to respond to that grace in thought, word and deed, not only will they not be saved, but they will be the more severely judged." (*Church*, 14).

790. "God's Word, by Whom all things were made, was Himself made flesh so that as perfect man, He might save all men and sum up all things in Himself. . . . He it is Whom the Father has raised from the dead, lifted on high and stationed at His right hand, making Him Judge of the living and the dead. Enlivened and united in His Spirit, we journey toward the consummation of human history, one which accords with the counsel of God's love: 'To re-establish all things in Christ, both those in the heavens and those on the earth' (Eph. 1:10).

"The Lord Himself speaks: 'Behold, I come quickly! And my reward is with me, to render to each one according to his works. I am the Alpha and the Omega, the first and the last, the beginning and the end' (Apoc. 22:12-13)." (*Modern World*, 45).

PURGATORY

791. It was not the purpose of Vatican II to explain the doctrine of Purgatory but it does give witness in three sections of the Dogmatic Constitution on the Church to the traditional teaching on the subject. It tells us that some of Christ's disciples have finished with this life and are being purified." (*Church*, 49). The Council "accepts with great devotion the venerable faith of our ancestors regarding the vital fellowship with our brethren . . . who are still being purified after death." (*Church*, 51).

792. Concerning prayers for the souls in Purgatory, the Council has this to say: "Very much aware of the bonds linking the whole Mystical

Body of Christ, the pilgrim Church from the very first ages of the Christian religion has cultivated with great piety the memory of the dead. Because it is 'a holy and wholesome thought to pray for the dead that they may be loosed from sins' (2 Mach. 12:46), she has also offered prayers for them." (*Church*, 50).

HEAVEN AND THE SAINTS

793. More numerous are the texts to be found in the conciliar documents concerning heaven and the saints. Especially rich in significance for all of us is the simple statement that God is "our goal." (*Non-Christian Religions*, 1).

794. God's plan for us will be realized "when all who share one human nature, are regenerated in Christ through the Holy Spirit and behold together the glory of God and can say: 'Our Father.' " (*Missions*, 7). Then we shall "communicate in life and glory" with God "who made all things," will be "all in all" (1 Cor. 15:28) and will procure "at one and the same time His own glory and our happiness." (*Missions*, 2).

795. It is by a gift of the Holy Spirit that some are called "to give clear witness to the desire for a heavenly home and to keep that desire green among the human family." (*Modern World*, 38). Through the Eucharist "a pledge of future glory is given to us" (*Liturgy*, 47) and it is "with hope of good things to come" that we perform "the task committed to us in this world by the Father and work out our salvation." (*Church*, 48). In heaven we shall appear "with Christ in the state of glory (Col. 3:4) in which we shall be like God since we shall see Him as He is (1 John 3:2)." (*Church*, 48).

THE COMMUNION OF SAINTS

796. "By reason of the fact that those in heaven are more closely united with Christ, they establish the whole Church more firmly in holiness, lend nobility to the worship which the Church offers on earth to God, and in many ways contribute to its greater upbuilding (1 Cor. 12:12-27). For after they have been received into their heavenly home and are present to the Lord (2 Cor. 5:8), through Him and with Him and in Him, they do not cease to intercede with the Father for us. Rather, they show forth the merits which they have won on earth through the one Mediator between God and man, Christ Jesus (1 Tim. 2:5). There they served God in all things and filled up in their flesh whatever was lacking

of the sufferings of Christ on behalf of His Body which is the Church (Col. 1:24). Thus by their brotherly interest our weakness is very greatly strengthened." (*Church*, 49).

797. "It is supremely fitting, therefore, that we love those friends and fellow heirs of Jesus Christ, who are also our brothers and extraordinary benefactors, that we render due thanks to God for them and 'suppliantly invoke them and have recourse to their prayers, their power and help in obtaining benefits from God through His Son, Jesus Christ, our Lord Who is our sole Redeemer and Savior' (*Trent*). For by its very nature every genuine testimony of love which we show to those in heaven tends towards and terminates in Christ Who is the 'crown of all saints.' Through Him it tends towards and terminates in God, Who is wonderful in His saints and is magnified in them." (*Church*, 50).

798. "As long as all of us, who are sons of God and comprise one family in Christ (Heb. 3:6), remain in communion with one another in perfect charity and in one praise of the Most Holy Trinity, we are responding to the deepest vocation of the Church and partaking in a foretaste of the liturgy of consummate glory. For when Christ shall appear and the glorious resurrection of the dead takes place, the splendor of God will brighten the heavenly city and the Lamb will be the lamp thereof (Apoc. 21:24). Then in the supreme happiness of charity the whole Church of the saints will adore God and 'the Lamb Who was slain' (Apoc. 5:12) proclaiming with one voice: 'To Him Who sits upon the throne, and to the Lamb, blessing and honor and glory and dominion forever and ever' (Apoc. 5:13-14)." (*Church*, 51).

799. "When we look at the lives of those who have faithfully followed Christ, we are inspired with a new reason for seeking the city which is to come (Heb. 13:14; 11:10). At the same time we are shown a most safe path by which, among the vicissitudes of this world and in keeping with the state in life and condition proper to each of us, we will be able to arrive at perfect union with Christ, that is, holiness. In the lives of those who shared in our humanity and yet were transformed into successful images of Christ (2 Cor. 3:18), God vividly manifests to men His presence and His face. He speaks to us in them, and gives us a sign of His kingdom to which we are powerfully drawn, surrounded as we are by so many witnesses (Heb. 12:1) and having such an argument for the truth of the gospel." (*Church*, 50).

800. "In various ways and degrees we all partake in the same love for God and neighbor, and all sing the same hymn of glory to our God. For all who belong to Christ, having His Spirit, form one Church and cleave together in Him (Eph. 4:16). Therefore the union of the wayfarers with the brethren who have gone to sleep in the peace of Christ is not in the least interrupted. On the contrary, according to the perennial faith of

the Church, it is strengthened through the exchanging of spiritual goods." (*Church,* 49).

THE RESURRECTION

801. Vatican II reminds us that "at the end of the world 'they who have done good shall come forth unto resurrection of life; but they who have done evil unto resurrection of judgment' (John 5:29; Mt. 25:46)." The Council then goes on to say: "We reckon therefore that 'the sufferings of the present time are not worthy to be compared with the glory to come that will be revealed in us' (Rom. 8:18; 2 Tim. 2:11-12). Strong in faith we look for 'the blessed hope and glorious coming of our great God and Savior, Jesus Christ' (Tit. 2:13), 'Who will refashion the body of our lowliness, conforming it to the body of His glory' (Phil. 3:21), and Who will come 'to be glorified in His saints and to be marveled at in all those who have believed' (2 Th. 1:10)." (*Church,* 48).

802. In the Pastoral Constitution on the Church in the Modern World Vatican II tells us that "man is obliged to regard his body as good and honorable since God will raise it up on the last day." (*Modern World,* 14). The Council adds that through the Holy Spirit "Who is 'the pledge of our inheritance' (Eph. 1:14), the whole man is renewed from within, even to the achievement of 'the redemption of the body' (Rom. 8:23). 'If the Spirit of Him Who raised Jesus from the death dwells in you, then He Who raised Jesus Christ from the dead will also bring to life your mortal bodies because of His Spirit Who dwells in you' (Rom. 8:11)." (*Modern World,* 22).

Conclusion

803. As stated in the Introduction, direct quotations from Vatican II account for about nine-tenths of this book's contents. As an ecumenical Council, Vatican II was not only the latest but also the most authentic and authoritative expression of the Church, her life and her spirituality ever given to our generation. Unfortunately many of our contemporaries seem to think that the Council is already out of date and irrelevant. This is certainly not the opinion of the present Holy Father of whom some have predicted that he will be hailed by future historians as "Pope Paul the Great." In fact, Pope Paul VI has been quoted as saying that he regards it as his principal duty in life to see that the ideas and ideals of Vatican II be carried out.

804. In the General Audience granted by the Pope on July 15, 1970, the Holy Father said: "We cannot say that the Council ended with its closure, as happens with so many events which time passes over, buries, and leaves to students of past events to keep their memory alive. The Council was an event which is lasting, living on not only in memory but also in the Church's life; it is destined to last for a long time yet, inside and outside the Church." (*L'Osservatore Romano,* July 23, 1970).

805. Earlier in that same year, on February 4, 1970, His Holiness said: "We are still meditating on the Council's teachings. For we are convinced that they constitute a *Summa* for our time, a very rich, authoritative compendium of doctrine and guidance for its needs. . . . (*L'Osservatore Romano,* February 12, 1970).

806. "The teachings of Councils used to end regularly by stating an error, then deploring it, finally condemning it with the classic phrase, *Anathema sit.* But the methods of the Second Vatican Council are intended to throw light upon what is to be praised, appreciated, done and hoped for." (*Ibid,* p. 1).

807. More severe is the judgment passed on critics of the Council by the same Holy Father on July 15, 1970, when he urged his hearers to be

faithful to the Council, to the Church and to Christ. He declared that "many who talk about the Council do not really know its marvelous documents. Some who are more concerned with contestation, with hasty and subversive change, dare to insinuate that the Council is already finished with. They dare to think that it served only to tear down, not to build up. But any one who is willing to see the Council as the work of the Holy Spirit and the Church's responsible organ, will assiduously and respectfully take up the Council's documents and use them as nourishment and law for his own soul and for his community. We should remember the theological terms adopted by the very first Council of Jerusalem: *Visum est . . . Spiritui Sancto et nobis'* (Acts 15:28): 'It has seemed good to the Holy Spirit and to us.'

808. "The second kind of fidelity is fidelity to the Church. We ought to understand her, love her, serve her and develope her both because she is the sign and the means of salvation, and because she is the object of Christ's immolated love. *'Dilexit Ecclesiam et se ipsum immolavit pro ea.* He loved the Church and gave himself up for her' (Eph. 5:25). We are the Church, that Mystical Body of Christ of which we are vital members and in which we ourselves shall have our everlasting reward.

809. "This fidelity to the Church, as you know, is betrayed by many today; it is debated, interpreted according to private views, and minimized. Its deep and authentic meaning is not understood, and the Church is not given that respect and generosity which she deserves, not for our humiliation but rather for the sake of valuable experience and honor.

810. "Finally, fidelity to Christ. Everything is contained in that. We will only repeat to you the words of Simon Peter, whose unworthy yet true successor we are and above whose tomb we are at this moment. He said: 'Lord, to whom shall we go? Thou alone hast the words of eternal life' (John 6:69).

811. "Fidelity to Christ. This is what the post-Conciliar period should be, dearest brothers and children. With Our Apostolic Benediction." (*L'Osservatore Romano,* July 23, 1970).

General Index

NOTE In order to bring the teachings of Vatican II about God and His work for us into clearer perspective, the principal references to Him in this index are given first in the following sequence: God in General; Trinity; God the Father; God, the Son, Word, Christ; Holy Spirit. Cross references, however, are given in the alphabetical index.

NOTE 2 Numerals in this index refer to paragraph numbers — not to pages. References as to what is contained in the Introduction are indicated by Introd. a, Introd. b, etc.

Our home, 11

193

His priestly, prophetic and royal office shared even by laity in mission to world. 182

Liturgy is an exercise of His priestly office. 611

CHRIST WORKING IN MEN AND IN SACRAMENTS Always at work for salvation of all men, 470

"Draws all men to Himself." 88

Himself leads and nourishes the "sheep," i.e., us. 131

Is at work in hearts of men through energy of Holy Spirit. Fosters desire for heaven and for better world here. 558

Is principal agent in the sacraments. 526

Offers Himself in Mass through ministry of priests. 611

Present by His power in sacraments. 611

Present to people in their bishops. Through them He preaches, administers sacraments, incorporates new members; directs and guides the people. 272

Sitting at right Hand of His Father is continually active in Church leading men to her, joining them to Himself. 209

Wills to continue His witness and serve through the laity so He shares His life, mission, priesthood with them. 493

GOD THE HOLY SPIRIT Calls priests, raises them up for a divine work. 290

Dwells in the faithful as in a temple; prays in them. 29

He Who raised Christ from the dead will also bring life to your mortal bodies because of the Spirit Who dwells in you. 678

His identity, 4

Is the pledge of our inheritance. 541

Prays in hearts of the faithful; bears witness that they are adopted sons. 147

Priests receive Him at ordination. 309

Through Him men are to be united with Father and Son. 79

Through His gift man can contemplate and appreciate the divine plan. 546

With marvelous Providence works towards sound social order. 746

HOLY SPIRIT ACTING IN INSTITUTIONAL CHURCH By communicating His Spirit to His brothers, Christ made them into His Body. Holy Spirit strengthens "organic structure" of Church and unfailingly preserves form of government established by Christ in Church. 248

Constantly strengthens organic structure and inner harmony of Church. 260

Gives Church unity, fellowship, gifts — vivifies ecclesiastical institutions as a kind of soul; instills the mission spirit which animated Christ Himself. 249

HOLY SPIRIT AND CHRIST Calls all men to Christ and stirs in
    their hearts the obedience of faith. 710

Christ completed His work by death, resurrection, ascension and
    sending of Holy Spirit. 80, 158

Christ impelled to work of His ministry when Holy Spirit descend-
    ed upon Him. 80

Christ sent Him from His Father to carry on saving work inwardly.
    144

Having the first fruits of the Spirit we groan and desire to be with
    Christ. 710

Sent by Christ to be "advocate, Who, as Lord and life-giver would
    abide with them forever." 687

Sent by Christ to inspire us from within to love God and neighbor.
    534

Through Him Christ seeks to stir us to work for temporal and eter-
    nal welfare. 558

Through His action Son became man to save men. 80

United with Christ, the Faithful are led by Holy Spirit on their
    journey to kingdom of the Father. 744

HOLY SPIRIT AND CHURCH Christ made "His whole Mystical
    Body share in the anointing by the Holy Spirit with which He
    Himself had been anointed." 211

Church made manifest by outpouring of Holy Spirit. 141

Church made one through Him. 140

"Does in the whole Church what the soul does in all the members
    of one body." (St. Augustine) 214

Dwells in believers, rules the Church, joins us to Christ and is prin-
    ciple of Church's unity. 215

Dwells in Church and hearts of the faithful as in a temple. Allots
    gifts, fits them for their tasks. 147

"Existing as one and the same Being in the Head and in the mem-
    bers, vivifies, unifies and moves the whole body," as soul
    does in man's body. 214

His work and that of Christ in the Church, 209-223

Men possess Him to measure of their love for Church (St. Augus-
    tine). 443

Prompted by Him, Church must walk Christ's road of poverty,
    obedience, service, sacrifice. 191

Renews and purifies Church constantly. 670

Sent by Christ, gives Church unity, gifts, grace. 258

Through Him Church was established. 133

To impel Church towards her proper expansion, 144

To sanctify the Church so that all believers may have access to the

Alphabetical Index

vary, tabernacle. 90-91

God wants us to understand it so we can have confidence in Him and love Him. 90-91

AUGUSTINE, ST. Aim of ministry is that whole society of saints be offered as sacrifice to God through Christ so we may be Body of so exalted a Head. 311

Holy Spirit does in Church what soul does in man's body. 214

Men possess Holy Spirit to measure of their love for Church. 443

Says Mary is mother of the members of Christ. 585

"What I am for you (bishop) terrifies me. What I am with you (Christian) consoles me." 286

AUTHORITY Cf. Religion and civil authority.

Educators should form men who will respect and obey lawful authority. 769

Political authority must be exercised within limits of morality and on behalf of the dynamically conceived common good. 764

Public authority is to be exercised for common good according to a juridical order enjoying legal status. Citizens are bound in conscience to obey. 764

The State and public authority are based on human nature and hence belong to a divinely foreordained order. 764

To be respected and, insofar as it is lawful, must be obeyed. 769

AUTHORITY OF BISHOPS As representatives of Christ calls for obedience among laity. 489

As teachers endowed with authority of Christ. 273

As vicars of Christ is proper, ordinary, immediate but regulated by supreme authority. 280-281

Is divinely conferred. 278

Shares in authority of Christ. 285-286

AUTHORITY OF CHRIST Vested in bishops, 244

AUTHORITY OF CHURCH Given by God. 410

Lord has appointed some as visible rulers in the Church. Those with power are servants. 255

Laymen and all disciples of Christ should accept with ready Christian obedience whatever their sacred pastors, as representatives of Christ, decree in their roles as teachers and rulers in the Church. 247

Priests should be united with those whom the Lord has appointed as visible rulers in the Church. 358

AUTHORITY OF GOD Is absolute. No human activity can be withdrawn from His dominion. 732

AUTHORITY OF POPE Is full, immediate and universal. He has primacy over all churches. 259

199

AUTHORITY OF RELIGIOUS SUPERIORS. As God's represent-
atives, 404
In seminary to be accepted from personal conviction, 452
They should listen to subjects. 434
Used in spirit of service. 432
AUTHORITY OF STATE Christ and apostles recognized that author-
ity, coming from God. 765
Christians must show how authority can be harmonized with free-
dom. 767
AVARICE Cause of man's misery. Christ carried on redemptive work
in poverty. 98
BAPTISM A patent of nobility for God's children given in name of Fa-
ther, Son and Holy Spirit. 33
All must be incorporated into Christ by baptism and into the
Church. 165
By it we are formed in the likeness of Christ. 619
In the baptismal font the Holy Spirit begets to a new life those who
believe. 618
In the name of the Father, the Son and Holy Spirit. 156
Incorporates believers into Mystical Body. 618
It is Christ Who baptizes. 611
Men are justifed in Christ through baptism sought in faith, become
sons of God and sharers in divine nature. 112
BAPTISM AND CONFIRMATION Through these sacraments all are
commissioned to apostolate by Christ Himself. 497
BAPTISM AND PREACHING By these the Church brings forth chil-
dren conceived of Holy Spirit and born of God. 138
BEATITUDES By charity, by avoiding sin and thus leading men to
Christ, laity can express spirit of beatitudes. 477
Laymen must spread spirit of beatitudes. 504
Religious state shows world cannot be offered to God without
spirit of the beatitudes. 408
Spirit of beatitudes recommended for men working for socio-
economic development. 753
BETTER WORLD For its creation, Vatican II calls for cooperation
even with those who harass the Church. God is Father of all
and we are brothers. 762
Man's effort to better it is in accord with God's Will. 60-64
Social justice and charity a primary duty of everyone to create a
better world, 759
Cf. Temporal Order.
BISHOPS 269-287
Appointed by Holy Spirit. 270

ator. 51

To be esteemed because created by God and destined for resurrection. 52

Vatican II on those who idolize or undervalue the body. 49 ff.

BODY OF CHRIST Cf. Christ's Body.

BONAVENTURE, ST. How theology should be studied. 459

BREVIARY 563-571

An obligation. Ordinaries can dispense their subjects or commute the obligation for just reason. 570

By it Church praises God and intercedes for salvation of the world. 564

By it day and night are sanctified as Christ and Church address the Father. 565

Even laity urged to recite it all or in part. 571

Even priests not bound to office in choir are urged to recite parts in common. 571

Must be said by clerics in major orders unless dispensed. 380

Vespers should be recited publicly in church on Sundays and major feasts. 571

Will be recited well by priests if they realize words of St. Paul: "Pray without ceasing." 379

BROTHERHOOD Christ urged sons of God to treat each other as brothers. He died for all of us. 134

God has fatherly concern for all. He wants all men to be one family treating each other as brothers. 27

Laity should promote it nationally and internationally. 747

Since God is origin and purpose of all men we are all brothers and must work for peace. 762

BROTHERS Cf. Brotherhood.

CELIBACY 363-365

By it priests are consecrated to Christ in a new way — hold fast to Him with undivided heart — devote themselves to God and men. 363

Its advantages for the clergy — a gift from God. 456

Why confirmed by Vatican II. 364

CELIBACY Means for preserving it, 365

Seminarians should be trained for it. 456-457

Stimulates pastoral love and is fountain of spiritual fruitfulness. 363

CHARACTER FORMATION For seminarians, 451 ff.

CHARISMATIC GIFTS Cf. Gifts.

CHARITY All are called to perfection of charity — need Christ's help — can mold selves on Christ in seeking God's Will. 535

And faith. By such witness especially the People of God share in prophetic office of Christ. 203

As bond of perfection rules all the means of attaining to holiness — gives life to them — makes them work. 684

By charity, prayer, example and works of penance, the Church becomes a mother of souls to be saved. 697

Eucharist communicates the charity that is soul of all apostolate. 494

Fostered by evangelical counsels. 390

Infused by Holy Spirit into those who practice evangelical counsels. 301

Poured forth into our hearts by Holy Spirit. 477

Sacraments dispose faithful to practice it. 617

CHARITY — FRATERNAL All are obliged to help form public opinion on justice, charity, virtue, vice, etc. 760

Laity to love people of their milieu with same love with which God loves us. 517

Priests to teach people that they should not live for themselves alone but must administer to others the grace they receive. 686

Reveals God's presence. 670

CHARITY A sign of the Church in every age, 698-699

By works of charity, piety and apostolate, the faithful become the light of the world and give glory to God. 696

Church sees likeness of Christ in the poor and suffering and tries to help them. 695-696

Claimed by Church as a duty and right that she holds in special esteem. 698-699

Duties of justice must be fulfilled before gifts can be considered as charity. 701

If Eucharistic celebration is to be sincere, it must be followed by works of charity, mutual help and mission activity. 635

Preference to be given to works that will make beneficiaries able to meet own needs. 701

Work must pay attention to image of God and of Christ in each person. Freedom and dignity of each beneficiary to be respected. 701

Work to be favored by laity locally and internationally, 702

Work to extend to every person and every need — food, clothes, health, etc. Duty rests on every prosperous person and nation. 700

Workers to share burdens of others, 756

Works of, 695-702

Cf. Love.

Cf. Social.

CHASTITY Vowed for heavenly kingdom is great grace — liberates heart — fosters love for God and men — good witness to Christ. 402

Means to be used to preserve it. Easier to practice where fraternal love thrives. 403

CHILDREN And Parents, 657-660

To be welcomed from God, 656

CHILDREN In Christian family to know and worship God and love neighbor, 657

To contribute to holiness of parents and support them, 660

CHRISTIANS Cf. People of God.

CHURCH As Mystery. A reality inbued with hidden presence of God. 139-140

God planned to assemble in the Holy Church all who believe in Christ. 141

Grows by the power of God. 136

To reveal mystery of God Who is ultimate goal of man. She thus opens up to man the meaning of his existence. 155

Triumphant, militant, suffering united in love for God and neighbor. 230, 778

CHURCH COMES FORTH From Father's love — founded by Christ — made one in Holy Spirit. Her purpose to be fully achieved in next world. 140

CHURCH ESTABLISHED By Christ Who gave apostles and successors the duty of teaching, sanctifying and ruling. 258

By virtue of Christ, the one, holy, catholic and apostolic Church gathers together (St. Augustine). 625

Christ gives her gifts so we can serve each other by His power unto salvation. 124

Through her, Christ communicates truth and grace to all. 126

Through her, Christ is born and grows in hearts of the faithful. 587

Through it we abide in Christ without Whom we can do nothing. 130

CHURCH AND HOLY SPIRIT Church organically united in Holy Spirit with same faith, sacraments and government but differing rites. 218

Constantly renewed and purified by Holy Spirit. 670

Established through gift of Holy Spirit. 133

Gets unity, fellowship, gifts, etc. He vivifies ecclesiastical institutions as a kind of soul — gives mission spirit which motivated Christ Himself. 149

206

To teach, sanctify and rule with authority of Christ, 286

CLERGY To recognize dignity of laity, use their prudent advice, encourage their initiative. 489

And laity have different but unifying function. Cooperation needed. 254

CLERICS Not yet deacons are "called by the Lord and set aside as His portion." Must bring hearts and minds in accord with their splendid calling. 246

COMMAND Cf. Mission Command.

COMMON GOOD Christians as members of political community must promote common good. 767

Demands social justice as primary duty for all. 759

Determined in basic sense by eternal law. 761

In today's world becoming more complex and universal. Involves rights and duties with respect to whole human race. 758

Laity should promote it nationally and internationally. 747

Public authority must be exercised in behalf of common good. 764

To be considered in fixing wage scales. 755

COMMUNICATIONS MEDIA Men have a right to pertinent information but what is communicated must be true and as complete as charity and justice allow. 773

Must use honorable and appropriate means in harmony with moral law — must respect rights and dignity of man. 773
Cf. Public Opinion.

COMMUNION By it Christ is consumed, mind is filled with grace and pledge of glory is given to us. 626

By it we are taken into communion with Christ and one another and are made members of Christ and of each other. 638

"The partaking of the Body and Blood of Christ . . . transforms us into what we consume" (St. Leo). 625

COMMUNION OF SAINTS 224-236; 796-800

By it we can be co-redeemers. 121

Fosters charity, joins us to Christ. 574

Gives us chance to be partners in work of redemption. 172

Is a way in which God accepts spiritual offerings of all for the work of redemption. 111

Our union with those who have died in the peace of Christ is not interrupted but is strengthened through exchange of spiritual goods. 800

People on earth, in heaven and in Purgatory are filled with love for God and neighbor and share their spiritual goods. 230
Cf. Saints.

COMMUNITY By charity, prayer, example and works of penance the

Church community becomes mother of souls to be saved. 697

By reason of Eucharistic sacrifice community is on way with Christ to the Father. 530

If faithful exercise priestly, prophetic, royal office given them by God they become signs of God's presence. 530

No Christian community possible except on basis of Eucharist. Education in spirit of community must begin here. 486

CONFIDENCE God wants us to have confidence in Him. 90-91

Priests to rely on power of God, 361

CONFIRMATION Binds us more intimately to the Church. 622

By it Holy Spirit strengthens us. 621-622

CONFORMITY The elect are predestined from eternity to be conformed to the Son of God. 78

CONFORMITY WITH CHRIST With His help we can mold ourselves on Him, seek Father's will in all things, give glory to God and serve men. 535

Cf. Love of Conformity.

CONSCIENCE 716-721

Christians must be guided in civic affairs by Christian conscience. 768

Daily examination of conscience helps priests to turn heart to God. 381

"Freedom of conscience" is based on subjectivism and the term is therefore dangerous. 721

In forming one's conscience one must attend to Church's teaching. Christ made her the teacher of truth and it is her duty to declare the principles of moral order which have their origin in human nature itself. 720

Is a law not made by man that holds him to obedience. It is a law written by God and to obey it is the dignity of man. By it he will be judged. 716

Is most secret sanctuary of man. There he is alone with God Whose voice echoes in his depths. 716

Man is bound in conscience but stands under no compulsion. 718

Man must follow it in order to come to God for Whom he was created. 717

Man must seek religious truth so as to form true judgments of conscience. 73

Non-Christians can be saved under certain conditions by following conscience. 162

Often errs by invincible ignorance without losing its dignity. This is not true of man who cares little for truth and goodness and is blinded by habitual sin. 719

Often out of balance with practical thinking, 68

People who use communications media should make judgments about them according to well-formed conscience. 760

When public authority is exercised under due conditions, citizens are bound in conscience to obey. 764

CONTEMPLATION By it religious adhere to God in mind and heart. 423

Church herself is devoted to contemplation. 548

Downgraded by some; defended by Vatican II even for active communities so they may adhere to God.

In the Church, action is subordinated to contemplation. 128

Preaching the fruit of one's contemplation is highest form of life, adopted by Christ Himself. 549

Priests in preaching fruit thereof gain profit. 318

Religious to combine it with apostolic love, 423

Cf. Religious.

Cf. Plan of God.

CONVERSION All must be converted. 165 ff.

Contemplative communities important for conversion of souls, 414

Contemplative life urged even for mission lands as means to conversions. 548

Converts are called into personal relationship with God. 530

Must not be forced, 42

Priests to summon all men to conversion and holiness, 314

Priests to try to convert people to Church, 349

Cf. Sinners.

CONVERTS Cf. Conversions.

COOPERATION WITH GOD Cf. Partnership.

CO-REDEEMERS By apostolic love, religious associate selves with work of redemption. 423

Our role as, 107-111

People of God "used as an instrument for the redemption of all." 201

COUNSELS Cf. Evangelical Counsels.

CREATION All things come from God through the Word and go back to Him in the same way. 53

All things, even material universe, were created through the Word and give men an enduring witness to God. 722

Due to God's goodness, 7

Through the Word of God, 8

What God made is good, takes on special dignity through relationship with human person for which they were made. 54

CREATION OF MAN 8 ff.

Man by his labor unfolds the Creator's work. 754

Man would not exist if he had not been created by God's love and constantly preserved by it. 676

Cf. Creatures.

CREATURES Give witness to God. 13

As gifts of God are to be loved and respected, 537

Cf. Creation.

CROSS Christ's Passion reminds us we must carry our cross. 558

We must follow narrow way of the Cross to extend Kingdom of God. 205

Cf. Stations of the Cross.

CULTURAL SPHERE Its spiritual aspect, 758-760

Studies can lead to better understanding of God's Wisdom, to contemplation of Creator. With added help of grace man can acknowledge God. 771

Studies plus grace of God enable man to acknowledge Word of God, the true light that enlightens every man. 771

CULTURE And revelation. God, revealing Himself, spoke according to the culture proper to different ages. 772

And science if properly promoted can serve as preparation for the gospel. 772

By studying history, philosophy, etc., men can elevate human family to better understanding of God's Wisdom. 771

Laity must give witness to Christ, live the "new" life in their cultural sphere so as to perfect the culture itself. 516

DARKNESS Struggle with powers of darkness is age-old. Need grace to survive. 708

DEACONS Virtues to be practiced by them, 450

With priests and bishops exercise divinely established ministry, 244

DEAD Church cultivates memory of the dead and prays for them. 231

Doctrine of survival after death gives hope for ourselves and deceased relatives. 232

DEATH 783-785

"Beggars description" but through Christ and in Christ the riddles of sorrow and death grow meaningful. 783

Christ destroyed death by His death and resurrection. 785

God is with us to free us from darkness of sin and death — to give us eternal life. 94

Grows meaningful through Christ. 26

Its date is uncertain so we must stand guard. 788

Made holy and gets new meaning through Christ's sufferings. 85

Man seeks its meaning. Only God can answer. 69

Solid faith keeps us united in Christ with dear ones taken in death.

Will be vanquished when man is restored to wholeness by an almighty and merciful Savior. 784

DEFINITIONS OF DOCTRINE Cf. Infallibility.

DEMOCRACY Priesthood harmed by exaggerated democracy. 288

DESTINY Of man
   Cf. Man.
   Cf. Heaven.

DETACHMENT From worldly concerns leads to docility to divine voice in every day life. 351

DEVELOPMENT Christians who help socio-economic development and defend justice can do much for human welfare and peace. 753

Individuals and governments to provide individuals and peoples with means to develope themselves. 750

DEVIL By shedding His Blood Christ freed us from bondage to devil. 94

Christ overthrows his dominion. 180

People who deny existence of devils, 572

Through Christ, God aimed to snatch men from power of Satan. 81

We put on armor of God that we may stand against his wiles. 710

DEVOTIONAL PRACTICES For priests, 375 ff.

DEVOTIONS Popular devotions to be encouraged; should be in harmony with liturgical seasons. 601

Seminarians to practice devotions recommended by Church; live the gospel, 440

To angels and saints, 572 ff.
   Cf. Mary.
   Cf. Piety, Exercises of.
   Cf. Saints.

DIGNITY OF MAN Cf. Man.

DIRECTOR Cf. Spiritual Director.

DISCIPLINE In seminary, 452

DISSENTERS Ignore Church as Mystical Body; stress idea of "People of God" and criticize institutional Church. 206, 208

DOCILITY To divine Voice aided by detachment from worldly concerns. 351

By faith and grace priests can become more docile to mission given them by Holy Spirit. 378

DOCTRINE Main concern of Vatican II was to guard and teach more effectively the sacred deposit of doctrine. 663-664

New ways of preaching it to be studied through modern literary forms. 664

To be guarded by Vatican II; embraces the whole man composed of body and soul. Commands him to tend always toward heaven. 775

EARTH And all it contains to be subjected by man to himself and governed with justice and holiness. 754

And all it contains is intended for the use of every person and people. 750

To be subdued by man; creation to be brought to perfection. 730

ECONOMIC ORDER Its spiritual aspects, 748-753

Activity to be carried on according to its own laws but within limits of morality. 749

    Cf. Productivity.

EDUCATION Congregation for Catholic Education in Rome gives rules regarding seminarians' training. 462, Note 2

Educators are to form men who respect and obey lawful authority. 769

Of children devolves primarily on parents. 658-659

Vatican II favors wider diffusion of knowledge. 770

ELECT Foreknown and predestined from eternity by the Father to be conformed to the Son. 78

ELLIOTT Father Walter. On Confession, 645

EMOTIONS A stimulant for spiritual love to share in God's love, 53

ENEMIES To be loved, 693

EQUALITY In Christ and in Church. There is no inequality of race, nationality, social condition or sex. 199

ERROR To be repudiated but the person in error does not lose his dignity as a person, 693

ETERNAL LIFE Consists in knowing true God and Jesus Christ Whom He has sent. 506

For all as goal of mission work, 176

God is with us to raise us up to eternal life. 94

John XXIII says earthly goods must not prejudice eternal happiness. 531

Law of love impels faithful to promote God's glory and obtain eternal life for others. 506

Laity to give account to others concerning hope for eternal life that is in them. 492

Possible for those who did good after Adam's sin. 76

ETERNITY While living in history, man maintains his eternal vocation. 781-782

EUCHARIST 623 ff.

A meal of brotherly solidarity, 623

A pledge of hope and strength, 623

A renewal of the covenant between God and man. It inspires love for Christ, imparts grace, sanctifies men and glorifies God. 641

A sacrament of love, sign of unity, bond of charity and paschal banquet, 626

And the Church, 632-636

Bond of union, 637-641

Bread and wine changed into glorified Body and Blood of Christ, 623

By it Church constantly lives and grows. 275

Center and summit of the sacraments, 186

Communicates charity which is soul of entire apostolate. 494

Contains Christ, the entire spiritual wealth of Church. 624

Fount and apex of whole Christian life. We must offer ourselves along with the divine Victim. 205

Fountain of grace, 612

If its celebration is to be sincere it must lead to works of charity, mutual help and mission work. 635

In this sacrament the unity of believers who form one Body of Christ is expressed and brought about. 632

Is source and apex of whole work of preaching gospel. 636

Is the very heartbeat of the congregation of the faithful. Priests to teach people to offer selves along with it. 634

No Christian community can be built except on basis of Eucharist. Education in community must begin there. 635

Offers life to men, challenges them to offer selves, their labors and all creation with Christ. 624

Other sacraments and whole apostolate of Church are directed towards Eucharist. 624

Partaking of Body of the Lord we are taken up into communion with Him and with one another. 223

Priestly ministry deals principally with it as a means for perfecting the Church. 326

Shows Christ's deep humility, 100

The faithful by its reception are fully joined to the Body of Christ. 636

Through it we have pledge of future glory in heaven. 795

EUCHARIST Cf. Communion.

EUCHARISTIC SACRIFICE Cf. Mass.

EVANGELICAL COUNSELS A call to live for God alone and renounce world. 395

A divine gift, 389

Based on words of Christ. Practice regulated by Church under inspiration of Holy Spirit. 389

Beneficial to personal development, charity and Christ-like life, 398

By them men free themselves from obstacles to charity and perfection, consecrate selves to God. 394

Foster charity and union with Church. 390

Practiced since earliest times under influence of Holy Spirit. 388

Their practice is governed by hierarchy. 393

Those who make profession must seek God above all, develop life hidden in Christ, love neighbor. 396

EVANGELIZATION Cf. Mission.

EVE Her disobedience brought death. 101

Her disobedience, lack of faith corrected by Mary. 105

EVIL Christian must battle against it through tribulations and even to death if necessary. 674

Inclinations of heart not to be served by body, 52

Man has to struggle constantly. 67

Man is inclined to evil. 66

Man unable to battle successfully but God gives strength. 93

EXAMINATION OF CONSCIENCE Cf. Conscience.

EXAMPLE Apostolate of example, 507 ff.

First duty of all towards spread of faith is to lead profoundly Christian life. 189

Of Christ has redemptive value. 96-100

Of Christian life can draw men to God. 508, 510

Of parents, a means to lead children to maturity and holiness. 658

Of profoundly Christian life and charity will make the Church a "sign," light of world, salt of earth. 507

Of Saints makes us desire heaven and shows us how to become holy, i.e., united with Christ. 799

EXEMPT COMMUNITIES Cf. Religious.

EXTREME UNCTION Cf. Sick, Sacrament of the.

FAITH 663-672

As supernatural act, God's help needed for it; impossible unless God draws a man. 42, 59

Church must preach faith and repentance to ignorant, careless Catholics. 178

God in ways known to Himself can lead the inculpably ignorant to the faith without which we cannot please God. 168

God planned to assemble in the Holy Church all who believe in Christ. 141

Grace and help of Holy Spirit needed to move the heart, turning it to God, opening mind and giving joy. 668

Holy Spirit calls all men to Christ and stirs in their hearts the obedience of faith. 667

Holy Spirit opens hearts of non-Christians so they can believe. 160

It is through gift of Holy Spirit that man comes by faith to contemplate the divine plan. 666

The doctrine is one thing. Ways of presenting it is another and these should be improved. 664

The obedience of faith must be given to God Who reveals. By it man entrusts his whole being to God, offering full submission of intellect and will to God Who reveals. 668
> Cf. Doctrine.

FAITH, EFFECTS Gives hope in memory of Christ's cross and resurrection. 675

God the Father and Christ made "present" and "visible" by living faith, e.g., of martyrs and people who really live their faith in charity. 670

Holiness can be achieved if we accept circumstances of life in faith from hand of God. 536

If solid, provides answer to anxiety about future. Helps us to be united with deceased relatives, etc. 671

Mary's faith loosed what Eve's unbelief bound. 105

Men are justified through baptism sought in faith, become sons of God and sharers in the divine nature. 112

Proves its fruitfulness by penetrating believer's entire life, especially by charity. 670

Salvation to be achieved through faith in Christ and His grace. 153

FAITH, NECESSITY Always stressed by Vatican II. 59

And Baptism. Christ says both are necessary. 165

FAITH, QUALITIES Like that of Abraham urged for priests, etc. 367

Must be a free act. Nobody to be forced to accept, but no one can give adherence unless God draws him. 42

Of many anemic because of excessive humanism. Introd.

FAITH, SPREAD OF First duty of all towards spread of faith is to lead profoundly Christian life. 189

Laity can be powerful heralds of faith if, aided by sacraments, they live their faith and talk about it. 509-510

FAITH, TO BE NOURISHED It begins in hearts of unbelievers by hearing Word of God. Is fed in the hearts of believers. 313

Meditation on God's word needed to recognize God always and everywhere and to seek His will or make judgments. 545

Nourished by priests through spiritual reading. 378

Nourished by right reading, singing, praying or acting. 672

Nourished by sacraments. Faithful should understand the sacramental signs. 617

Seminarians to search for solutions of human problems in light of revelation, 460

FAITHFUL Are not of this world but are light of the world, give glory to God. 467

Must all aim at perfection so Church may be purified and renewed. 490

Owe exalted status not to self but to special grace of Christ. 557

Should be to world what soul is to the body. 504

To grow into manhood according to mature measure of Christ, 480
Cf. People of God.

FAMILY, CHRISTIAN By a truly Christian life, it becomes nursery for vocations. 661

Even a "relatively large family" is commended. 655

Husbands and wives to be witnesses and cooperators in grace to each other and their children, 502

Is first cell of society; must be sanctuary of Church through prayer, mutual love, etc. 502

Its meaning, dignity and duties, 649

Prayer is a means to help children to maturity and holiness. 658

Proclaims kingdom of God and hope for heaven. 653

Should be first school of social virtues. 659
Cf. Children.
Cf. Husband and Wife.
Cf. Parents.

FAMILY OF GOD Apostles were ordered to preach gospel so that whole human race should become family of God. 89

As sons of God we are one family in Christ. 226

Christ made whole human race into a family. 688

FEASTS Of Saints. Reason for observing them, 576

FELLOWSHIP God invites man to fellowship with Himself. 58, 86

FINANCIAL SUPPORT For Church's work. It is duty of honor for people to return to God a share of good things received from Him. 502

FLESH Its weakness can be overcome by power of Christ. 709

FOLLOWING OF CHRIST Cf. Imitation of Christ.

FORGIVENESS Of injuries demanded by Christ. 693

Since we all offend in many things we must pray for forgiveness. 620

FOUNDERS Their spirit to be safeguarded by members of community, 437

FREE WILL 37 ff.

By it man chose self instead of God. Could still choose God instead of self. 76

Cause of imaginary debate in Trinity, 44

Damaged by sin. Grace needed. 41

For men, theoretically a cause for conflict in Trinity, 43

Given so men could earn greater share in God's life, love, and happiness. 75

Given to us so we can cooperate with God in saving self and others. 120

Needed for doing good. Often abused. 39

Needed for faith. 42

Of Eve brought death; that of Mary, life. 101

One of God's greatest natural gifts, 38

Why God gave it. 40

FREEDOM Dignity of sons of God. These are heritage of sons of God. 197

God has regard for human person. Man is to be guided by his own judgment and enjoy freedom. 718

Religion. That doctrine which destroys religious liberty of citizens must be rejected. 768

Cf. Free Will.

FREEDOM OF RELIGION Christians as citizens must show how civil authority can be harmonized with freedom. 767

Many pressures now curb freedom but many are inclined to use freedom as excuse to reject authority. All, especially educators, should form men who respect moral order and obey lawful authority. Responsible freedom to be fostered. 769

Social order must be based on truth, justice, charity, freedom, etc. 746

Source of conflicts, 43

Vs. Freedom of conscience. Church's declaration on freedom of religion is not based on freedom of conscience since this term is based on subjectivism and is dangerous. 721

FRUITS Of the Holy Spirit to be possessed in holiness, 620

FULFILLMENT By sinning man sought fulfillment apart from God. 65

Christ was crucified and rose again so world might be fashioned anew and reach its fulfillment. 714

Only God can really provide it. 70

Sin blocks its path. 93

GIFTS, CHARISMATIC: Are to be used not only for Church but for good of mankind. 734

Granted for apostolate. Laity to be "free" to use them but judgment as to nature and use is to be made by pastors. 498

Their genuineness and proper use to be judged by those who preside over Church. 251

GIFTS OF HOLY SPIRIT Charismatic and hierarchical, 249-251

Differ. Some keep alive desire for heaven; others promote service to men for time and eternity. 543

GLORY Given to God in Eucharist. 641

GLORY OF GOD Church is to spread the Kingdom of Christ for the glory of God the Father and to save men. 157

Purpose of ministry. It consists in this: that men knowingly, freely, gratefully accept what God has achieved through Christ. 300

Through mission work that plan of God is fulfilled to which Christ was obediently devoted for the glory of the Father. 154

We must devote ourselves to it with all our being. 535

GOD Cf. Initial pages of this Index.

GOOD Cf. Common Good.

GOOD WORKS 695-702

GOODNESS OF GOD Reason for creation, 7

GOODS Men are obliged to give relief to the poor and not only out of their superfluous goods. 750

Of earth to be justly distributed, 750

Of earth to be used in a way that will not prejudice man's eternal happiness, 775

Cf. Justice.

GOSPEL For all time the source of all life for the Church, 193

Cf. Preaching.

GOVERNMENT, CIVIL Cf. Authority of State.

Cf. State.

GOVERNMENT OF CHURCH By divine institution the Church is structured and governed with wonderful diversity. 252

Holy Spirit "unfailingly preserves the form of government established by Christ in His Church." 248

Cf. Authority.

Cf. Church.

GRACE All of it comes from Christ. 574

And truth among non-Christians described as a "secret presence of God." 180

Apostolate is designed to manifest Christ's message and communicate His grace. 153

Channeled through Liturgy, especially Eucharist. 641

Flows from Passion, Death and Resurrection of Christ. 616

If sons of the Church do not respond to it they will not be saved but judged more severely. 137

HELL We must live so as not to enter eternal fire. 788

HIERARCHY Through it Christ exercises His prophetic office. Hierarchy teaches in His name, with His authority. 245

To govern practice of evangelical counsels, 393

HOLINESS All of us called to it in the Church which Christ loved and made into His Body, 540

Charity as the bond of perfection rules all the means of attaining holiness, gives life to them and makes them work. 684

Christ is author and finisher of holiness since He sent Holy Spirit to inspire us from within to love God and man. 534

Fifth Chapter of Dogmatic Constitution on Church is entitled "Call of the whole Church to holiness." It is like a litany of virtues needed for perfection. 662

Fruits of the Spirit to be possessed unto holiness, 620

Identified with union with Christ. 577

Imparted by Eucharist. 641

Laity to help each other lead holier lives, 475

Love of conformity constitutes its very essence. 550

Men become holy in Christ through baptism sought in faith; become sons of God, sharers in divine nature; must complete this holiness. 533

Obtained in the Church through grace of God. 167

One and the same holiness is cultivated by all who are moved by Holy Spirit and obey the Father. 544

Promotes a more human life in earthly society. 685

Through Christ and in Christ, Trinity is fountain of all holiness. 420

To be achieved by workers through own work, 756

Cf. Sanctification.

HOLINESS OF PRIESTS Demanded especially by consecration of Orders and as instruments of Christ. 359

Is great help in ministry. God desires to manifest wonders through those who are particularly docile to Holy Spirit. 360

Priests to summon all to conversion and holiness. 314

HOLINESS IN LAITY They can achieve it through circumstances of life if they accept all with faith from hand of God and cooperate with His Will. 536

HOLY SPIRIT Cf. God, Holy Spirit.

Cf. Fruits of the Spirit.

Cf. Gifts of Holy Spirit.

HOPE 673-675

A source of strength as we realize that sufferings here cannot compare with glory to come. 675

By it we can "make the most" of present conditions, turn to God in difficulties. 473

By sharing in Father's love and witnessing to the truth we can arouse hope among men that they may get to heaven. 689

Derived from faith concerning Cross and Resurrection of Christ. 675

Faith arouses the hope that the dear departed have found true life with God. 784

For a better world and eternal life a characteristic of Vatican II. 673

For eternal riches makes men try to spread God's kingdom and make a better world here. 475

For heaven is a gift of the Holy Spirit. 689

Laity to give account to others concerning hope of eternal life that is in them. 492

Mary is a sign of hope. 597

Of others raise an echo in hearts of Christ's followers. 744

Stirred by promise of Redemption after first sin. 76

We perform the task committed to us by the Father "with hope of good things to come." 786

HUMAN RACE Belongs to the Church (Paul VI). 287

To become family of God through preaching of gospel, 89

HUMAN SOLIDARITY Cf. Solidarity.

HUMANITY Cf. Human Race.

HUMILITY And obedience. Christ emptied self, redeemed men by obedience. 355

Imitating Christ's humility men seek to please God rather than men. 472

In priests conscious of own weakness, testing what is God's Will in a kind of captivity to Holy Spirit. 357

Of Christ shown in Eucharist. 100

HUNGRY "If you do not feed the man dying of hunger, you have killed him" (Gratian). 750

HUSBAND AND WIFE 652-656

Are witnesses to Christ for each other and children. 653

In spirit of sacrifice to fulfill duty of procreating but this is not sole aim of matrimony. 655

Strengthened by sacrament of matrimony to fulfill duties and practice, needed virtues. 654

Two in one flesh. Mutual aid and fidelity needed. 652

HUSBANDS Cf. Family.

IMAGES Of Christ, Mary and Saints to be venerated, 595

Of Saints venerated, 580

If sons of Church do not respond to grace, they will not be saved but will be more severely judged. 137

Man must render account to God concerning good and evil he did. 41

Son of God has been made Judge of living and dead. 790

Will be according to conscience. 716

JUSTICE, SOCIAL A person in extreme need can take what is needed for life from others. "Feed the man dying of hunger, for if you have not fed him, you have killed him" (Gratian). 750

By it created goods should be available to all so that each can support self and family. 750

Christian encouraged to assist in socio-economic development and defend justice. Can make great contribution to human welfare and peace. 753

Duties of justice must be satisfied before thinking merely of charity. 701

Essential to the common good today. A primary duty for everyone, 759

Everyone is obliged to help form public opinion on justice, virtue, vice, etc. 760

Groups to respect needs and legitimate aspirations of other groups, 758

Laity to work for more just distribution of goods, 64

Social order must be based on justice, truth, charity, etc. 746

Some nations rich, others deprived of necessities of life. This scandal must be eliminated. 752

JUSTIFICATION Cf. Sanctification.

KINDERGARTEN Universe is God's kindergarten. 17

KINGDOM OF GOD Begun by God Himself is goal of People of God. 779

Established on earth by Christ. 538

KINGDOM OF CHRIST Identified with Church, 136

LABOR Benefits self and society and thus unfolds Creator's work. 61, 62, 64

By it man becomes associated with redemptive work of Christ Who also worked. 755

By it man supports family, serves fellowmen, can exercise charity, becomes partner in work of bringing God's creation to perfection. 755

By subjecting the earth to himself as God commanded and governing it in justice and holiness, man provides for his family, benefits society, unfolds Creator's work. 754

Contributes to realization of divine plan. 61-62

Each of us can have impact on all men and contribute to salvation of whole world by offering up labor and hardships. 706

Man has duty to work and also a right. Society must help people find work. Just wages needed to enable man and family to live decently. 755

Partnership with God, 60, 61, 62, 64

Spiritual aspects, 754-756

Superior to other elements of economic life. It comes immediately from the person who stamps his seal on things of nature. 755

Workers to perfect themselves, help others, raise society and even creation to better mode of existence. 756

Workers to share each other's burdens by charity, imitate Christ and achieve greater apostolic charity. 756

LABOR UNIONS 757

Laborers have basic right to form unions that will represent them, promote formation, promote economic and social welfare. 757

LABORERS Cf. Labor.

Cf. Wages.

LAITY Are called to produce fruits of the Spirit; their work, prayer, suffering, recreation are sacrifices acceptable to God. 493

As members of living Christ must cooperate in expansion and growth of the Body of Christ. 478

By doing everything even in secular affairs according to God's Will can grow in union with Christ. 471

By reason of Eucharistic Sacrifice, community of faithful proceeds with Christ to the Father. 484

Called by Christ out of darkness into His light. 495

Clergy and laity have different but unifying functions. Cooperation needed. 254

Clergy are not to shoulder whole saving mission of Church alone; must get laity to cooperate. 483

Dignity of, 464-468

Essential if Church is to be perfect sign of Christ — only through them can gospel be imprinted on life of a people, 482

Even in beginning of a mission greatest attention to be paid to raising up a mature Christian laity, 482

Have Christ and clergy for brothers. 465

Have means to arrive at union with Christ. 614

Have noble duty of extending divine plan of salvation to all men of all times. 519

Have right to spiritual benefits of Church and to reveal their wishes and opinions concerning the Church. 474

Laity called to holiness and to sanctify others. 469 ff.

Laity to be aided by clergy, trained in responsibility for all men; taught the mystery of Christ and shown practical methods, 518

Laity to help each other lead holier lives even in daily occupations, 475

Missionaries to form congregations who exercise priestly, prophetic, royal offices. Thus laity become sign of God's presence. 484

Pastors to recognize their dignity, use their prudent advice, encourage their initiative, 489

People of God and Body of Christ, 478 ff.

Since their energy is a gift from God, they should use it for growth and continuous sanctification of Church. 479

To cling to Bishop as Church does to Christ, 488

To cooperate with pastors who must judge nature and proper use of gifts received from Holy Spirit, 498

To learn deepest meaning and value of all creation — relate it to God, 475

To obey Church authorities after example of Christ Whose obedience gave us liberty of children of God, 489

To work along with hierarchy, 482

Urged to recite parts of Breviary. 563, 571

Used by God as instrument of redemption for all. 110

        Cf. Family.
        Cf. Humility.
        Cf. Husband and Wife.
        Cf. Laborers.
        Cf. Matrimony.
        Cf. Parents.
        Cf. Patience.
        Cf. Poverty.
        Cf. Priesthood of laity.
        Cf. Suffering.
        Cf. Temporal Order.

LAITY AND SOCIAL MILIEU Have principal role in permeating world with Spirit of Christ. 475

This apostolate is so much the responsibility of laity that it can never be properly carried on by others. 763

To love people in their milieu as God loves them, 517

To make Christ known to their milieu in which many can come to know Christ only through them, 515

LAITY ASSIGNED TO APOSTOLATE BY CHRIST HIMSELF

Mary a perfect example of lay apostolate. 503

Their apostolate is participation in saving mission of Church. 497

LAW OF GOD For People of God is new commandment to love as Christ loves us. 204

Highest norm of life. By it God governs universe. 73

LAWS OF CHURCH Priests to submit in all things to God's will as expressed in laws of Church. 354

LAYMEN Cf. Laity.

LIFE

A pilgrimage, 675

Both individual and collective is struggle between good and evil because of sin. 93

Divine. Man called so that with his entire being he may be joined to God in endless sharing of divine life. 528

In God. Holy Spirit was bestowed on us by the Father "that living the life of God we might love God and the brethren." 681

Its highest norm is divine Law. 73

Its meaning understood in mystery of God Who is goal of man. 71

Made holy and gets new meaning through Christ's sufferings. 85

Man seeks its meaning. Only God can answer. 69

Ministry of priests to contribute to divine life in men, 300

Priests cannot be ministers of Christ unless they are witnesses and dispensers of supernatural life. 346

Theocentric, 527 ff.

Through faith we learn meaning of our temporal life. 786

Cf. Eternal Life.

Cf. Spiritual Life.

LIFE OF CHRIST A common love urges us to live more for Christ Who died for us and rose again. 710

Flows from Christ into His members, is a reason why mission work is necessary. 163

Of People of God issues from Christ. 574

Poured into members of Mystical Body. 619

Through Christ we live. 539

We must bear in our bodies the dying of Jesus so that the life of Jesus may be manifest in us. 704

LIFE OF FAITHFUL To live the new life in Christ and thereby raise the culture in which they live. 516

LIFE THROUGH HOLY SPIRIT By preaching and baptism Church brings forth to a new life children conceived by Holy Spirit and born of God. 185

Christ promised to send Holy Spirit as advocate "Who as Lord and life-giver would abide with them forever." 687

Holy Spirit is Spirit of life. Through Him the Father gives life to men dead from sin. 542

In baptismal font Holy Spirit begets to a new life those who believe in Christ. 146

LOVE FOR GOD Emotional love often impossible but spiritual love is imperative. 694

God wants our love. 90-91

If it is to be fruitful, we must hear word of God and with help of His grace try to fulfill His Will. 679

Those who say we can love God only in neighbor forget distinction between emotional and spiritual love. 694

LOVE FOR GOD AND NEIGHBOR Christ is Author of holiness for He sent Holy Spirit to inspire men with love for God and neighbor. 680

First and most necessary gift is that charity by which we love God above all and neighbor because of God. 679

For God and mankind inspired by Holy Spirit, 501

Fostered by evangelical counsels, 393

Greatest commandment. Christ enriched love of neighbor by identifying Self with every human being making whole race one family. 688

Impels faithful to promote glory of God and obtain eternal life for men. 506

Is greatest commandment. The two cannot be separated. In a world growing more and more interdependent this is of paramount importance. 682, 741

Those who obey Christ to seek kingdom of God first, will receive stronger, purer love for helping neighbor. 753

LOVE FOR NEIGHBOR A sign of Christ's disciples, 688

As Christ loved neighbor, 534

Christ taught us that law of love is basic law of human perfection. Love not restricted to great affairs but must be shown in ordinary affairs of life. 743

For God as driving force impelling men to share spiritual goods with all men now and eternally through mission work. 176

Is "new" commandment given by Christ. 687

Its basis is love for God: we must love neighbor "because of God." 677, 679

The commandment to love as Christ loved us is the law of the People of God. 204

Union of men in truth and charity somewhat similar to union of Three Persons in Trinity. 683

We cannot in truthfulness call on that God Who is Father of all if we do not treat others as brothers. 690

LOVE OF CHRIST FOR US Each can say: "The Son of God loved me and gave Himself up for me." 783

LOVE OF CONFORMITY Conforms our minds, hearts and wills to

Christ's mind, heart and will. Restores divine likeness which
was marred by sin. 112, 113, 114
Core of ascetical theology, sanctity, 550
In pastors. World entrusted to them is world God so loved as to
give His Son to save it. 114
Many forms of love, e.g. gratitude, benevolence, friendship. Great-
est is love of conformity. 112
Purpose of revelation is to conform our minds to God's mind
Christ's example urges conformity of heart and will. 114
With God in mind, heart, will is highest form of love. 694
LOVE OF GOD FOR US And of Christ known through gifts of Holy
Spirit. 133
Father wishes us to recognize Christ as our Brother and love Him.
By giving witness to the truth we share mystery of the Fa-
ther's love. 689
God's love for men reason why He gave free will. 75
Mission of Church rooted in decree from "fountain of love" within
God the Father. 150
We would not exist if we had not been "created by God's love and
constantly preserved by it." 529
LOYALTY To Christ cannot be divorced from loyalty to Church. 354
MAGISTERIUM Not above Scripture and tradition but serves them
by explaining them faithfully, 264
Pope, Bishops, 258-268
Scripture scholars to be guided by it, 263
So linked with Scripture and tradition that one cannot stand with-
out the other, 265
MAN Cf. Body.
Cf. Brotherhood.
Cf. Free Will.
Cf. Heart.
Cf. Heaven.
Cf. Intellect.
Cf. Revelation.
Cf. Sin.
Cf. World.
MAN AND CREATURES Appointed master of earthly creatures by
God. 24
Has divine mandate to subject earth to self and govern it in justice
and holiness, 60 ff.
Has mandate to relate self and world to Creator, 60
MAN AND GOD A revelation of God, 13
"As a son in the Son can call God 'Father.' " 26

Called to communion and to converse with God. 529
Called to converse with God. 30
Can know, love God. 24
Created by God to God's image, has God for his goal. 532
Destined to communion with God. 8
God is his goal. 27
God the Father is the origin and purpose of all men. 27
His relations with the Trinity, 78-81
Man's relationship with God, 55-59
To have access to Father through Christ in Spirit and to share in divine nature, 58
To live the life of God, 9
Trinity his home, 11
When image of God was marred in him, the Son as Image of Father was sent to restore it. 78

MAN AND GOD IN THIS WORLD
A citizen of earth and of heaven, must tend towards heaven. 775
A partner of God, 60 ff.
All men are called to union with Christ from Whom we go forth, through Whom we live, towards Whom we go. 539
Drawn by Christ to Himself. 88
God waits in man's heart. 35
Human race to be made into family of God, 140
Is not restricted to the temporal sphere. While living in history, he maintains his eternal vocation. 781
Made of body and soul, must always tend towards heaven. 775
Made to participate in divine law. Must form conscience according to religious truth. 73
Whole human race made a family by Christ. 688

MAN CREATED BY GOD'S LOVE All men are created in image of God and are to be a family living in spirit of brotherhood. God is goal of all. 724
And sustained by God's love.30
Cannot live fully according to truth if not devoted to Creator. 30
Created for God. 717
Created to likeness of God. 5, 10
Formed in image of God, 24

MAN, HIS DESTINY IN GOD
Adopted as son of God by baptism. 28
Called through Christ to be God's adopted son. 42
God calls him so that with his entire being he may be joined to God in endless sharing of divine life. 776
His destiny, Cf. Heaven

Cooperated in redemption and is its most excellent fruit. 589

Cooperates in "birth and development" of Christ's brethren. 106

Co-Redemptrix consented to sacrifice of Christ. 104-105

Death through Eve, life through Mary. 105

Devoted herself wholly to redemption of men. Priests to honor her as protectress of ministry. 387

Her saving influence derived from Christ. 103

Mediatrix, 102 103

Perfect example of spiritual and apostolic life. Even in heaven she has maternal care for brethren of her Son. 503

Sinless, devoted self to work of Christ and served mystery of redemption. 590

Suffered with Jesus and united herself to His sacrifice, consenting to His immolation. 591

MASS A sacrifice offered in name of whole Church, 323

By it Church prays and labors to make whole world into People of God, Body of Christ, etc. In Christ, honor and glory is given to the Creator. 630

By it the work of our redemption is carried on. 632

In it Christ offers self through ministry of priests. 611

In it the sacrifice of Christ on Cross is celebrated. 632

In it we are united with Saints in heaven in worship of God. 233

Instituted to "perpetuate the sacrifice of the Cross" and as memorial of Christ's death and resurrection. 626

Realizes prophecy of Malachy about name of God being great among peoples and sacrifice being offered everywhere. 630

Taking part in Eucharistic sacrifice is a condition for extending the Kingdom of God. 205

The one sacrifice of the New Testament, viz. the Sacrifice of Christ offering Himself once and for all to His Father as a spotless Victim, 305

Through hands of priest and in name of whole Church, the Lord's sacrifice is offered in unbloody and sacramental manner. 628

       Cf. Communion.

       Cf. Sacrifice of Faithful.

MASS AND PEOPLE

During its celebration all sacrifices of laity are offered to the Father. 493

Eucharistic Sacrifice is fount and apex of whole Christian life. Faithful to offer self along with divine Victim. 627

Eucharistic action is heartbeat of the congregation of faithful. Pastors to teach people to offer divine Victim and themselves with it. 634

MYSTICAL BODY All members are members of one another —
    render service to each other. 220
    All members have part in mission of whole Body. 221
    All members in communion with each other. 219
    Believers are incorporated in it by baptism. 618
    Christ at work in His Body. His life poured into believers, 216
    Christ formed it to give us chance to share in whole work of re-
        demption. 111
    Christ made His whole Mystical Body share in the anointing by the
        Holy Spirit with which He Himself had been anointed. 211
    Christ offered Self for us that we might be body of so exalted a
        Head (St. Augustine). 631
    Church as the Mystical Body, 206-208
    Gets its increase from Christ. 483
    In it we can become co-redeemers. 121
    It was by communicating His Spirit to His brothers that Christ
        made them into His Body. 248
    Members are incorporated into Christ and made like unto Him by
        baptism, confirmation and Eucharist. 217
    Members to be molded into Christ's image until He is formed in
        them. 222
    The Holy Spirit "existing as one and the same Being in the Head
        and the members, vivifies, unifies, and moves the whole
        body" like soul in human body. 214
    This name for the Church seems to stress Christ's action in
        Church. 207
    Was established to give us chance to cooperate in work of salva-
        tion. 172
        Cf. Church.
MYSTICAL INTERPRETATION OF MAN'S BODY Through it
    the material world praises God freely. 554
MYSTICISM Laity to learn deepest meaning and value of creation.
    475
    Regarding human body, 50, 51, 53, 54
    To be fostered even in missions and adapted to seeds already plant-
        ed there by God, 426
        Cf. Mystic.
NATURE Since nature as assumed by Christ was not annulled it was
    raised to divine dignity in our respect also. 112
NEIGHBOR Every man is our neighbor — foreign laborers, refugees,
    illegitimate children, etc. 691
        Cf. Love.
NON-CHRISTIANS Cannot be saved if they know Church is neces-

239

sary and refuse to enter. 165

God in ways known to Himself can lead the inculpably ignorant to the faith without which we cannot please God. 168

Missioners to search out the "treasures a bountiful God has distributed" among them. 181

Saved under certain conditions. 162

OBEDIENCE By it Christ achieved redemption, gave His life as ransom for many. 95

Christ by obedience and humility emptied Self and redeemed mankind. 355

If love is to be fruitful we must willingly hear word of God and with help of His grace try to fulfill His Will. 679

Man's tragedy due to disobedience to God. Redeemed through Christ's obedience. 97

Of Abraham based on his faith, 367

Prompted by Holy Spirit, Church must follow Christ's road of poverty, obedience, service, sacrifice. 705

Through mission work that plan of God is fulfilled to which Christ was obediently devoted. 154

OBEDIENCE OF FAITH Cf. Faith.

OBEDIENCE OF LAITY In institutional Church laity and all disciples of Christ should accept with Christian obedience whatever sacred pastors as representatives of Christ decree in their role as teachers and rulers in the Church. 247

Let laymen follow example of Christ Who by His obedience even at cost of death opened way of liberty to children of God. 247

OBEDIENCE OF MARY A cause of salvation, 105

Brings life. Disobedience of Eve, death, 101

Brought salvation (St. Irenaeus), 583

Untied knot of Eve's disobedience, 105

OBEDIENCE OF PRIESTS As freely vowed likens men to Christ. 400

By this vow, religious sacrifice selves, are united to saving will of God and follow Christ. 405

Leads to a more mature freedom — but must submit to authority. 356

One of most necessary virtues for priests is to seek not own will but Will of Him Who sent them. 352

One of their most necessary virtues, 290

Religious urged to show active, responsible obedience. 434

Seminarians to be trained in priestly obedience. 453

They are to imitate Christ Whose meat was to do Will of Him Who sent Him. 353

To build unity of own lives priests must submit in all things to

241

PASSIONS Man must free self from their captivity. 41

PASTORAL LOVE Flows mainly from Eucharistic sacrifice which is center and root of priestly life. 362

PASTORS Asceticism proper to them; seeking profit of people, not one's own, 551
        Cf. Clergy.

PATIENCE By making the most of all circumstances, men can practice patience, express hope by turning to God. 473
    Taught by God, 14

PATRIARCHS Gave people knowledge of God. 76

PAUL VI Calls Church a mystery, a reality imbued with the hidden presence of God. 139
    Calls Mary Mother of the Church. 585
    His prayer at Bogota Eucharistic Congress for priests, 107
    On duty of priests to foster vocations by their own example, 524
    On Vatican II, 803 ff.
    Says dominant thought of Vatican II was pastoral. 287
    Says Vatican II documents good for spiritual reading and meditation. 600

PEACE For its establishment, respect for persons and peoples, brotherhood are necessary. Hence peace is also fruit of love. 761
    Results from harmony built into society by its divine Founder as actualized in line wih justice, control of passions and lawful authority. 761
    Since God is origin and purpose of all men, we should all work together for peace. 762

PENANCE, SACRAMENT OF 329-331, 642-645
    As Sacrament helps priests to be united wit Christ. 381
    Bishops to urge people to offer penance and prayer for evangelization of world. 192
    By works of penance, prayer, etc., the Church community becomes a mother to souls to be saved. 697
    Church is holy but embraces sinners; needs always to be purified by penance. 712
    Excellent means for correcting faults. 645
    People must be taught that essence of virtue of penance is hatred for sin as an offense against God. 715
    Priests reminded of benefits they can obtain from it and from daily examination of conscience. 644
    Priests to be ready to hear confessions. 644
    Priests to urge people to confess their sins — get closer to Christ. 642

PEOPLE OF GOD Its law is the new commandment of love. Its goal is kingdom of God which will be brought to perfection at end of time. 779

Sanctified by Holy Spirit, can offer selves as sacrifice, living, holy, pleasing to God. 466

Social nature willed by God. 487

Cf. Faithful.

PERFECTION All members of People of God are called to it. 199

All of the faithful are called to perfection of charity. 534 ff.

By assuming role of Good Shepherd priests will find bond of pastoral perfection in their work. 362

Christ taught us that law of love is basic law of human perfection and lies open to everyone. 743

Every Catholic to aim at it so Church may be purified and renewed. 490

Fifth Chapter of Dogmatic Constitution on Church is like a litany of virtues needed for perfection. 662

In order to attain to it, faithful must use their strength as a gift from Christ. Then they can mold selves on Christ and seek God's will in all things. 535

Of love for God and neighbor fostered by evangelical counsels. 393

Religious community life is aid to it. 429

PERFECTION OF CHARITY Cf. Charity.

Cf. Holiness.

PERSON Does not lose dignity even when in error, but error is to be repudiated. 693

God has regard for the dignity of human person. Man is guided by his own judgment and is to enjoy freedom. 718

Goodness of creatures is shown by relationship with human person for which they were made. 54

Impossible for an individual to grasp all knowledge but we must preserve view of the whole person with his values of intellect, will, conscience, etc. These values are all rooted in the Creator and elevated by Christ. 745

PERSON IN THE NATION AND THE WORLD 746-747

Dignity and total vocation of person must be honored in socio-economic realm. 748

Economic productivity must serve all men of all races in their intellectual, moral, spiritual and religious life. 749

His labor is superior to other elements of economic life because it comes immediately from the person who stamps his seal on things of nature. 755

One of its basic rights is to form labor unions. 757

Peace cannot be preserved unless personal values are safeguarded.

Religious submission of will and mind must be given to his authentic teaching authority even when he is not speaking ex cathedra. Judgments must be adhered to. 268
> Cf. Infallibility.

POVERTY Of Christ, a factor in redemption of avaricious sinner, 98
> Of spirit. Men following the poor Christ are not depressed by poverty nor puffed up by riches. 472
> Priests urged to embrace voluntary poverty. 350
> Prompted by Holy Spirit Church must follow Christ's road of poverty, obedience, service, sacrifice. 705
> Vow of poverty in imitation of Christ gives precious witness to Him. 400-401

PRAYER 559 ff.
> By charity, prayer, etc., the Church community becomes a mother to souls to be saved. 697
> Each of us can have impact on all men and contribute to salvation of world by prayer, penance, etc. 706
> For Souls in Purgatory offered by Church, 792
> Is companionship and conversation with God. 559-560
> Missioner to be a man of prayer, 371
> Necessary because "without me you can do nothing," 562
> Should be response to relationship with God by adoration, praise, thanks, love, confidence, petition, etc. 561
> To be response to our relationship with God our Father, Creator, Benefactor, Helper, Guide, etc., 560
> To go with Scripture reading. By prayer we talk to God. We hear Him when reading Scriptures (St. Jerome). 610
> Urged upon priests along with spirit of adoration as means towards union with Christ. 376
>> Cf. Family Prayer.
>> Cf. Priests.
>> Cf. Seminarians.
>> Cf. Union with God.

PRAYER OF PETITION Bishops to train people, especially the suffering, to offer prayer, penance, suffering for evangelization. 192
> People must be exhorted to pray for sinners. 715
> Priests to lead faithful to ever improved spirit of prayer, 328
> Saints in heaven pray for us. 796
> Through merits of saints Church pleads for God's favors. 234
> To be addressed to Mary, 597
> To the saints is traditional. 573

PREACHING 309-320

Aim is that people rooted in faith, hope and charity may grow in Christ. 314

Aim is to make whole human race into family of God. 89

By it and by baptism the Church brings forth children who are conceived of Holy Spirit and born of God. 138

By it and by sacraments mission work brings about presence of Christ. 186

It is God Who opens hearts. Sublime utterance comes from Him. 317

The gospel is one of principal means of spreading faith, preparing people for baptism, incorporating them in Christ. 183

Through it the Holy Spirit calls men to Christ, stirs obedience of faith. 146

Through saving word, faith begins in unbelievers, is fed in believers. 313

PREACHING GOSPEL IS PRIMARY DUTY OF PRIESTS Because none can be saved who has not believed. 312

Eucharist is the center and apex of whole work of preaching the gospel. 187

Fruit of contemplation is profitable to preacher. 549

Scripture needed if one is not to be "empty preacher" (St. Augustine). 316

To be nourished and ruled by sacred Scripture, 184

"Woe is me if I do not preach the gospel" (St. Paul). 508, 510

PREDESTINATION Sons of God through the Word, 8

The elect predestined from eternity to be conformed to Son of God. 78

PRIDE The first sin. Christ gave supreme example of humility in the Eucharist. 100

PRIESTS Cf. Celibacy.

        Cf. Devotional Practices.

        Cf. Holiness of Priests.

        Cf. Mass.

        Cf. Missioner.

        Cf. Orders, Sacrament of.

        Cf. Penance as Sacrament.

        Cf. Prayer.

        Cf. Priesthood.

        Cf. Scripture Reading.

        Cf. Spiritual Reading.

        Cf. Visits to Blessed Sacrament.

PRIESTS AND SACRAMENTS 326-331

Admonished to examine conscience often and be ready to hear

304
Of Christ, Cf. Priests.
Priests mold and rule the priestly people, offer Mass in the name of
all the people. 491
Today like pre-Reformation clergy in Europe, 288
Under attack, 288
PRIESTHOOD OF LAITY 464, 491 ff.
A result of regeneration by baptism, anointing of Holy Spirit. By it
they offer selves as sacrifice pleasing to God. 492
And clergy essentially different but interrelated as participation in
Christ's priesthood, 491
By it they join in Eucharistic offering, receive sacraments, practice
self-denial, charity, 491
By it they offer spiritual sacrifices to God and consecrate the world
itself. 493
By it they proclaim Christ's perfection. 495
Christ, the Great Prophet, exercises this office through laity also,
provides the needed gifts. 500
Laity share role of Christ as Priest, Prophet and King; lead people
to Church; cooperate in catechetical instruction; help mis-
sions financially. 502
They are consecrated so as to offer spiritual sacrifices and witness
to Christ. 494
PRISONERS An object of charitable work, 700
PRO-CREATION Share in God's creative work, 63
PRODUCTIVITY Purpose must not be mere multiplication of goods
or profit but must serve man — the whole man. 749
Cf. Person.
PROFESSORS Cf. Seminary Professors.
PROPERTY, PRIVATE Has a social quality based on communal na-
ture of earthly goods. To overlook this leads to greed and dis-
turbances. 751
Should benefit not only owners but others. 750
PROPHECY Christ the Great Prophet exercises this office through
laity also. For this He gives needed gifts. 500
Every member of Christ to give witness to Him in spirit of prophecy. 481
PROPHETIC OFFICE OF CHRIST Exercised by Him through hierarchy who teach in His name and with His authority. Also
through laity. 245
PROPHETIC OFFICE OF PEOPLE Spreads living witness to Christ
by means of faith and charity and by offering sacrifice of
praise to God. 203

If the Spirit of Him Who raised Jesus from death dwells in you,
then God will bring to life your mortal bodies because of His
Spirit. 802

Man is obliged to regard his body as good since God will raise it up
on last day. 802

Of the dead when Christ appears, 226

Through Holy Spirit the Father gives life to men dead from sin
until at last He revives in Christ even their mortal bodies. 145

To life or to judgment at end of the world, 788

When Christ appears and the glorious resurrection takes place, the
splendor of God will brighten the heavenly city. 798

RETREATS Gladly undertaken by priests, 376

REVELATION 12 ff.

And culture: God in revealing Himself spoke according to the culture proper to each age. 772

By deeds and words shows deepest truths about God and salvation
of men. 58

Concerning man, 24

Enables us to go into Mind and Heart of God and see why He values us. 36

God speaking to men, 20

God reveals Self and His Will to men, speaks to men, lives among
them, invites them to fellowship. 58

Is preserved and faithfully expounded in Church through action of
Holy Spirit. No new public revelation admitted. 266

Its prime purpose is to conform men's minds to God's. 114

Perfected in Christ, 22

Son was sent not only to tell men "the innermost realities of God"
but also to show that God is with us to free us from the darkness of sin and to raise us to eternal life. 782

Source of certainty, 13

Cf. Faith.

RIGHTS Cf. Justice.

ROSARY Mistakenly depreciated, 602

Recited in Chapel a means to obtain plenary indulgence. 605

RULES Of religious communities endorsed by hierarchy. 393

SACRAMENTALS Draw power from Christ's passion, death and resurrection. 616

SACRAMENTS 616 ff.

Are all linked with and directed towards Eucharist. 624

As signs instruct. They also nourish faith and impart grace. Faithful should understand the signs. 617

By them and by preaching, mission work brings about presence of

Christ. 186

Christ present in them by His power. It is He Who baptizes. 611

Dispose faithful to receive grace fruitfully, to worship God and practice charity. 617

Draw their power from passion, death and resurrection of Christ. 616

Entrusted in special way to clergy but laity also have important role in them. 188

Pastors to labor to see that faithful are nourished with spiritual food through devout reception of sacraments. 633

Their purpose is to sanctify men, build up Body of Christ and give worship to God. 617

      Cf. Baptism.

      Cf. Confirmation.

      Cf. Eucharist.

      Cf. Mass.

      Cf. Matrimony.

      Cf. Orders.

      Cf. Penance.

      Cf. Sick.

SACRIFICE Faithful to offer selves as a sacrifice, living, holy, pleasing to God, 466

Missioner, in spirit of sacrifice to carry in himself the dying of Jesus, 373

Of the faithful to be made perfect in union with the sacrifice of Christ through ministry of priests, 328

Priests also to mortify themselves. 374

Sanctified by Holy Spirit, people can offer selves as a sacrifice, living, holy, pleasing to God. 310

      Cf. Mass.

SACRIFICE OF CHRIST Its aim is that the entire commonwealth of the redeemed, i.e., the society of saints, be offered as a universal sacrifice to God through the High Priest Who in His Passion offered His very self for us that we might be the body of so exalted a head (St. Augustine). 631

Prompted by Holy Spirit, Church must walk Christ's road of poverty, obedience, service, sacrifice. 191

SADNESS Cf. Suffering.

SAINTS Cherished not only for their example but that whole Church be strengthened in charity. 227

Companionship with them joins us to Christ. 227

Our union with them best expressed in united worship of God, e.g., Mass, 233

establishing Mystical Body and Communion of Saints. 172
Cf. Elect.

SALVATION, CHURCH A PARTNER Church alone has fullness of
means of salvation. 125
Church commissioned to bring it to every man. 153
In whole work of salvation. 122
Its history worked out by God through mission. 152

SALVATION, HOLY SPIRIT Sent by Christ to do His saving work
inwardly — forever sanctify the Church. 144-145

SALVATION OF NON-CHRISTIANS Impossible for those who
know Church is necessary and refuse to enter or to stay in the
Church. 165
Possible under certain conditions. 162

SALVATION ONLY THROUGH CHRIST "Achieved by faith in
Christ and by His grace." 153
Christ came to save men from sins and make them holy. 711
Christ distributed in His Body "gifts and ministries through which,
by His own power, we serve each other unto salvation." 213
God offered help to all by virtue of Christ after Adam's sin. 75
Impossible by our own strength alone. Christ did for us what we
could not do — expects us to do what we can with His help.
120-121, 171
Offered before time of Christ. 75-76
Son of God was sent to be source of salvation for all. 156

SANCTIFICATION And growth of Church. Laity to use their God
given energy for this purpose. 479
Christ was delivered up for our sins and rose for our justification.
197
Christ's work for our sanctification, 112 ff.
Is not automatic. Men are justified in Christ through faith, bap-
tism, etc. 112
Ministry is principal means for sanctification of shepherds of souls.
283
Pastors are servants of Christ, stewards of God's mysteries, wit-
nesses to God's power to make men just. 332
Through the Holy Spirit, 542-544

SANCTITY OF PRIESTS Bishop responsible for, 279
Cf. Holiness.

SATAN Cf. Devil.

SAVED, THE Cf. Elect.

SCIENCE A copy of order God ordained for universe, 17
And culture, if properly promoted, can serve as a preparation for
the gospel. 772

257

Favored by Vatican II, 770

If scientists think their methods of investigation are alone valid, they can be led into agnosticism but true science confers many benefits culturally, etc. 772

SCIENTISTS Cf. Science.

SCRIPTURE Gives knowledge of Christ. "Ignorance of Scripture is ignorance of Christ" (Jerome). Prayer to go with reading. 610

In it God meets His children, speaks to them. 608

It is support of Church, food for souls, source of spiritual life. 608

SCRIPTURE AND TRADITION A mirror in which Church looks at God. 609

One deposit of word of God. Magisterium of Church not above Scripture and tradition but serves them by explaining them faithfully. 264

Tradition and magisterium so linked that one cannot stand without the others, 265

SCRIPTURE READING "By prayer we talk to God. Reading word of God we hear Him" (St. Jerome). 610

To nourish People of God, enlighten minds, strengthen wills, inflame hearts, 607

Urged for priests to become more perfect disciples of Christ. 377

SCRIPTURE SCHOLARS Studies in seminaries to be soul of theology, 458

Urged to study Fathers of East and West as also various liturgies, all under care of magisterium. 263

Without using it priest would be "empty preacher" (St. Augustine). 316

SELF-DENIAL Giving is only way in which man can find himself. 683

Sacrifice — Church must walk this road like Jesus did. 705

Seminarians to be trained in it, 453

Urged for all the faithful. 684

SEMINARIANS 438-463

Devotions and virtues to be practiced, 440

Kind of discipline needed, 452

Should by prayer live in companionship with Father, Son and Holy Spirit and identify own lives with that of Christ. 559

Spiritual, doctrinal, pastoral training to be linked. 439

To be dismissed if unsuitable, 455

To be trained for apostolate even during holidays, 449

To be trained for celibacy, 456-457

To learn how to represent Christ Who came to serve. 446

To live in companionship with Father through Christ in Holy Spirit, 439

259

God's help man is unable to keep up the battle. 93

Blocks path to fulfillment. 93

By himself man cannot save self from sin. Needs Christ. 556

By shedding His Blood, Christ freed us from bondage of sin. 94

Christ came not only to save men from sin but to make them holy.
112, 711

Christ was delivered up for our sins and rose for our justification.
197

Christ was sinless but came to expiate sins of all. 712

Disrupted man's relationship with own goal, with himself and with
others. He is split within himself. 93

Father sent His Son to free us from "darkness of sin." 782

God is with us to free us from darkness of sin and death. 94

God offered help to all by virtue of Christ after Adam's sin. 75

Man by original sin set himself against God; mind was darkened.
65

Not a surprise to God, 75

Only a divine person could make adequate atonement for it. 101

Original, 10

People must not only be taught social consequences of sin but that
essence of virtue of penance is hatred of sin as an offense
against God. 715

Priests to offer gifts and sacrifices for sin, 299

Since we all offend in many things, we need God's mercy and must
say: "Forgive us our debts." 533

Though world is entangled with many sins it gives Church living
stones to be built up into dwelling place for God. 723

Through Holy Spirit, Father gives life to men dead from sin. 542

World was created by God's love but fell into bondage of sin and
was emancipated by Christ. 714

     Cf. Evil.

     Cf. Sinners.

SINNERS Baptism adds new title of nobility by reason of price God
paid in ransom for sinners. 92

Church is holy but embraces sinners and needs always to be purified by renewal and penance. 712

God sent Son to establish peace and communion with sinners. 83

"If we say we have not sinned, we make Christ a liar and His word
is not in us" (St. John). 713

People must be exhorted to pray for sinners. 715

Through Holy Spirit the Father gives life to men dead from sin.
145

To become sons through "Blood of the Cross," 83

SOCIAL Action — laity urged to favor charitable and social welfare work in local, national, international spheres. 702

Aspect of property, Cf. Property.

Justice, Cf. Justice, Social.

Life — groups now have better access to fulfillment and more rights and duties with respect to human race. 758

Nature of People of God willed by God. 487

Order, Cf. Temporal Order,

Sphere — its spiritual aspects, 758-760

Virtues essential for common good and better world, 759

Virtues of family is first school for acquiring them. 659

Welfare. All must look on every neighbor as another self, taking into account life of the other and means for him to live with dignity. 742

Welfare work — Christian charity works to reach out to every one and every need. Every prosperous person and nation has this duty. 700

Work should aim at enabling beneficiaries to become independent of charity. 701

Work, Cf. Charity, Work of.

SOCIETY And religion. Christians to distinguish clearly their duties as members of Church and duties as members of human society. 768

Benefitted by man's labor. 754

Peace results from harmony built into society by its divine founder and actualized by justice, lawful authority, etc. 761

Priests to teach people to seek God's will in all things, not live for themselves alone but must administer the grace they receive to others. Thus they fulfill duty to society. 686

The Church being made up of men must be leaven and kind of soul for society which is family of God. 733

Welfare of the whole of society must be advanced in economic order also. 748

SOCIO-ECONOMIC DEVELOPMENT Cf. Development.

SOLIDARITY Laity should promote solidarity both in national and international spheres. 747

SONS OF GOD As such we are one family in God. 226

Holy Spirit dwells in them, prays in them, bears witness that they are sons of God. 147

Men are called through Christ to be adopted sons of God. 669

To treat each other as brothers. Christ died for all of us. 134

We are such through being joined to Christ in the Church and being signed by Holy Spirit. 133

Made one with Christ's suffering as the body is with the head, we
endure with Him that with Him we may be glorified. 222
Men following Christ are willing to endure all and take up
their cross. 472
Suffering on behalf of the Church, the apostles supplied what was
wanting of the sufferings of Christ. 705
Those who suffer poverty, sickness, etc., are united with the suffering Christ for the salvation of the world. They are "blessed."
703
We must carry in our bodies the dying of Jesus so that the life of
Jesus may be manifest in us. 704
> Cf. Martyrs.
> Cf. Sick.

SUPERIORS To be docile to God's Will and use authority in spirit of
service, show charity, 432
To give religious a chance to perfect themselves spiritually, doc-
trinally, professionally, 433
To listen willingly, but authority is not to be weakened, 434

SUPERNATURAL LIFE Given by Holy Spirit. 501
Hierarchy has right to decide what is needed in temporal affairs to
protect and promote supernatural order. 737
Order. Promoting it was main purpose of Vatican II but it must
reflect its efficacy in natural order too. 735

TECHNOLOGY Favored by Vatican II, 770
Used to meet needs of humanity carries out plan of God. 729-730

TEMPORAL ORDER According to God's plan, 731-740
Christ through His Spirit fosters not only hope for heaven but also
for more human life here. 725
Cooperation with God in this order, 727-730
Earthly affairs have an autonomy of their own that is in harmony
with will of God Who created all things and gave them laws
and order. 731
Even charismatic gifts are to be used not only for Church but for
good of all mankind. 734
First duty of Christian is eternal salvation but faith adds emphasis
to their duty to work for a more human world. 727
Hierarchy must teach moral principles to be followed in temporal
affairs. Has right to judge whether these affairs conform with
moral principles. 737
In fulfilling her mandate for salvation, Church must be concerned
with whole man including his earthly life insofar as it has a
bearing on his heavenly calling. 726
Its elements help us achieve ultimate goal and also have value of

Is fostered by all work done according to God's Will. 471

Is holiness. 577

Is source of apostolic results. 415

Laity get their right and duty concerning apostolate from this union. 496

Led by Holy Spirit, the faithful go forward in union with Christ to kingdom of the Father. 744

Priests achieve unity of own lives by uniting selves with Him in doing Father's will. 298

Through it apostolate of religious flourishes, 418

Through the Church we abide in Christ without Whom we can do nothing. 130

Urged for priests and people. 376

UNIONS Cf. Labor Unions.

UNITY Among priests through spending selves in even lowly tasks assigned to them, 358

Brought about by Eucharist, Cf. Eucharist.

Of people of God: There is neither Jew nor Greek, slave nor free man, male nor female — all are one in Christ (St. Paul). 199

Priests' lives built on imitation of Christ in ministry. 353-354

UNIVERSE A book about God, 14

A "portrait" of God, 15

Created through the Word, gives man an enduring witness to God. 722

God's "kindergarten," 17

God's work of art to show to His children, 18

Governed by divine law. 73

Is sacred and destined to share in man's eternal destiny. As represented by man's body it will reach its crown through him and give free praise to God. 722

Prepared during billions of years to be our home. It is a book to learn about God. 74

Valued by God, 16

Cf. Earth.

Cf. World.

VATICAN I Vatican II adheres to its doctrines. 664

VATICAN II "A *summa* for our time, a rich, authoritative compendium of doctrine and guidance for its needs" (Paul VI). 805

Appeals to scholars, 19

Characterized by hope for better world and eternal life. 673

Destined to last a long time both within and outside the Church (Paul VI). 804

Did not condemn like other Councils but threw light on what

ought to be praised, appreciated, done and hoped for (Paul VI). 806

Documents good for spiritual reading and meditation (Paul VI). 600

Its critics don't know the documents and seek hasty and subversive change (Paul VI). 807

Its main concern was to guard deposit of doctrine and explain it more efficaciously (John XXIII). 663-664

Misinterpreted due to exaggerated anthropocentrism. 239

Most spiritual of all Councils? Introduction, m.

On spiritual strengths and weaknesses, 56

One of its aims was to give Church a chance to contribute more effectively to solution of modern problems. 735

Out of date? Some think so. Not so Paul VI. He is quoted as saying his main task in life is to bring ideas and ideals of Vatican II to realization. 803

Paul VI says its dominant thought was pastoral. 287

Paul VI says people who see the Council as work of the Holy Spirit use the documents as nourishment for own souls and own community. 807

Stresses reverence for man. Every man, 691

Was latest, most authentic and authoritative expression of Church, her life and spirituality given to our day. 803

VESPERS Cf. Breviary.

VIRGINS Veneration of sainted virgins, 573

VIRTUES Demanded in believers, mercy, kindness, humility, meekness, patience, 620

Fifth Chapter of Dogmatic Constitution on Church is like a litany of virtues necessary for sanctification. 662

Moral and social virtues to be cultivated for the common good and a better world. 759

Needed by laity for social apostolate. 763

Needed for sanctification. 112 ff.

(Social) family is first school for acquiring them. 659

Cf. Humility.

Cf. Obedience.

VIRTUES FOR DEACONS AND OTHER CLERICS For seminarians — both natural and supernatural. 451

For seminarians — faith, hope, charity, prayer, etc. 440

VIRTUES FOR MISSIONERS Faith, hope, love, prayer, self-discipline, 371

Listed, 369

Zeal, love for God and neighbor, obedience, 372

Church is "compelled by Holy Spirit to do her part towards full realization of God's will." 157

Holiness possible if we accept life situations with faith as coming from God and show in our actions the love God has for men. 536

Is that men through Christ should have access to Father in Holy Spirit and share in divine nature. 58

Only by faith and meditation on God's word can we seek His will in every event. 545

Only those who do it will enter kingdom of heaven. Father wishes us to recognize Christ as our brother and love Him. 689

Permits an autonomy in earthly affairs. Created things and societies have own laws and values conferred by God. 731

Priests to teach faithful to see what is God's will in all things. 686

To achieve perfection of charity we must seek God's will in all things. 535

To be detected through spiritual reading and faith by priests, 378

To unify their lives priests should submit to God's will in all things. 354

> Cf. Obedience.

WISDOM OF GOD By cultural studies men can raise humanity to better understanding of God's Wisdom. 771

Shown in universe, 19

WITNESS By living witness we exert prophetic office and become sign pointing out Christ to others. 173-174

Every member of Christ to give witness to Him in spirit of prophecy. 481

Laymen must witness to the resurrection and life of Christ and be sign that God lives. 504

WIVES Cf. Family.

WORD, MINISTRY OF Cf. Preaching

WORK Done in Holy Spirit is sacrifice acceptable to God. 493

Of every kind done according to God's will leads to union with Christ. 471

Of Priests, 299-303

Ineffective without God's help. Hence prayer is necessary. 562

> Cf. Labor.

WORKS, GOOD 695-702

WORLD Becoming more interdependent, 758

Consecrated to God by works and sacrifices of laity. 493

Each of us can have impact on all men and contribute to world's salvation by offering our prayers, penance, hardships, etc. 706

Father sent Son to save it. 80

God gave us to save it. 348

In pejorative meaning refers to spirit of vanity and malice which transforms into instrument of sin, energies intended for service to God. 722

Is to be related to God by divine mandate. 60 ff.

Laity called by God to work like leaven for sanctification of world in which they live and make Christ known to others. 514

Laity have principal role in permeating world with spirit of Christ. 475

Of men is the one God loved so much as to give own Son to save it. Though entangled with many sins it has many talents and gives the Church living stones to be built into dwelling place of God. 347

Priests and, 345-351

Renounced by vows. 395

Vatican II concerned with whole world which was created by God's love but has fallen into bondage of sin. 714

What soul is to body, Christians should be to world. 504

Which is intimately related to man and achieves its purpose, through him will be perfectly re-established in Christ. 787

Cf. Better World.

Cf. Temporal Order.

Cf. Universe.